T0339277

An excellent, helpful, and practical introduction to the topic for beginners.

—Peter J. Gentry, Donald L. Williams Professor of Old Testament
Interpretation, The Southern Baptist Theological Seminary

With this handbook Anderson and Widder provide a clear and helpful introduction to Old and New Testament textual criticism. In a time of increasing specialization and fragmentation, a handbook that takes what the two fields have in common—in particular scribal habits—as the starting point is very welcome. Clear explanations, definitions of keywords, lucid tables, and illustrating examples make this introduction particularly suitable for the beginning student.

—Tommy Wasserman, professor of biblical studies,
Ansgar Teologiske Høgskole, Kristiansand, Norway

Anderson and Widder's accomplished overview of the concept, purpose, history, and practice of textual criticism opens the field to a wide audience. With its step-by-step case studies and the transliterated Greek and Hebrew texts, this is an excellent introduction for the novice in textual criticism. The generous footnotes and valuable bibliography will also make it a favorite reference book for pastors and students of the Bible who need to refresh their skills and update their knowledge of the discipline.

—Sylvie T. Raquel, associate professor of biblical studies,
Trinity International University

What a valuable, versatile, and much-needed resource to orient beginners in the discipline of textual criticism! Those who teach Greek courses or deal with textual variants of Scripture in any setting will find this work absolutely engaging and worthwhile.

—Viktor Roudkovski, chair, Department of Theology, associate professor of
theology, School of Theology and Vocation, LeTourneau University

Bible and theology students as well as English Bible readers will welcome Amy Anderson's excellent addition to this readable volume. Her years of detailed manuscript work combine with a teacher's sensitivity to make an intimidating subject easy to grasp. This is a book for the novice that will set them on the right path to making sense and making use of New Testament textual criticism.

—Peter J. Gurry, assistant professor of New Testament, Phoenix Seminary

Although textual criticism can be an intimidating subject for students new to biblical studies, Anderson and Widder provide a well-balanced manual that addresses all the main issues and more. Students will appreciate greatly their thorough, step-by-step guidance through the critical apparatuses and their judicious introduction to text criticism.

—Kevin Chau, senior lecturer, Department of Hebrew,
University of the Free State, South Africa

Finally, a university resource clear enough to be used in churches! Many people are interested in the Bible and the art and science of textual criticism. As a pastor I am pleased to discover a book that is so well-written, accurate, and engaging. I will be using it in my church as a text to introduce the wonderful world of textual criticism. The authors have produced a masterful resource that will have a broad appeal for years to come, since its approach is unique and its prose is exceedingly lucid.

—Rev. Dr. Jac D. Perrin, Eden Prairie Assembly, Minnesota;
University of Birmingham, England

Anderson and Widder have written a readable introduction to the textual issues of both the Hebrew Bible and the Greek New Testament. Beginners will find this a helpful and handy approach to issues that can otherwise be quite complicated. The authors have introduced not just the time-honored procedures that have grown to become the standards over the past several centuries but also the newer methods which continue to change and shape the field and the text.

—Jeff Cate, professor of New Testament, California Baptist University

Writing an introductory textbook for a complicated field in a responsible way is a daunting task that few accomplish, but Anderson and Widder have done so in an admirable manner in this work. The information is up-to-date on scholarship yet understandable for both students and non-students alike. This is an ideal text-book for college-level courses that want to introduce students to textual criticism, whether the students have studied Greek and Hebrew already or not. The book includes resources for further study via an annotated bibliography at the end of each major section, plus a wonderful quick-reference glossary of the key terms in the fields of Old Testament and New Testament textual criticism is included as an appendix at the end of the book. The work has a logical flow from the larger field of textual criticism to the subfields of Old Testament and then New Testament textual criticism and even includes an overview of the textual criticism approaches of some of the major English translations. Numerous variants are analyzed in each of the sections so that students can see firsthand the dominant methodology for resolving the textual information and arriving at the earliest attainable text of the passage. In brief, this is a work that is easy to recommend to others and that I'll be using myself in some of my classes.

—Bill Warren, director of the H. Milton Haggard Center for New Testament Textual Studies, Landrum P. Leavell II Chair of New Testament and Greek, New Orleans Baptist Theological Seminary

TEXTUAL CRITICISM OF THE BIBLE

LEXHAM METHODS SERIES

TEXTUAL CRITICISM OF THE BIBLE

—

REVISED EDITION

Amy Anderson and Wendy Widder
Edited by Douglas Mangum

LEXHAM PRESS

Lexham Methods Series: Volume 1: Textual Criticism of the Bible, Revised Edition
Copyright 2018 Lexham Press

Lexham Press, 1313 Commercial St., Bellingham, WA 98225
www.lexhampress.com

Print ISBN 9781577996637
Digital ISBN 9781577997047

Lexham Editorial Team: Claire Brubaker, Erin Mangum
Design: Brittany Schrock
Typesetting: ProjectLuz.com

CONTENTS

LIST OF TABLES

SERIES PREFACE

T he Lexham Methods Series introduces a variety of approaches to biblical interpretation. Due to the field's long history, however, the coverage is necessarily selective. This series focuses on the major areas of critical biblical scholarship and their development from the nineteenth century to the early twenty-first century. While we recognize that theological approaches to interpretation have played an important role in the life of the Church, this series does not engage the wide variety of hermeneutical approaches that arise from specific theological readings of the biblical text.

The methods discussed here include the broad movements in biblical criticism that have helped define how biblical scholars today approach the text. Understanding the basics of textual criticism, source criticism, form criticism, tradition history, redaction criticism, linguistics, social-scientific criticism, canonical criticism, and contemporary literary criticism (rhetorical, structural, narrative, reader-response, poststructural) will help illuminate the assumptions and conclusions found in many scholarly commentaries and articles.

Each approach to biblical interpretation—even those that are not explicitly theological—can be defined according to a guiding presupposition that informs the method.

- **Textual criticism**: Comparing ancient manuscripts to determine the *earliest form of the text* and study how the text was transmitted throughout history

- **Source criticism**: Reading the text to find the *written sources* the author(s) used

- **Form criticism**: Reading the text to find the *oral traditions* the author(s) used

- **Tradition-historical criticism**: Reconstructing the *historical development of the traditions* identified by form criticism

- **Redaction criticism**: Reading the text to understand *how it was put together* and what message the text was meant to communicate

- **Canonical criticism**: Reading the final form of the text *as Christian Scripture*

- **Rhetorical criticism**: Analyzing the text for the *rhetorical effect of the literary devices* the writers used to communicate and persuade

- **Structural criticism**: Analyzing the text *in terms of contrast and oppositions*, recognizing that contrast is believed to be the essence of meaning within a cultural, linguistic, or literary system

- **Narrative criticism**: Reading the text *as a narrative* and paying attention to aspects including plot, theme, and characterization

- **Linguistic approach**: Analyzing the text *using* concepts and theories developed by *linguistics*

- **Social-scientific approach**: Analyzing the text *using* concepts and theories developed in the *social sciences*

The Lexham Methods Series defines these approaches to biblical interpretation, explains their development, outlines their goals and emphases, and identifies their leading proponents. Few interpreters align themselves strictly with any single approach. Contemporary Bible scholars tend to use an eclectic method that draws on the various aspects of biblical criticism outlined above. Many of these methods developed in parallel, mutually influenced each other, and share similar external influences from literary theory and philosophy. Similarly, ideas and questions arising from one approach often directly influenced the field as a whole and have become common currency in biblical studies, even though the method that generated the concepts has been radically reshaped and revised over the years.

In introducing a variety of methods, we will address each method as neutrally as possible, acknowledging both the advantages and limitations of each approach. Our discussion of a particular method or attempts to demonstrate the method should not be construed as an endorsement of that approach to the text. The Lexham Methods Series introduces you to the world of biblical scholarship.

ACKNOWLEDGMENTS

The authors would like to express their gratitude for the exceptional help of colleagues in the production of this book. We'd like to especially thank Doug Mangum for his careful editorial work throughout, but particularly in the Old Testament portion of the text. We also deeply appreciate Peter Gentry's suggestions on Old Testament textual transmission. With respect to the New Testament portion, we owe particular gratitude to James Leonard, Timothy Mitchell, Greg Paulson, and Daniel Wallace for reading the text with meticulous care and making important suggestions for refinement of wording and factual accuracy. Additional thanks to Peter Gurry and Tommy Wasserman for valuable comments on particular sections. Such generous assistance has raised the quality bar tremendously.

ABBREVIATIONS

REFERENCE WORKS

AYBD   *Anchor Yale Bible Dictionary* (formerly *Anchor Bible Dictionary*).
D. N. Freedman. 1992.

BDAG   W. Bauer, F. W. Danker, W. F. Arndt, and F. W. Gingrich. *A
Greek-English Lexicon of the New Testament and Other Early
Christian Literature.* 3rd ed. 1999.

BDB   *Enhanced Brown-Driver-Briggs Hebrew and English Lexicon.*
Logos Bible Software. 2000.

DPL   *Dictionary of Paul and His Letters.* G. F. Hawthorne and R. P.
Martin. 1993.

EDB   *Eerdmans Dictionary of the Bible.* D. N. Freedman. 2000.

HALOT   *The Hebrew and Aramaic Lexicon of the Old Testament.* L.
Koehler, W. Baumgartner, and J. J. Stamm. 5 vols. 1994–2000.

LBD   *Lexham Bible Dictionary.* J. D. Barry. Logos Bible Software.
2012.

LSJ   H. G. Liddell, R. Scott, and H. S. Jones. *A Greek-English Lexicon.*
9th ed. with rev. supp. 1996.

NBD   *New Bible Dictionary,* 3rd ed. D. R. W. Wood. 1996.

NIDOTTE   *New International Dictionary of Old Testament Theology and
Exegesis.* W. A. VanGemeren. 5 vols. 1997.

OTP   *Old Testament Pseudepigrapha.* J. H. Charlesworth. 2 vols.
1983–85.

ZEB   *The Zondervan Encyclopedia of the Bible.* Moisés Silva and M.
C. Tenney. 5 vols. 2009.

COMMENTARIES

AYBC	Anchor Yale Bible Commentary (formerly Anchor Bible Commentary)
CCS	Continental Commentary Series
ICC	International Critical Commentary
NAC	New American Commentary
NICNT	New International Commentary on the New Testament
NIGTC	New International Greek Testament Commentary
NIVAC	The NIV Application Commentary
PNTC	The Pillar New Testament Commentary
WBC	Word Biblical Commentary

JOURNALS

BSac	*Bibliotheca Sacra*
JBL	*Journal of Biblical Literature*
JETS	*Journal of the Evangelical Theological Society*
JNSL	*Journal of Northwest Semitic Languages*
NovT	*Novum Testamentum*
VT	*Vetus Testamentum*
WTJ	*Westminster Theological Journal*

BIBLE VERSIONS

AMP	The Amplified Bible. 1987.
ASV	American Standard Version. 1901.
BHK	*Biblia Hebraica.* R. Kittel. 1905–1973.
BHQ	*Biblia Hebraica Quinta.* A. Schenker. 2004–.
BHS	*Biblia Hebraica Stuttgartensia.* K. Elliger and W. Rudolph. 1977–1997.
CEV	Contemporary English Version. 1995.
ESV	English Standard Version. 2001.
GNB	Good News Bible. 1992.
GNT	Greek New Testament
HCSB	Holman Christian Standard Bible. 2009.
JPS	Jewish Publication Society. 1917.
KJV	King James Version
LEB	Lexham English Bible. 2012.

LES	Lexham English Septuagint. 2012.
LHB	Lexham Hebrew Bible. 2012.
LXX	Septuagint
MSG	*The Message.* 2005.
MT	Masoretic Text
NA27	Nestle-Aland, *Novum Testamentum Graece.* 27th edition. 1993.
NA28	Nestle-Aland, *Novum Testamentum Graece.* 28th edition. 2012.
NAB	New American Bible. 1970.
NASB	New American Standard Bible. 1995.
NCV	New Century Version. 2005.
NET	New English Translation. 2005.
NETS	*A New English Translation of the Septuagint.* A. Pietersma and B. Wright. 2009.
NIV	New International Version. 2011.
NIV84	New International Version. 1984.
NKJV	New King James Version. 1982.
NLT	New Living Translation. 2007.
NRSV	New Revised Standard Version. 1989.
RSV	Revised Standard Version. 1971.
SBLGNT	*The Greek New Testament: SBL Edition.* 2011.
THGNT	*The Greek New Testament Produced at Tyndale House, Cambridge.* 2017.
TR	Textus Receptus
UBS3	United Bible Societies' *Greek New Testament.* 3rd edition. 1975.
UBS4	United Bible Societies' *Greek New Testament.* 4th edition. 1998.
UBS5	United Bible Societies' *Greek New Testament.* 5th edition. 2014.

1

INTRODUCTION TO TEXTUAL CRITICISM

1.1 INTRODUCTION

A longtime Christian and student of the Bible posted the following comment about Romans 8:1:

> View the difference in versions here! You may want to add this to your NIV. I have an NIV Bible, but when I study, I *always* compare it to the KJV:
>
>> "Therefore, there is now no condemnation for those who are in Christ Jesus" (Rom 8:1 NIV).
>>
>> "There is therefore now no condemnation to them which are in Christ Jesus, *who walk not after the flesh, but after the spirit*" (Rom 8:1 KJV).
>
> Big difference, huh?

This comment concerns an issue that surfaces throughout the Bible: differences in Bible versions that may affect the meaning. While some Bibles include footnotes to indicate when such differences exist, these notes are not always helpful for readers with no background knowledge of the preservation and transmission of the Bible from its original authors to the current day.

What should we think when we find disagreement between English versions? Which translations are right? Why would translators "change" the biblical text? How can readers make good decisions about these discrepancies between versions?

These questions are important for every student of the Bible, and textual criticism contributes part of the answer. In this chapter we will describe what textual criticism is and why it is necessary. Then we will consider the goal of textual criticism and some of the basic principles for practicing it. Finally, we will evaluate the benefits and limitations of this discipline.

1.2 WHAT TEXTUAL CRITICISM IS—AND IS NOT

Textual criticism can explain some of the differences people notice between their English versions, such as the omission of "who walk not after the flesh, but after the Spirit" in the NIV of Romans 8:1 above. However, other variations in translation are not text critical in nature; instead, they reflect translation technique and decisions made by translation committees. Understanding the differences between text-critical issues and translation issues is an important first step in the study of textual criticism because it helps explain why translations differ and determine when textual criticism will *not* be helpful.

1.2.1 TRANSLATION TECHNIQUE AND UNCLEAR MEANING

Before a single word of the biblical text is translated, the translation committee, denomination, or other group commissioning the translation decides what their translation philosophy will be. Do they want to produce a "literal" translation, a paraphrase, or something in between? Many variables factor into the translation philosophy, but in general, translators must decide whether they want to preserve the *form* of the source language as closely as possible or the *meaning* of the source language as the translator understands it. It is impossible to reproduce languages exactly because the grammar and syntax of each language is different. The rules of the **source language**—Greek and Hebrew, in the case of the Bible—differ from the rules of English, the **target language**. Since each language has its own rules, translation requires adapting the rules of the source language to fit into the rules of the target language. Consider the following translations of Isaiah 19:16:

Table 1.1: Translation Options for Isaiah 19:16			
NASB	**NLT**	**NIV**	**MSG**
In that day the Egyptians will become like women, and they will tremble and be in dread because of the waving of the hand of the LORD of hosts, which He is going to wave over them.	In that day the Egyptians will be as weak as women. They will cower in fear beneath the upraised fist of the LORD of Heaven's Armies.	In that day the Egyptians will become weaklings. They will shudder with fear at the uplifted hand that the LORD Almighty raises against them.	On that Day, Egyptians will be like hysterical schoolgirls, screaming at the first hint of action from GOD-of-the-Angel-Armies.

The differences between these translations of the same Hebrew words illustrate the difficulty of representing information given in one language in a second language.

Translation committees decide whether they want to represent in English every *word* of the Greek or Hebrew, or whether they want to represent in English the *meaning* of the Greek or Hebrew text. The first option results in what is usually called a "word-for-word" translation or a "literal" translation (though both are impossible in an absolute sense). This approach to translation is called **formal equivalence**, and translations that aim to be "formally equivalent" try to translate the *forms* in the source language into equivalent *forms* in the target language as much as possible. A literal translation can give the reader a good sense of the structure of the underlying Hebrew or Greek, but it can also create an awkward sentence flow and even lead to a failure to grasp the author's intended meaning. English Bible versions that strive for a word-for-word translation include the LEB, NASB, KJV, and ESV.

With the second approach, translators still make a real attempt to represent the Greek or Hebrew accurately, but they are more willing to "smooth out" the text so that it reflects more readable, idiomatic English. This approach is called **dynamic equivalence**. The goal is to "produce the

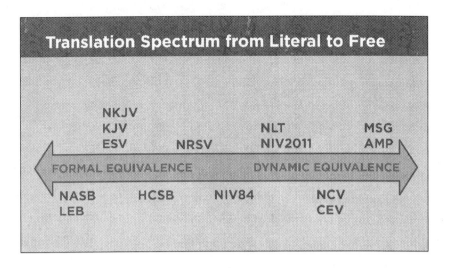

same effect on readers today that the original produced on its readers."[1] English versions that employ dynamic equivalence include the NIV, NLT, CEV, and NCV.[2]

Practitioners of a third translation approach may add explanatory words or phrases that are not in the original text, and they are more likely to rework word order and other aspects of the structure. This option is typically called "paraphrase" (often described as "putting things into your own words") because the adjustments make significant changes to the structure of the original Hebrew or Greek: "They tend to explain rather than translate."[3] In this method, the translator tries to give the text fresh impact for contemporary readers. Popular English paraphrases include the AMP and MSG.

Thus, the various English versions of the Bible all fall along a spectrum between "highly literal" and "highly paraphrastic."[4] According to New Testament scholar David Alan Black, most important differences in

---

1. William W. Klein, Craig L. Blomberg, and Robert L. Hubbard, *Introduction to Biblical Interpretation* (Nashville: Thomas Nelson, 2004), 126.

2. While we include the NIV in the category of dynamic equivalence for the purposes of this book, others prefer to see it as a "balanced or mediating type" between the formal and dynamic equivalence translations. See, for example, Kenneth Barker, *The Balance of the NIV: What Makes a Good Translation* (Grand Rapids: Baker, 2000), 42–43.

3. J. S. Duvall and J. D. Hays, *Grasping God's Word: A Hands-On Approach to Reading, Interpreting, and Applying the Bible* (Grand Rapids: Zondervan, 2005), 168.

4. Klein, Blomberg, and Hubbard, *Introduction to Biblical Interpretation*, 125.

English translations can be accounted for by the translation technique a committee adopts.[5]

The translation committee makes their translation decisions based on the translation theory they have chosen.[6] However, when the translators encounter a passage where the grammar or syntax of the source language is ambiguous, they still must decide how to best render the text in English. Consider the following translations of 1 Timothy 3:6, a verse identifying qualifications for an overseer:

Table 1.2: Translation Options for 1 Timothy 3:6			
KJV; compare NRSV	NASB	NIV	NLT
Not a novice, lest being lifted up with pride he fall into the condemnation of the devil.	Not a new convert, lest he become conceited and fall into the condemnation incurred by the devil.	He must not be a recent convert, or he may become conceited and fall under the same judgment as the devil.	An elder must not be a new believer, because he might become proud, and the devil would cause him to fall.

This is an example of a sentence that has some ambiguity in meaning. The highlighted phrases translate the Greek clause εἰς κρίμα ἐμπέσῃ τοῦ διαβόλου (eis krima empesē tou diabolou):

εἰς κρίμα	ἐμπέσῃ	τοῦ διαβόλου
eis krima	empesē	tou diabolou
into condemnation	**he might fall**	**of the devil**

---

5. David Alan Black, *New Testament Textual Criticism: A Concise Guide* (Grand Rapids: Baker, 1994), 13.

6. In practice, translators may make decisions that fall at various points along the spectrum, regardless of the translation committee's official position. For particular sentences and phrases, a literal version such as the ESV may translate more idiomatically than the NIV. Bible translator Dave Brunn has catalogued many examples of this type in his book *One Bible, Many Versions: Are All Translations Created Equal?* (Downers Grove, IL: InterVarsity, 2013), 51–57.

The phrase literally translates as "[lest] he might fall into the condemnation of the devil." The first part of the verse clearly indicates that new converts are at risk of falling (ἐμπέσῃ, *empesē*), but where they might fall is less clear: "into the condemnation of the devil." In Greek, as in English, this expression could mean the condemnation *caused* by the devil (NLT) or the condemnation *received* by the devil (NASB, NIV). Some translations make an interpretative decision (e.g., NLT, NASB, NIV), while others leave it to the reader to sort out (or ignore) the ambiguity (KJV, NRSV). Normally the intended meaning of a text is clear from the context, but sometimes readers—and translation committees—must make these types of interpretative decisions.

1.2.2 TEXTUAL CRITICISM IS NOT TRANSLATION

Both of the issues described above—translation technique and uncertain meaning—are important factors in explaining why translations vary. But they are *translation* issues, not *textual* issues. That is, they are concerned only with transferring a particular passage from the source language into the target language. In an analogy from the world of education, teachers are like translators. Using textbooks and other resources, teachers try to find the best possible way to translate (transfer) the information to their students. The teachers' primary concern is not establishing the validity of their resources; they have placed trust in scientists, linguists, mathematicians, and historians—the experts who are continually updating and adjusting the information in textbooks. The teachers' primary concern is communicating the text to their students effectively. Thus, by way of general comparison, scholars are like textual critics, the experts who establish the sacred text, and teachers are like translators, those who communicate the meaning of the text.

1.2.3 TEXTUAL CRITICISM DEFINED

The word "criticism," which today often connotes negativity, derives from an older usage, meaning "to analyze or investigate." **Textual criticism** involves analyzing the manuscript evidence in order to determine the oldest form of the text. Such analysis also reveals historical evidence about the transmission of the text, scribal habits, theological biases, and more. Biblical scholars engage in this discipline, as do scholars in the broader field of literature. For example, the writings of most ancient authors, such as Plato or Shakespeare, may be published as a "critical edition," in which scholars have sifted through manuscripts to identify errors that may have crept into the text and to determine the author's original intention.

Because the original biblical manuscripts (called **autographs**) have not survived, we must depend on handwritten copies, none of which agree with each other 100 percent. The task of the **textual critic** is to resolve variations in the readings of these ancient manuscripts by identifying and "removing all changes brought about either by error or revision."[7] When successful, textual criticism results in the best representation of the *Ausgangstext*, or the ancient form of the text that is the ancestor of all extant copies, the beginning of the manuscript tradition.[8]

1.3 LOOKING AHEAD

In the following chapters, we will both define and illustrate textual criticism. If you have studied biblical languages and are familiar with textual criticism, this resource will refresh your knowledge and further develop your ability to understand discussions that hinge on text-critical questions. It will also prepare you to take on some textual issues yourself. If you have never studied Hebrew or Greek and are unfamiliar with textual criticism, this volume will introduce you to a new world. It will equip you to study your Bible more effectively by presenting why English versions differ and helping you decipher footnotes that explain variations in word choice. This resource will increase your awareness of the challenges faced by biblical

---

7. D. W. Gooding, "Texts and Versions: The Septuagint," *NBD* 1172.

8. In recent decades textual scholars have tended to avoid using the term "original text" since it implies less complexity than the actual situation of most ancient documents. For example, we might suspect that Luke wrote several drafts of his Gospel before "publishing" it by making it available to the public. Which of these drafts is the "original text"? Or Luke may have made several copies and sent them to different addressees. As lengthy handwritten texts, they would have had some differences in wording. The German term *Ausgangstext* is often translated as "initial text," but it is preferable to use the German since the English translation is easily misunderstood as "original text" by nonexperts. When a nonexpert encounters the German, however, he or she will not presume to know what it means without obtaining a definition. For more on original text versus *Ausgangstext*, see Eldon J. Epp, "The Multivalence of the Term 'Original Text,'" in *Perspectives on New Testament Textual Criticism: Collected Essays, 1962–2004* (Leiden: Brill, 2005); and Michael W. Holmes, "From 'Original Text' to 'Initial Text': The Traditional Goal of New Testament Textual Criticism in Contemporary Discussion," in *The Text of the New Testament in Contemporary Research: Essays on the Status Quaestionis*, ed. Bart D. Ehrman and Michael W. Holmes, 2nd ed. (Leiden: Brill, 2012), 637–88.

scholars in their work with the text and increase your appreciation for the text that has been so carefully preserved for us.

Chapter 2 provides an overview of the field of textual criticism for both the Old Testament and the New Testament and introduces the types of variation that occur in biblical manuscripts. It identifies the goals and limitations of textual criticism, and it also outlines some basic principles for practicing textual criticism. Chapters 3 and 4 focus on the Old Testament and New Testament respectively, outlining the history of textual criticism in each Testament, detailing the manuscript evidence, and working through examples. Finally, in Chapter 5, we further discuss the significance of textual criticism and English translations and explore how textual criticism relates to various understandings of the doctrine of Scripture.

Throughout the book, we have marked key terms in a **bold** typeface, usually when they first appear in a chapter. You will find a definition for these words in the glossary at the back of the book. The technical nature of textual criticism presents a steep learning curve with new terminology. We have attempted to use jargon sparingly, but, at the same time, an introduction to textual criticism should introduce you to the terminology of the discipline. Since a glossary term will not always appear in bold, if it appeared earlier in the chapter, for example, you should check the glossary if you come across an unfamiliar term.

1.4 RESOURCES FOR FURTHER STUDY

Although this book focuses on textual criticism, Bible translation is an important and closely related subject. The following resources provide additional information and lines of inquiry:

Beekman, John, and John Callow. *Translating the Word of God: With Scripture and Topical Indexes.* Dallas: SIL International, 2002.

Beekman and Callow's *Translating the Word of God* is a how-to manual for the serious translator, but it also includes information that can be helpful for understanding the difficulties of translation and the decisions translators make.

Duvall, J. Scott, and J. Daniel Hays. "Approaches to Translating God's Word." Pages 166–70 in *Grasping God's Word: A Hands-On Approach* to *Reading, Interpreting, and Applying the Bible.* Grand Rapids: Zondervan, 2005.

Duvall and Hays provide a helpful discussion of the inherent difficulties of translation in any language. They also explain and illustrate formally and functionally equivalent Bibles, as well as some that are periphrastic. Their work is a popular textbook for introductory hermeneutics courses.

Klein, William W., Craig L. Blomberg, and Robert L. Hubbard. "Techniques of Translation." Pages 125–26 in *Introduction to Biblical Interpretation.* Nashville: Thomas Nelson, 2004.

Klein, Blomberg, and Hubbard's *Introduction to Biblical Interpretation* includes a brief section on translation techniques. While their text covers the same basic content as Duvall and Hays, their treatment is shorter and includes fewer examples.

Nida, Eugene A. *Toward a Science of Translating.* Leiden: Brill, 1964.

Eugene Nida was a pioneer in Bible translation theory and linguistics and is best known among Bible students for his joint project with Johannes Louw, *A Greek-English Lexicon of the New Testament Based on Semantic Domains.* Nida is widely associated with the theory of dynamic equivalence.

2

—

AN OVERVIEW OF TEXTUAL CRITICISM

2.1 WHY IS TEXTUAL CRITICISM NECESSARY?

The Bible was written at a time when the means for sharing documents were far different from the technology we have today. When the church in Thessaloniki received a letter from the Apostle Paul in the mid-first century, the believers there would have read it aloud in their gatherings, and then devoted followers who recognized the value of Paul's words would have produced handwritten copies of the letter to pass around to a wider audience. By the end of the first century, Paul's letters were being copied as a collection. Hand-copying of the Pauline corpus continued through the centuries, until Johannes Gutenberg invented movable type in fifteenth-century Germany. With some variation, this process of repeated hand-copying happened with every book in the Bible—the New Testament books in Greek, and the Old Testament books in Hebrew and Aramaic.

In addition to these original language manuscripts, Christians translated their sacred texts into other languages. The Old Testament documents were translated into Greek, Latin, Coptic, and Syriac, and the New Testament documents were translated into Latin, Coptic, and Syriac, followed later by Gothic, Armenian, Georgian, Ethiopic, Slavonic, and Arabic. The Bible was repeatedly recopied within each of these languages. Further, Jewish and Christian scholars quoted the sacred texts in their own writings, which others also copied and translated to dispense and preserve.

This proliferation of hand-copied texts resulted in thousands of manuscripts, no two exactly alike. **Textual criticism** is the discipline that guides

scholars in establishing what the authors of the Bible wrote. This is especially important for those who value the Bible as God's Word. While most Christians may never study the original languages or engage in advanced textual criticism, the work of textual critics enables us to know with confidence what God has said through the human authors.

Familiarity with the process of textual criticism can also help make sense of marginal notes that appear in many English versions—such as the footnote for Romans 8:1 in the ESV: "Some manuscripts add *who walk not according to the flesh (but according to the Spirit)*." This footnote points out a place in the text where there is variation in the wording of the ancient manuscripts. In textual criticism, this is called a **variation unit**, and each different reading at that point is called a **variant**.

Though there are thousands of variation units in the text of the Bible, the text is remarkably reliable. Old Testament scholar Bruce Waltke says the most recent **critical edition** of the entire Old Testament (*BHS*) has no significant variation in 90 percent of the text.[1] Of the thousands of instances of variation in the Bible, nearly all of them concern spelling, word order, synonyms, and other elements that do not affect meaning at all. Those variation units that affect the meaning of a biblical text are found in

---

1. Bruce K. Waltke, "Textual Criticism of the Old Testament and Its Relation to Exegesis and Theology," *NIDOTTE* 1:65. On *BHS*, which stands for *Biblia Hebraica Stuttgartensia*, see §3.2.1.c.2.

the footnotes of any good English Bible. Even these variants do not affect doctrine or theology.[2]

2.1.1 DIFFERENCES AMONG TEXTUAL WITNESSES

The types of variation that appear in biblical manuscripts share important similiarities, regardless of which Testament the **textual critic** is working in (see §2.1.2 Errors and Changes in Transmission). Thus, both Old Testament (OT) and New Testament (NT) textual critics can follow the same general process when determining which variant readings are the most accurate. The present chapter discusses this process, and later chapters deal more specifically with textual criticism in the OT (see chapter 3 on OT textual criticism) and the NT (see chapter 4 on NT textual criticism).

However, the textual evidence for each Testament is quite different. Basic knowledge of these differences establishes the groundwork for understanding the task of the textual critic. The OT developed over a long period and is largely silent on issues of authorship, audience, purpose, and time of writing. By contrast, the documents of the NT were written during a period of less than one hundred years, and many books explicitly identify authors, audiences, and even the reason for composition. Based on historical knowledge of the first and second centuries AD, scholars can also make reasonable assumptions about the date of most NT books. Another significant difference between the Testaments that affects the textual critic is the quantity and quality of manuscripts available. Many of the available biblical manuscripts are in **codex** form. The codex is the predecessor of the modern book—sheets of **papyrus** or **parchment** were folded in half and sewn together along the fold. Both sides of the page were used for writing. The codex format is known to have existed by the late first century AD (from a reference by the Roman poet Martial, c. AD 85), but it was not widely used until the fourth century.[3] The other usual format for ancient biblical manuscripts was the scroll, a long roll of papyrus or parchment

---

2. See, for example, Biblical Hebrew textual critic Shemaryahu Talmon, who says that few differences affect the "intrinsic message" of the OT texts ("Old Testament Text," in *Cambridge History of the Bible*, ed. P. R. Ackroyd and C. F. Evans [Cambridge: Cambridge University Press, 1975], 1:161).

3. C. H. Roberts and T. C. Skeat, *The Birth of the Codex* (Oxford: Oxford University Press, 1987), 25, 42–44.

with text written in columns. A scroll could be quite long and had to be read by unrolling the next column and rolling up the finished column.[4] For these reasons (and others), scrolls usually had text on only one side. This distinction between manuscripts with writing on both sides and writing on one side is important for understanding the textual evidence. A fragment of a manuscript may only represent part of a page from a codex, so the text on one side may be near the beginning of a chapter, while the text on the other may be later in the same chapter or come from a later chapter altogether. The issues surrounding the quality and quantity of biblical manuscripts are discussed further below.

2.1.1.a Old Testament Witnesses

If some OT writings date as far back as Moses, then parts of it were copied by hand for almost three thousand years before the printing press appeared. One challenge for OT textual critics is that few fragments of any early writings have survived. Two small scrolls dating to the sixth or seventh century BC contain a version of the priestly blessing found in Numbers 6:24–26, but this provides limited material for textual critics.[5] A second challenge for OT textual critics is that the few available manuscripts are a considerable distance from the original writing. For most of the history of biblical scholarship, the oldest and best available manuscripts of the Hebrew Bible dated to the tenth and eleventh centuries AD—far removed from the original writing. The **Leningrad Codex** (AD 1009) is the only complete manuscript of the Hebrew Bible, but the **Aleppo Codex** (AD 925), the **Cairo Codex of the Prophets** (AD 896), and others contain significant portions. In 1947 the discovery of the **Dead Sea Scrolls** revolutionized the study of OT textual criticism when Hebrew manuscripts from as early as the first century BC surfaced. However, even these manuscripts are a considerable distance from the original writing of the OT books.

---

4. For example, the Great Isaiah Scroll from the Dead Sea Scrolls is around twenty-four feet long or over seven meters (Alison Schofield, "Dead Sea Scrolls, Isaiah," *LBD*).

5. Emanuel Tov, *Textual Criticism of the Hebrew Bible*, 3rd ed. (Minneapolis: Fortress, 2012), 111; Paul D. Wegner, *A Student's Guide to Textual Criticism of the Bible: Its History, Methods and Results* (Downers Grove, IL: InterVarsity, 2006), 26, 140–42.

Table 2.1: Important Hebrew Manuscripts			
BHS Sigla	**BHQ Sigla**	**Name**	**Date**
ꟴ		Biblical texts from Qumran (Dead Sea Scrolls)	c. 100 BC
C	M^C	Cairo Codex of the Prophets	AD 896
	M^A	Aleppo Codex	AD 925
L	M^L	Leningrad Codex	AD 1009

2.1.1.b New Testament Witnesses

Unlike the OT manuscript evidence, which is meager and far removed from the actual composition of the books, the NT has thousands of surviving manuscripts, many of which were copied within three centuries of when the books were written.[6] A few can even be safely dated as early as the mid-second century.[7] The NT manuscripts also exhibit greater textual variation than their OT counterparts, in part because of the historical setting of their transmission. Bruce Metzger explains, "In the early years of the Christian Church, marked by rapid expansion and consequent increased demand by individuals and by the congregations for copies of the Scriptures, the speedy multiplication of copies, even by non-professional scribes, sometimes took precedence over strict accuracy of detail."[8] In addition, scholars have discerned that manuscripts often share typical variant readings and have sorted them into textual groupings, labeled the **Alexandrian text-type**, the **Byzantine text-type**, the **Western text-type**, and the so-called **"Caesarean" text-type**.[9]

---

6. David Alan Black, *New Testament Textual Criticism: A Concise Guide* (Grand Rapids: Baker, 1994), 18.

7. See Pasquale Orsini and Willy Clarysee, "Early New Testament Manuscripts and Their Dates: A Critique of Theological Palaeography," *Ephemerides Theologicae Lovanienses* 88.4 (2012): 443–74.

8. Bruce M. Metzger, *Manuscripts of the Greek Bible: An Introduction to Greek Paleography* (New York: Oxford University Press, 1981), 21.

9. Originally these designations were associated with geographical areas. For example, the Alexandrian text-type was so named because of a presumed connection to Alexandria, Egypt, while the Western text-type was associated with Italy, Gaul, and North Africa, and the Byzantine text-type with the empire of that name centered in Asia Minor. More recently these geographical connections are seen as tenuous, but the names of the text-types remain. In reality, many important manuscripts defy easy categorization as any single "**text-type**."

2.1.2 CHANGES AND ERRORS IN TRANSMISSION

Because all biblical documents were copied by hand for nearly three thousand years, it is not surprising that the manuscripts contain differences. While there is a range in degree and nature of the variants, several common scribal mistakes account for the majority of the differences in the biblical manuscripts. Some mistakes are similar to the kind anyone would make when copying a text by hand, but others are unique to the ways ancient Greek or Hebrew were written.

Because the earliest Greek manuscripts were written in **scriptio continua** (all capital letters with no spaces between words), and Hebrew does not distinguish between upper- and lowercase letters[10] and was originally written without vowels, a number of difficulties can arise in determining the actual wording and sentence structure intended by the original author. In addition, for the most part, neither language incorporated punctuation, paragraphing, section headings, or end-of-the-line hyphenation. Some manuscripts were written down by scribes as the text was read aloud to them, increasing the possibility for misunderstanding. The combination of these features resulted in a challenging task for copyists—even those working in their first language—as well as for translators working in a second (or third or fourth) language.

The following English versions of Genesis 1:1–2 in the OT and John 1:1 in the NT, presented in a style similar to ancient Hebrew and Greek, will give you a sense of the situation scribes and translators encountered:

Genesis 1:1–2	John 1:1–2
n th bgnnng gd crtd th hvns nd th rth nw th rth ws frmlss nd mpty nd drknss ws vr th fc f th dp nd th sprt f gd ws hvrng vr th srfc f th wtrs	INTHEBEGINNINGWASTHE WORDANDTHEWORDWASWITH GODANDTHEWORDWASGOD THISONEWASINTHE BEGINNINGWITHGOD

---

10. The Hebrew does use a different final form for some letters. Many assume that Hebrew manuscripts were also written without division between the words, but the earliest available manuscripts do not support this. However, scholars have discovered variants that reflect improper division of words, so it is possible that words were not divided in earlier stages of the written language. We do not have direct evidence to prove this (Tov, *Textual Criticism* [3rd ed.], 196–97, 234–35). See also Ellis R. Brotzman and Eric J. Tully, *Old Testament Textual Criticism: A Practical Introduction*, 2nd ed. (Grand Rapids: Baker, 2016), 23–25.

The process of copying and recopying such texts resulted in many unintentional errors of spelling, omission, and addition. Manuscripts also reflect intentional changes that scribes and translators made to the text to smooth out syntax, clarify meaning, or add information. Every change—intentional or not—resulted in textual variants for textual critics to sort out. The most common types of variants are discussed in the following pages.

2.1.2.a Omissions

During the process of copying, scribes sometimes inadvertently omitted letters, words, or even phrases that were in their source document or **exemplar**. Textual critics are able to discern the reason for many common errors, as we illustrate in the following sections. At the same time, some errors defy ready explanation. We illustrate these below as well.

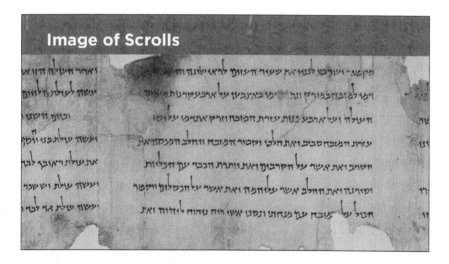

2.1.2.a.1 General Omissions

Three examples will suffice to demonstrate textual omissions that scholars cannot fully explain: Genesis 4:8; 1 Samuel 13:1; Ephesians 1:1.

Genesis 4:8 records that, in response to Yahweh's invitation to do what is right (Gen 4:6–7), Cain speaks to his brother. It goes on to state that when the brothers are in a field together, Cain kills Abel. The literal translation of the **Masoretic Text**, the traditional Hebrew text, is, "And Cain said to Abel, his brother. And it was when they were in the field, Cain rose up against Abel, his brother, and killed him." Ancient translations include

Cain's words, "Let us go out to the field" (see the **Septuagint**, **Peshitta**, **Samaritan Pentateuch**, and **Vulgate**), indicating that either something fell out of the Hebrew text or all the translations added something. Scholars are unable to explain how the phrase "Let us go out to the field" disappeared from the Hebrew.

Many English translations simply make the best of the Hebrew. Others incorporate the variant reading of the ancient translations and include a marginal note specifying that the quotation is not in the Hebrew. Compare the following English translations:

ESV	KJV	LEB	NIV
Cain spoke to Abel his brother. And when they were in the field, Cain rose up against his brother Abel and killed him.	And Cain talked with Abel his brother: and it came to pass, when they were in the field, that Cain rose up against Abel his brother, and slew him.	Then Cain said to his brother Abel, "*Let us go out into the field.*" And when they were in the field, Cain rose up against his brother Abel and killed him	Now Cain said to his brother Abel, 'Let's go out to the field.' While they were in the field, Cain attacked his brother Abel and killed him.

In a second example, 1 Samuel 13:1–2 summarizes the reign of King Saul, but the numbers in the verse are confused. Compare the following English translations:

ESV	NIV	NRSV	KJV	LEB
Saul lived for one year and then became king, and when he had reigned for two years over Israel.	Saul was thirty years old when he became king, and he reigned over Israel forty-two years.	Saul was ... years old when he began to reign; and he reigned ... and two years over Israel.	Saul reigned one year; and when he had reigned two years over Israel.	Saul was thirty years old at the beginning of his reign, and he reigned forty-two years over Israel.

The NRSV translates the Masoretic Text most literally, but many English translations deduce a number based on the fuller narrative. The Septuagint does not help in this case since many Greek manuscripts lack the entire verse. Other Greek manuscripts have "thirty," while still others reflect the Masoretic Text.[11]

A final example is found in Paul's letter to the Ephesians. In Ephesians 1:1, Paul identifies himself as the author of the letter and addresses his audience of saints. The vast majority of English translations say that Paul wrote to the saints *in Ephesus* (e.g., ESV, NASB, KJV, NIV, NRSV), but a handful do not specify Ephesus as the letter's destination (e.g., RSV). The phrase "in Ephesus" is not in the earliest and best manuscripts.[12] The difference in the English translations reflects a textual variant in the Greek.

2.1.2.a.2 Haplography

Some omissions of text occur when a copyist missed a portion of a repeated sequence of letters or words. The result is a **haplography**—a "single writing" in place of a "double" repetition present in the exemplar. Such oversight could be caused by the scribe's eyes skipping from one word or letter combination to another word or letter combination that is similar or identical. For example, an English typist could easily type "to th ends of the arth," unintentionally skipping one *e* where there were two intended.[13] Haplography often occurs because of *homoeoteleuton* (literally, "same ending"), when two lines in the exemplar end in the same way. This type of error occurs in both Testaments, as illustrated below.

---

11. Tov, *Textual Criticism* (3rd ed.), 10–11.

12. Thus, this may be an issue of addition rather than omission. It could be, for example, that Paul intended the letter as an encyclical, to be circulated among a group of churches in the region. The words "in Ephesus" may have been added to the copy that was sent to that city, which then became the main (but not only) copy to be reproduced. This is more broadly discussed by, e.g., C. E. Arnold, "Ephesians, Letter to The: Destination," DPL 244–45; F. F. Bruce, "Nature and Purpose of Ephesians," in *The Epistles to the Colossians, to Philemon and to the Ephesians*, NICNT (Grand Rapids: Eerdmans, 1984), 240–46; and Andrew T. Lincoln, "Setting and Purposes," in *Ephesians*, WBC (Dallas: Word, 1990), lxxiii–lxxxvii. See also Derek R. Brown, "The Letter's Destination," in *Lexham Bible Guide: Ephesians* (Bellingham, WA: Lexham Press, 2013).

13. Obviously, the use of *scriptio continua* in the early Greek manuscripts would make haplography even more likely.

Old Testament Examples

Judges 20:13. In the Masoretic Text, the end of Judges 20:13 says, "But Benjamin [בנימן, *bnymn*] were not willing to listen." The plural verb "were" with the singular subject "Benjamin" hints that something is not right in this text. The marginal notes of the Masoretic Text (the **qere**) indicate that the text should read, "But the sons of Benjamin [בני בנימן, *bny bnymn*] were not willing to listen." The mistake occurred when the **scribe** missed the word בני (*bny*, "sons of") because the very next word (בנימן, *bnymn*, "Benjamin") repeats the three letters בני (*bny*). This same error occurs elsewhere in the OT (e.g., 1 Chr 7:6).

1 Samuel 9:16. The Masoretic Text of 1 Samuel 9:16 reads, in part, "And you shall anoint him to be prince over my people [עמי, *'ammi*] Israel, and he will deliver my people [עמי, *'ammi*] from the hand of the Philistines for I have seen my people [עמי, *'ammi*]." Nearly every English translation follows this reading. However, the final clause in the Septuagint has, "I have seen the affliction of my people." The otherwise unnecessary addition of the phrase "the affliction of" in the Greek suggests that a word has fallen out of the Hebrew. Two factors could have contributed this. First, "my people" occurs three times in the short span of this verse, making it a prime candidate for haplography. Second, the Hebrew word for "the affliction of," עני (*'ani*), shares two Hebrew letters with עמי (*'ammi*, "my people"), suggesting that the scribe missed the word עני (*'ani*) because of its similarity to עמי (*'ammi*, "my people"), which he was already writing three times.

New Testament Example

1 Thessalonians 2:7. In 1 Thessalonians 2:7, Paul compares his ministry work in Thessalonica to a mother caring for her children. Some Greek manuscripts say he and his colleagues "became gentle" (compare ESV, NASB, KJV, NIV), while others say, "we became infants" (compare NET, NLT). The expression "became gentle" reflects the Greek phrase ἐγενήθημεν ἤπιοι (*egenēthēmen ēpioi*), while "we became infants" is from the Greek phrase ἐγενήθημεν νήπιοι (*egenēthēmen nēpioi*). The only difference between these two expressions is the *nu* (or *n*) at the beginning of the second word. New Testament textual critic David Black considers the latter to be correct and says the first reading developed by haplography: The scribe skipped over the *nu* at the beginning of νήπιοι (*nēpioi*) because the preceding word, ἐγενήθημεν (*egenēthēmen*), ended with an *nu*.[14]

2.1.2.a.3 Parablepsis

The term **parablepsis** applies to scribal errors caused by the eye skipping from one part of the text to another. It is similar to haplography in that it often involves an omission of text caused by repeated letters, words, or phrases. However, parablepsis is not just the omission of the repeated element; it involves jumping from one repeated element to another and omitting everything in between. When copying a manuscript, the scribe's eyes skipped "from one letter or cluster of letters to a similar looking line," unintentionally leaving out the material between the two.[15] Technically, parablepsis could also be responsible for textual additions if the scribe loses his place on the page or in the line and writes a word or phrase over again (see §2.1.2.b.1 Dittography below). Examples of omission by parablepsis are present in both Testaments.

Old Testament Examples

1 Samuel 14:41. The Masoretic Text of 1 Samuel 14:41 says, "And Saul said to Yahweh, God of Israel, 'Give a perfect lot.' And Jonathan and Saul were captured, but the people escaped." Several English translations reflect this reading (e.g., NASB, JPS, NIV, LEB). However, in other English translations, Saul's speech is significantly longer: "Then Saul said, 'O LORD God of Israel, why have you not answered your servant today? If this guilt is in me or in my son Jonathan, O LORD God of Israel, give Urim; but if this guilt is in your people [Israel], give Thummim.' And Jonathan and Saul were indicted by the lot, but the people were cleared" (NRSV; compare NET, ESV). These longer translations are based on the Septuagint's translation of 1 Samuel 14:41, in which the word "Israel" occurs three times (the English translations do not reflect these three occurrences). It appears that in the Masoretic Text, the scribe's eyes skipped from the first occurrence

---

14. Black, *New Testament Textual Criticism*, 60. See also Derek R. Brown, "Were They Gentle or Infants?," in *Lexham Bible Guide: 1 Thessalonians* (Bellingham, WA: Lexham Press, 2012). This example is covered in more detail in §4.3.4.b 1 Thessalonians 2:7.

15. Matthew S. DeMoss, *Pocket Dictionary for the Study of New Testament Greek* (Downers Grove, IL: InterVarsity, 2001), 92.

of "Israel" to the third (indicated in brackets in the NRSV translation here), and he omitted everything in between.[16]

1 Kings 8:16 and 2 Chronicles 6:5-6. Much of the material in 1–2 Chronicles is parallel to earlier texts in Samuel and Kings, and comparisons of parallel passages sometimes reveal instances of parablepsis. Consider the following verses:

1 Kings 8:16	2 Chronicles 6:5-6
From the day that I brought out my people Israel from Egypt I have not chosen a city from all the tribes of Israel to build a house where my name might be, but I have chosen David to be over my people Israel.	From the day that I brought my people out of the land of Egypt I did not choose a city among all the tribes of Israel to build a house in order for my name to be there. Nor did I choose a man to be leader over my people Israel. But I have chosen my name to be there in Jerusalem, and I have chosen David to be over my people Israel.

The omitted section in 1 Kings 8:16 falls between two occurrences of the Hebrew word שָׁם (šām, "there"), shaded above (note that in Hebrew, the phrase "in Jerusalem" falls before "there"). It appears that the scribe's eyes skipped from the first "there" (שָׁם, šām) to the second, and he inadvertently omitted everything in between.

New Testament Examples

John 17:15. In **Codex Vaticanus**, a strange reading in Jesus' high priestly prayer—οὐκ ἐρωτῶ ἵνα ἄρῃς αὐτοὺς ἐκ τοῦ πονηροῦ (ouk erōtō hina arēs autous ek tou ponērou, "I do not ask that you should take them from the evil one")—is almost certainly due to *homoeoteleuton* in its exemplar. Two lines may have ended with the same words, and the scribe's eye skipped from the first to the second, causing the text in between to be accidentally omitted. The exemplar of Vaticanus probably looked like this:

---

16. P. Kyle McCarter Jr., *Textual Criticism: Recovering the Text of the Hebrew Bible*, Guides to Biblical Scholarship Old Testament (Philadelphia: Fortress, 1985), 41.

ΟΥΚΕΡΩΤΩΙΝΑΑΡΗΣ**ΑΥΤΟΥΣΕΚΤΟΥ**
ΚΟΣΜΟΥΑΛΛΙΝΑΤΗΡΗΣΗΣ**ΑΥΤΟΥΣΕΚΤΟΥ**
ΠΟΝΗΡΟΥ...
I do not pray that You should take **them from the**
[world but that You should keep **them from the**]
evil one...

1 John 2:23. Nearly all English translations of 1 John 2:23 reflect a Greek text that has two occurrences of "has the father" (τὸν πατέρα ἔχει, *ton patera echei*), each phrase ending its clause in the Greek: "Everyone who denies the Son does not have the Father; the one who confesses the Son has the Father also." However, some manuscripts lack the last clause entirely. In these cases, the scribe's eye jumped from the first occurrence of τὸν πατέρα ἔχει (*ton patera echei*)i to the second, and he thought he had completed the verse.[17]

2.1.2.b Additions

2.1.2.b.1 Dittography

In contrast to skipping over letters, words, or sections, scribes sometimes unintentionally wrote things twice. This "double writing" or **dittography** could involve a single letter or several words. Emanuel Tov notes that the components in some manuscripts may not even be identical, "since at a later stage one of the two words was sometimes adapted to the context."[18] Examples from both Testaments are below.

Old Testament Examples

Jeremiah 51:3. In the Masoretic Text, Jeremiah 51:3 reads, "Let not the archer draw draw his bow," with the word "draw" (ידרך, *yidrokh*) appearing twice. The Septuagint, the Targums, the Peshitta, and the Vulgate all omit the second occurrence. The **Masoretes** recognized the error and left the second word unvocalized—that is, they did not mark vowels to go with the consonants.[19]

---

17. Black, *New Testament Textual Criticism*, 60.

18. Tov, *Textual Criticism* (3rd ed.), 224.

19. McCarter says it is possible that Jer 51:3 is not dittography but a combination of two readings: "let him not draw" and "let him draw" (*Textual Criticism*, 30n3).

Leviticus 20:10. The laws of Leviticus 20 in the Masoretic Text include the following sentence for adulterers: "If there is a man who commits adultery with the wife of a man who commits adultery with the wife of his neighbor, he shall be put to death" (compare NASB, ASV, JPS, KJV). Many translations consider the second occurrence of "a man who commits adultery with the wife of" (אִישׁ אֲשֶׁר יִנְאַף אֶת־אֵשֶׁת, 'îš 'ăšer yin'ap 'et- 'ēšet) to be dittography and omit it (see, e.g., ESV, NAB, NRSV).

New Testament Examples

Mark 3:16. In Mark 3:16, **Codex Sinaiticus**, Codex Vaticanus, and several other manuscripts insert "And he appointed the twelve" in front of "and he gave the name Peter to Simon." Paul Wegner says the phrase "and he appointed the twelve" (καὶ ἐποίησεν τοὺς δώδεκα, *kai epoiēsen tous dōdeka*) may represent dittography with the same phrase from Mark 3:14.[20] However, the NET Bible's explanation illustrates the difficulty of determining what kind of textual error occurred. The NET says that haplography has occurred:

> The first word of the clause in question is καὶ (*kai*), and the first word after the clause in question is also καὶ. And the first two letters of the second word, in each instance, are ἐπ (*ep*). Early scribes most likely jumped accidentally from the first καὶ to the second, omitting the intervening material. Thus, the clause was most likely in the original text.[21]

Metzger reports that the editorial committee of the United Bible Societies' (UBS) and Nestle-Aland (NA) Greek texts recognized the possibility of dittography but felt the words should be kept in the main text:

> The clause seems to be needed in order to pick up the thread of ver. 14 after the parenthesis ἵνα ... δαιμόνια. In order to reflect the balance of both external evidence and internal considerations, the Committee decided to retain the words within square brackets.[22]

---

20. Wegner, *Student's Guide*, 48.

21. Mark 3:16, note 32, in *The NET Bible: First Edition Notes* (Richardson, TX: Biblical Studies Press, 2006), https://net.bible.org/#!bible/Mark+3:16.

22. Bruce M. Metzger, *A Textual Commentary on the Greek New Testament*, 2nd ed. (Stuttgart: Deutsche Bibelgesellschaft , 1994), 69.

Acts 19:34. In Codex Vaticanus, the cry of the townspeople, "Great is Artemis of the Ephesians!" is written twice. In all other manuscripts, it is only written once. This dittography could have resulted from the immediately preceding word for "crying," which has the same ending letters as "of the Ephesians." It looks like this: κράζοντων μεγάλη ἡ Ἄρτεμις Ἐφεσίων (*krazontōn megalē hē Artemis Ephesiōn*).

2.1.2.b.2 Conflation

Sometimes scribes combined elements found in two or more manuscripts and created a longer reading. This combination is called **conflation**. Conflation may have resulted when the scribe was unwilling to choose between the two variants and thus included both. Some instances of conflation could have been unintentional errors, when a scribe inadvertently added something from another text in his memory, such as a wording difference from the Gospel of Luke that naturally flows out of the scribe's memory when copying the same story in Mark (see also §2.1.2.d.2 Harmonization below). Conflation may also have resulted when explanatory marginal notes or corrections in a manuscript were integrated—whether intentionally or not—into the running text in the new manuscript (see also §2.1.2.b.3 Glosses below).[23] Examples of conflation are present in both the OT and NT.

Old Testament Example

2 Samuel 22:38–39. In 2 Samuel 22:38–39, David boasts that he pursued his enemies and destroyed them. He declares that they did not turn back "until they were consumed. I consumed them" (ESV). The Hebrew of the Masoretic Text reads עד כלותם ואכלם (*'ad kallōtām wā'ekallēm*). However, a manuscript of 2 Samuel from the Dead Sea Scrolls (4QSam[a]) has simply "until they were consumed" (עד כלותם, *'ad kallōtām*), while the Septuagint reading, "until I (have) consumed them," indicates a Hebrew **Vorlage** that said עד אכלם (*'ad 'ekallēm*). McCarter asserts the Masoretic Text is a

---

23. Tov describes how a marginal note in Isa 36:11 of the Great Isaiah Scroll from Qumran could easily have been absorbed into the main text. See his discussion and the corresponding photographs of the manuscript (Tov, *Textual Criticism* [3rd ed.], 225, 385).

conflation, in which a scribe combined the variants represented in 4QSam[a] and the Septuagint.[24]

New Testament Example

Luke 24:53. Most English translations indicate that after Jesus' ascension, His disciples were continually in the temple "blessing" God (e.g., ESV, NRS, NET) or "praising" God (e.g., NASB, NIV, NLT). Some translations say the disciples were both "blessing" and "praising" God (e.g., KJV). These differences reflect variants in Greek manuscripts. The main Western **witness**, **Codex Bezae** (05), says the disciples were "praising" God (αἰνοῦντες, *ainountes*), but the Alexandrian manuscripts P75, Sinaiticus, Vaticanus, and several others have εὐλογοῦντες (*eulogountes*), which can be translated "praising" but normally means "blessing." The Byzantine text, which is prone to conflation, as well as a number of manuscripts included in the Caesarean grouping, have αἰνοῦντες καὶ εὐλογοῦντες (*ainountes kai eulogountes*, "praising and blessing").[25]

2.1.2.b.3 Glosses

In the course of using their copies of the Bible, early believers sometimes wrote explanations, interpretations of words or phrases, or commentaries of the church fathers in the margins of the manuscript or between the lines of text. An explanation of this type is called a **gloss**. In the case of the earliest OT texts transmission took place over hundreds of years, so that the manuscripts would have contained outdated references that were meaningless to a changing readership. As a modern example, if a researcher on the history of Rye Country Day School came across the name Barbara Pierce in copies of school documents, he might write "Bush" in the margin or above "Pierce" in the text. If others used his notes later in their own work, they might simply refer to "Barbara Bush," or they might even conflate the "variants" and refer to "Barbara Pierce Bush." When similar glosses occurred in handwritten biblical manuscripts, it was not always

---

24. McCarter, *Textual Criticism*, 37.

25. Black, *New Testament Textual Criticism*, 61. Black considers this to be conflation, but he admits that parablepsis may explain the difference instead (i.e., some manuscripts omitted one or the other of the words). For a more detailed discussion of this variation unit, see Metzger, *Textual Commentary*, 163–64.

clear to later copyists whether a marginal note was an addition or an accidentally omitted word inserted by the earlier scribe.[26]

Old Testament Examples

Genesis 14:3. In Genesis 14 Abraham engages in battle to rescue his nephew
Lot. According to Genesis 14:3, his opponents gathered in "the Valley of
Siddim (that is, the Salt Sea)." While we have no manuscript evidence in
which "that is, the Salt Sea" appears in a margin, it is plausible that this
short explanation was added during the transmission of the text to ensure
later readers knew where the Valley of Siddim was located.[27]

Joshua 20:3. Joshua 20 identifies who can take refuge in the new cities of
refuge in the promised land: "Anyone who kills a person by accident or
unintentionally." The Hebrew word here for "accident," שגגה (shegāgâ), is
somewhat obscure. The next word, "unintentionally," literally translates
"without knowledge" (בבלי־דעת, biblî-da'at). This second phrase is absent in
the Septuagint and the Vulgate, suggesting it was added in the Masoretic
Text to explain the obscure שגגה (shegāgâ, "[by] accident").[28]

New Testament Examples

Luke 23:17. You will find that most modern English translations do not
contain Luke 23:17. In the middle of Pilate's interaction with the Jewish
leaders concerning the fate of Jesus, after he offers to let Jesus go (Luke
23:16), the NKJV, however, says: "For it was necessary for him to release one
to them at the feast." Many witnesses contain this reading, including Codex
Sinaiticus. But Codex Bezae has it after verse 19. And it is not found at all
in P75, **Codex Alexandrinus**, Codex Vaticanus, half a dozen other Greek
manuscripts, one Vulgate (Latin) copy, and much of the Coptic evidence.
It can easily be imagined that an early Christian might have written an

---

26. Tov admits that "direct evidence for this practice is lacking for the Hebrew Bible,"
but scholars assume it occurred based on "parallels of marginal and interlinear additions in
Sumerian, Akkadian, Ugaritic, and other texts" (*Textual Criticism* [3rd ed.], 260).

27. Similarly, in Gen 14:14, Abraham is said to pursue the coalition "up to Dan." Dan was
known as Laish during the patriarch's time and didn't acquire the name Dan (after Jacob's son)
until sometime after the conquest (Josh 19:47; Judg 18:29). It appears that a scribe updated the
text of Gen 14:14 without preserving the original text, which likely said "Laish."

28. McCarter, *Textual Criticism*, 33.

explanatory gloss in the margin of Luke to explain why Pilate would offer to release a prisoner. Some copies incorporated this gloss after verse 16, and the ancestor of Codex Bezae put it after verse 19 because it was helpful for understanding. Otherwise it is difficult to explain, as Metzger writes, "its widespread omission and its presence at two different places. The verse is a gloss, apparently based on Mt 27.15 and Mk 15.6."[29]

John 5:3b–4. The NKJV for John 5:3-5 reads as follows: "In these lay a great multitude of sick people, blind, lame, paralyzed, *waiting for the moving of the water. For an angel went down at a certain time into the pool and stirred up the water; then whoever stepped in first, after the stirring of the water, was made well of whatever disease he had.* Now a certain man was there who had an infirmity of thirty-eight years" (compare KJV, NASB). However, the LEB of John 5:3-5 leaves out 3b–4 (italicized above) and reads: "In these were lying a large number of those who were sick, blind, lame, paralyzed. And a certain man was there who had been thirty-eight years in his sickness" (compare ESV, NIV, NRSV). Many late manuscripts, representing the Byzantine textual grouping, contain the longer reading, while the best and earliest manuscripts do not (e.g., P66, P75, Sinaiticus, Vaticanus, and Bezae). This suggests that John 5:3b–4 may have originated as an explanatory gloss written in the margin of one or more manuscripts to help the reader understand why people were lying in the porticoes of Bethesda. At some point during textual transmission, the gloss was incorporated into the text itself.

2.1.2.c Misspellings

A large number of textual variants are the result of spelling differences or errors. It may be that the spelling of a word changed over time. Some differences occurred when a scribe inadvertently switched letters, words, or sounds around in the course of copying. Others were the result of sloppy penmanship that made it difficult for a copyist to discern what his source manuscript read. Still others happened when scribes misheard manuscripts being read aloud for them to record. Consider a room full of English speakers asked to write the word "occurrence." Some might write "occurence," while others might write "ocurence" or "ocurrence."

---

29. Metzger, *Textual Commentary*, 153.

2.1.2.c.1 Metathesis

Metathesis is the accidental transposing of letters, words, or even sounds. Tov and Kyle McCarter define metathesis more narrowly as the inadvertent switching of two adjacent letters,[30] but David Black allows for entire words to metathesize,[31] and Matthew DeMoss says transposition of sequential sounds is also metathesis.[32] Both the OT and NT contain examples of metathesis.

Old Testament Example

Deuteronomy 31:1. English translations of Deuteronomy 31:1 differ in their understanding of Moses' actions prior to appointing Joshua as his successor (Deut 31:2-6). Some say he finished speaking, referring to his speech in the preceding chapters (compare NAB, RLT, NRSV); many others say he continued speaking (or "went and spoke"; compare ESV, NASB, NIV). This difference reflects two variants in the manuscripts. The Masoretic Text records, "And Moses went and spoke" (וילך משה וידבר, *wayyelek mōše wayədabbēr*), but the Septuagint reflects a Hebrew manuscript stating, "And Moses finished and he spoke" (ויכל משה וידבר, *wayəkal mōše wayədabbēr*). The difference between "and ... went" (וילך, *wylk*) and "and ... finished" (ויכל, *wykl*) is the arrangement of the last two consonants, *kāp* (כ/ך, *k*) and *lāmed* (ל, *l*). Whichever rendering is original, the variants clearly arose from metathesis.

New Testament Examples

Mark 14:65. When Jesus stood before the council of Jewish leaders, the guards "received him with slaps in the face" (LEB; compare ESV, NRSV, NASB). However, the KJV (compare NKJV) says the guards "did strike him with the palms of their hands." The texts agree in recording that the guards struck Jesus, but they disagree about whether the striking is represented by two words/phrases or whether one of the words/phrases is one of receiving. The difference here reflects the variant ἔλαβον (*elabon*, "received")

---

30. Tov, *Textual Criticism* (3rd ed.), 232–33; McCarter, *Textual Criticism*, 3.

31. Black, *New Testament Textual Criticism*, 59.

32. DeMoss, *Pocket Dictionary*, 84.

versus ἔβαλον (ebalon, "struck")—words in which the Greek letters β (beta, b) and λ (lambda, l) have been transposed.

John 1:42. In John 1, when Peter's brother, Andrew, brings him to Jesus, Jesus says, "You are Simon the son of John ['Ιωάννης, Iōannēs]" (LEB, ESV, NASB). In the NKJV, however, Jesus greets Peter and calls him the "son of Jonah ['Ιωνᾶς, Iōnas]" (compare "Jona" in KJV). This variant involves metathesis, as well as the omission of several letters. In Greek, here "John" is spelled 'Ιωάννου (Iōannou), while "Jonah" is spelled 'Ιωνα (Iōna). In this case, the α (alpha) and ν (nu) may have been transposed.[33]

2.1.2.c.2 Mistaken Letters

Other misspellings in manuscripts arose when scribes mistook letters for other, similar-looking letters. Such mistakes could have been caused by the exemplar—perhaps it was damaged or not written clearly—or they could have resulted from the copyist—he or she may have been working in poor light, may have suffered from poor eyesight, or may have failed to examine the exemplar carefully. For whatever reason, the scribe read the text as representing a different word or combination of words than intended. Examples from both Testaments are below.

Old Testament Examples

Genesis 10:4 and 1 Chronicles 1:7. The Table of Nations in Genesis 10 identifies a group of people known as the "Dodanim" (דדנים). However, 1 Chronicles 1:7 refers to the same group as the "Rodanim" (רדנים). Most scholars think 1 Chronicles 1:7 is correct and that Genesis 10:4 demonstrates a misreading of the Hebrew ר (resh, r) for the very similar looking ד (dalet, d).

Isaiah 63:6. In an oracle against Edom, Yahweh says he trampled nations in his anger and "made them drunk in [his] wrath" (LEB; compare NASB, NIV, KJV). However, the NRSV translates the same clause as "I crushed them

---

33. It is also possible that the author of John assimilated this reference to Matthew 16:17, where Jesus calls Peter "Simon Bar-Jonah." But note that different words for "son" are used in Matthew 16:17 (bar) and John 1:42 (huios). A further potential cause for confusion is that some minuscule manuscripts use a **nomen sacrum** for Ιωαννης (iōannēs), writing it as ιω̅ (iō).

in my wrath." The difference between "made them drunk" and "crushed them" is one Hebrew letter: "Made them drunk" translates the Hebrew verb שׁכר (*škr*), while "crushed them" translates the verb שׁבר (*šbr*). The letters כ (*kaph, k*) and ב (*bet, b*) are often confused.

New Testament Examples

Romans 6:5. Two ninth-century **majuscules**, 010 and 012,[34] which are normally representatives of the Western text of Paul's letters, apparently both descend from a common ancestor in which the double *lambda* of ἀλλα (*alla*, "but, yet, certainly") was confused with the letter *mu*, so that in this verse they both read ἁμα (*hama*, "together"). The meaning changes from "*certainly* we shall be in the likeness of his resurrection" to "*together* we shall be in the likeness of his resurrection."

1 Timothy 3:16. Paul begins his expression of the mystery of godliness with the words "*He who* was revealed in the flesh" (NASB; compare LEB, ESV, NIV, NRSV). However, the KJV begins, "*God* was manifest in the flesh" (compare NKJV).[35] The Greek pronoun behind the translation "He who" is ὅς (*hos*), while the Greek word behind the KJV translation "God" is θεός (*theos*). In most Christian documents, it was the norm to use the **nomen sacrum** for θεός, which is θ̅ς̅ (*ths*).[36] In the oldest manuscripts of the Greek New

---

34. A majuscule is a manuscript written in capital letters. These closely related manuscripts are also named, respectively, F (or Codex Augiensis) and G (or Codex Boernerianus) of the Paulines, not to be confused with F and G of the Gospels. (Because many manuscripts contained only a section of the Bible, one solution that was tried after scholars ran out of Latin letters for naming them was to give the same letter to a majuscule Gospel book and to a majuscule Pauline collection.)

35. The NLT translates "Christ was revealed in a human body," but not for the same reason the KJV and NKJV translate "God." The NLT is making explicit what the pronoun "he" or "who" implies. The KJV and NKJV read the proper noun "God," not a pronoun.

36. The Latin *nomen sacrum* (or the plural: *nomina sacra*, meaning "sacred names") is a common technical term for the Greek abbreviations found in NT manuscripts for words referring to sacred things. Their usage ranges from abbreviating the names "Jesus" and "Christ" to terms for sacred places such as Jerusalem or "heaven" to general words such as "savior," "son," or "father" when used in reference to God or Jesus. Scholars are not certain why Christians began to use *nomina sacra* to abbreviate a group of about fourteen words (such as "God," "Lord," "Christ," "Jesus," "Son," "Father," "Spirit," etc.), but one theory is that it is an echo of the Jewish practice of writing the Hebrew divine name "Yahweh" as יהוה (*YHWH*). For a thorough treatment of the *nomina sacra*, see Larry Hurtado, *The Earliest Christian Artifacts: Manuscripts and Christian Origins* (Grand Rapids: Eerdmans, 2006), 95–134. See also Metzger, *Manuscripts of the Greek Bible*, 33–38, and J. Scott Porter, *Principles of Textual Criticism, with Their Application to the Old and New Testaments* (London: Simms and M'intyre, 1848), 26.

Testament (GNT), which were written in majuscule script (all capital letters), without breathing marks or accents, the pronoun for "he who" (ΟΣ) could easily be confused with the *nomen sacrum* for "God" ($\overline{\Theta\Sigma}$).[37]

2.1.2.c.3 Homophony

Another type of spelling error resulted from **homophony**—confusion of words that sound alike but are spelled differently. A common English *homophone* is the trio of words "their," "they're," and "there." Even people familiar with the words can easily confuse them. In Greek, for example, there are a number of vowels and diphthongs (double vowels) for which the pronunciations came to be identical over time. These are η (*ē*), ι (*i*), υ (*y*), and ει (*ei*), and sometimes οι (*oi*) and υι (*ui*). Confusing these letters is referred to as **itacism**. In manuscripts of the Bible, itacisms and other mistakes of homophony could have occurred when a scribe copied from another manuscript, but they are more likely to have occurred when scribes wrote down texts that were read aloud to them.

Old Testament Examples

Isaiah 9:3. The Masoretic Text of Isaiah 9:3 speaks of the coming righteous king and what the nation will be like under his reign: "You have multiplied the nation; you have not increased the joy."[38] From early on scribes recognized an error of homophony here and wrote a correction in the margins so that the text would be read "You have multiplied the nation; you have increased its joy." The confusion is between the words לֹא (*lō'*, "not") and לוֹ (*lô*, "to it"). Most English translations follow the marginal correction of the Masoretes. The original KJV retains the error ("Thou has multiplied the nation, and not increased the joy"), but the NKJV makes the correction ("You have multiplied the nation and increased its joy").

1 Kings 1:18. English translations are fairly evenly divided in their rendering of the second half of 1 Kings 1:18. Some translations say "and now, my

---

37. That papyrus was used for writing material may have added to the likelihood of this textual change occurring. The fibers running through the text may have either caused an accidental change or even suggested to the mind of the scribe that $\overline{\Theta\Sigma}$ would be a helpful clarification for ΟΣ.

38. In the Hebrew, it is Isa 9:2.

lord the king" (compare LEB, NASB, KJV), while others say "and you, my lord the king" (compare ESV, JPS, NRSV). The difference is in the phrases ועתה (wəʿattâ, "and now") and ואתה (wəʾattâ, "and you"). The difference between these two pronunciations can be difficult to detect. In transliteration it is as slight as the direction of the apostrophe-like letter. In the first the letter is ע (ayin, ʿ), and in the second, the letter is א (aleph, ʾ); both are guttural (or **pharyngeal**) letters. While many English readers, unfamiliar with guttural letters (since English has none), pronounce these letters the same (namely, not at all), they also sounded similar enough to Hebrew scribes that at times they were confused.

New Testament Examples

Romans 5:1. Most English translations of Romans 5 include the statement "we have peace with God." This clause is translated from the Greek verb ἔχομεν (echomen, "we have") in the indicative form, which communicates that the idea of the verb is real—not simply possible. When a verbal form communicates that something is possible or intended, it is subjunctive. In the case of Romans 5:1, use of the subjunctive form, ἔχωμεν (echōmen), would mean, "Let us have peace with God." As you can see, the difference between the two verbal forms here is one vowel: "we have" is ἔχομεν (echomen), while "let us have" is ἔχωμεν (echōmen). The omicron (ο, o) and omega (ω, ō) are easily confused sounds. New Testament manuscripts attest both readings, though most English translations have chosen the indicative: "we have peace with God."

Revelation 4:3. This text reads in nearly all manuscripts:

ΚΑΙΠΡΙΣΚΥΚΛΟΘΕΝΤΟΥΘΡΟΝΟΥΟΜΟΙΟΣΟΡΑΣΕΙΣΜΑΡΑ
ΓΔΙΝΩ[39]
"and a rainbow encircled the throne, in appearance like an emerald"

However, Codex Sinaiticus and Codex Alexandrinus, as well as a tenth-century **minuscule**, 2329, have—independently—accidentally changed the meaning as a result of itacism:

---

39. καὶ ἶρις κυκλόθεν τοῦ θρόνου ὅμοιος ὁράσει σμαραγδίνῳ, kai **iris** kyklothen tou thronou homoios horasei smaragdinō

ΚΑΙΠΕΡΕΙΣΚΥΚΛΟΘΕΝΤΟΥΘΡΟΝΟΥΟΜΟΙΟΣΟΡΑΣΕΙΣΜΑΡΑ
ΓΔΙΝΩ[40]

"and priests encircled the throne, in appearance like an emerald"

2.1.2.d Intentional Changes

Most of the textual variation described above represents unintentional changes, although some may have been intentional. However, all of the textual changes in the sections to follow appear to have been intentional. Some of the scribes' changes were as innocuous as smoothing syntax, correcting bad grammar, or updating an older spelling. Other changes reflect a concern for accuracy and consistency between similar texts. Still others demonstrate scribal zeal for theological clarity where the text may have been ambiguous.

Textual criticism is never an exact science, and the identification of intentional changes along with the rationale behind such changes can be controversial. Nonetheless, the following examples illustrate the purposes behind some changes that appear to be intentional.

2.1.2.d.1 Spelling and Grammar

Languages change over time and location, a phenomenon that is obvious in the English language. For example, "colour" and "analyse" became "color" and "analyze" when they crossed the Atlantic Ocean, and "you all" or "all of you" became "y'all" when it moved south. The languages of the Bible also changed over time and location. Hebrew changed more than Greek since the composition and transmission of the OT took place over a much longer period of time than the NT. Scribes sometimes updated spellings and grammar to reflect changes in usage.

One of the most significant changes in written Hebrew was the addition of letters to help with pronunciation. Called **matres lectionis**, Latin for "mothers of reading," these extra consonants indicated when certain vowels should be read. The most commonly used *matres* were the *yod* (ʾ) to indicate a long *i* and the *waw* (ו) to indicate a long *u* or a long *o*. *Matres* were used in some of the earliest Hebrew writings we have, but their usage

---

40. καὶ ἱερεῖς κυκλόθεν τοῦ θρόνου ὅμοιος ὁράσει σμαραγδίνῳ, *kai* **hiereis** *kyklothen tou thronou homoios horasei smaragdinō*

increased after the exile—probably to reduce ambiguity and aid readers in deciphering the intended message. Most spelling changes are insignificant in textual criticism, but sometimes variation in spelling created ambiguity—and thus uncertainty for scribes.

Old Testament Examples

1 Samuel 1:24. After the birth of her miracle son, Samuel, Hannah returned to Shiloh to make an offering. In many English translations, she offers "three bullocks" (e.g., JPS, KJV, NET, LEB), while in others she offers a "three-year-old bull" (e.g., ESV, NIV, NRSV, NASB). This discrepancy reflects a difference between the Masoretic Text and the Septuagint, which agrees with a manuscript of Samuel from the Dead Sea scrolls (4QSamᵃ). The relevant phrase in the Masoretic Text is בפרים שלשה (bĕpārîm šĕlōšâ, "three bulls"), while the Septuagint reflects a Hebrew *Vorlage* (or parent text) that said בפר משלש (bĕpar mĕšulāš, "a three-year-old bull"). Two events probably occurred to create these variants. First, the letters בפרמשלש (bprmšlš) were divided differently in the manuscripts: בפר משלש (bpr mšlš) in the Septuagint *Vorlage*, and בפרמ שלש (bprm šlš) in the parent text of the Masoretic Text. Next, changes in Hebrew spelling resulted in the addition of two *matres lectionis* letters to the phrase in the Masoretic Text: to the phrase בְּפָרִם (bĕpārīm, "with bulls") was added a *matres lectionis yod* (י) with the i vowel, making בְּפָרִים (bĕpārîm, "with bulls"); and to the long a vowel in the word שְׁלֹשָׁ (šĕlōšā, "three") was added a *matres lectionis he* (ה), making שְׁלֹשָׁה (šĕlōšâ, "three").

Psalm 84:6. The Masoretic Text of the first half of Psalm 84:6[41] says, "The ones going through the Valley of Baca make it a spring." Most English versions reflect this understanding (e.g., ESV, NASB, JPS, KJV, NIV, NRSV). However, the NET Bible translates it, "As they pass through the Valley of Baca, he provides a spring for them"—a reading that more or less reflects the Septuagint. The NAB translation indicates that those passing through Baca "find spring water to drink." These translations derive from four variants of the verb that are based on the slightest differences in spellings that changed over time. The verb form in the Masoretic Text is ישיתוהו (yĕšîtûhû, "they make it"). This verb form has two *matres lectionis*: the *yod* (י) with the i

---

41. In the Hebrew text, Ps 84:6 is verse 7.

vowel (î), and the *waw* (ו) with the first *u* vowel (û). Without these "helper" letters, the verb form could mean something else. Without the first *waw* (ו), the form would be ישׂיתהו (*yĕśîtēhû*, "he makes it"). Without the second *yod* (י) in the Masoretic Text, the form would be ישׂתוהו (*yištûhû*, "they drink it"). Without both *matres lectionis*, the form becomes ישׂתהו (*yištēhû*, "he drinks it"). McCarter calls this an "extreme example," but it demonstrates how slight variations in spelling led to four different interpretations of virtually the same letters.[42]

New Testament Example

Matthew 1:7–8. In the oldest and best manuscripts of Matthew, the genealogy of Jesus identifies the son of Abijah and the father of Jehoshaphat as Asaph (Ἀσάφ). Later manuscripts identify the same person as Asa (Ἀσά). Although the OT includes a psalmist named Asaph, the man in Matthew's genealogy was a king of Judah, Asa. Other ancient documents indicate that the name Asa had variant spellings—including Asaph. The author and early copyists of Matthew would not have mistaken the psalmist Asaph for the king Asaph/Asa, but later copyists clarified by updating the spelling to the more commonly used name.

2.1.2.d.2 Harmonization

Several biblical books have similar, even parallel content. For example, much of the content of Samuel and Kings is repeated in the books of Chronicles. The three **Synoptic Gospels** (Mark, Matthew, and Luke) also share a lot of common material. In addition to these large-scale similarities, there are shorter parallel texts, such as David's victory song, which is recorded in both 2 Samuel 22 and Psalm 18. A significant amount of repetition can occur even with a single passage, as in Genesis 1. When they encountered parallel passages or significant repetition, scribes sometimes adjusted the text so that the details matched. This process is called **harmonization**. Examples from both Testaments are below.

---

42. McCarter, *Textual Criticism*, 53.

Old Testament Example

Genesis 1:7. The account of creation in Genesis 1 includes the repeated refrain "and God saw that it was good." This phrase is not present in the Masoretic Text (or most English translations) after the second day of creation (Gen 1:7–8). However, the Septuagint of Genesis 1:7–8 does include the refrain after God "called the vaulted dome 'heaven.'" The repetition in the passage and the presence of the phrase in the Septuagint has prompted the editors of *BHS* to suggest adding "and God saw that it was good" to Genesis 1:7 so that it corresponds to what is found in Genesis 1:4, 10, 12, 18, 21, 31. The Septuagint and the editors of *BHS* appear to be harmonizing the text.[43]

New Testament Examples

Matthew 19:17. In most English translations of Matthew's account of the rich young ruler, Jesus tells the man, "there is only one who is good" (ESV, NASB, NIV, NRSV). However, the KJV renders this phrase as "there is none good but one, that is, God" (compare NKJV). The Greek manuscripts on which the KJV is based appear to have harmonized Matthew's account with the same story in Mark, where Jesus declares, "there is none good but one, that is, God" (Mark 10:18 KJV; compare NRSV, ESV, NASB, NIV).

John 19:20. The Gospel of John specifies that the inscription over Jesus' cross was written in Hebrew, Latin, and Greek: καὶ ἦν γεγραμμένον Ἑβραϊστί, Ῥωμαϊστί, Ἑλληνιστί (*kai ēn gegrammenon Hebraisti, Rhōmaisti, Hellēnisti*). The parallel passage in Luke 23:38 has no such clause in the earliest Greek manuscripts (compare ESV, NASB, NIV, NRSV), but manuscripts that align with the Byzantine textual group include it. Most scholars believe that later scribes harmonized the text in Luke with the John passage by adding the phrase (compare KJV).

2.1.2.d.3 Theological Changes

Some changes in the biblical text seem to have been made for theological reasons, whether to protect the portrayal of God or to correct what seemed to be an error in the content. While most scholars agree that such

---

43. Issues such as this are two-sided: either one version added something, or one version omitted something. It can be difficult to decide which error is more plausible in a given text.

modifications took place, Tov contends that "the number of such changes is probably smaller than is usually assumed" since most scholars use the same handful of examples.[44] When variants appear that seem to be theological in nature, scholars speculate (and often debate) whether the changes were made intentionally.

Old Testament Examples

Tiqqune sopherim. The Masoretic Text includes eighteen slight changes that scribes made because they believed the text portrayed God in a bad light and was thus irreverent.[45] Called **tiqqune sopherim** ("corrections of the scribes"), these changes include omission, transposition, and changing of consonants, as well as alteration of word order. Kelley, Mynatt, and Crawford describe an example of the *tiqqune sopherim* from Genesis 18:22:

> The text states that "Abraham stood before Yahweh." The list of emendations tells us that the text originally stated that "Yahweh stood before Abraham." Since the idiom of "standing before" someone may also imply service before that person or homage, thus denoting a state of inferiority, this statement was deemed irreverent when applied to God. The word order was changed to have Abraham standing before Yahweh.[46]

---

44. Emanuel Tov, *Textual Criticism of the Hebrew Bible*, 2nd rev. ed. (Minneapolis: Fortress, 2001), 265. Detailed arguments using such examples can be found in Bart D. Ehrman, *The Orthodox Corruption of Scripture: The Effect of Early Christological Controversies on the Text of the New Testament*, 2nd ed. (Oxford: Oxford University Press, 2011).

45. This number of emendations is based on one Masoretic tradition. Other lists disagree on the number and the exact changes that were made (Page H. Kelley, Daniel S. Mynatt, and Timothy G. Crawford, *The Masorah of "Biblia Hebraica Stuttgartensia"* [Grand Rapids: Eerdmans, 1998], 37). Kelley, Mynatt, and Crawford provide a list of the eighteen *tiqqune sopherim* as well as additional comment on the phenomenon (*Masorah*, 37–40). The Masorah Magna on Ezek 8:17 and Zech 2:12 lists eighteen emendations. The corrections are referenced four other times in rabbinic literature, with lists numbering from seven to seventeen corrections (see Christian D. Ginsburg, *Introduction to the Massoretico-Critical Edition of the Hebrew Bible* [London: Trinitarian Bible Society, 1897], 347–50). For a detailed study of this phenomenon, see Carmel McCarthy, *The Tiqqune Sopherim and Other Theological Corrections in the Masoretic Text of the Old Testament* (Göttingen: Vandenhoeck & Ruprecht, 1981).

46. Kelley, Mynatt, and Crawford, *Masorah*, 38.

The *tiqqune sopherim* almost always relate to God, but one emendation involves a statement about Moses that the scribes perceived as irreverent (Num 12:12).[47]

2 Samuel 5:21 and 1 Chronicles 14:12. These parallel passages recount a battle between the Philistines and David's forces. Second Samuel 5:21 indicates that when they fled, the Philistines "left their idols there" (עצביהם, *ăṣabbêhem*, "their images, idols"; ESV, compare NRSV, NASB, KJV). In the later text of 1 Chronicles 14:12, the Philistines "left their gods there" (אלהיהם, *'ĕlōhêhem*, "their gods"; ESV, compare NRSV, NASB, KJV). The Septuagint and Vulgate also translate 2 Samuel 5:21 as "they left their gods there" (אלהיהם, *'ĕlōhêhem*, "their gods"). These variants within the Masoretic Text, combined with the witness of early translations, suggest "the scribe of the Masoretic Text in Samuel probably found cause for offense in that idols were referred to in this verse as *'ĕlōhêhem*, 'their gods,' usually employed for the god of Israel," and changed the word to *ăṣabbêhem* ("their idols").[48]

New Testament Examples

Mark 1:2. Mark 1:2–3 includes OT quotations from Malachi 3:1 and Isaiah 40:3. However, the earliest and best manuscripts of Mark introduce these quotations by saying, "As it is written in Isaiah the prophet," even though not all of the quotation is from Isaiah. The attribution to only Isaiah is reflected in most modern English translations (Mark 1:2 ESV, NASB, NRSV; compare NIV, NLT). However, later, mainly Byzantine, tradition corrected the confusion by changing the introductory sentence to "As it is written in the prophets"—a textual variant that is preserved in the KJV and NKJV (see §4.3.4.a Mark 1:2 for further discussion of this example).

1 John 5:6–8. If you compare a number of English translations of 1 John 5:6–8 you will find a complicated situation involving differences both in

---

47. According to scribal tradition, the phrases "his mother's womb" and "his flesh" in Num 12:12 originally read "our mother's womb" and "our flesh." The editors of the NET Bible note that the scribes changed them from first to third person because "apparently they were concerned that the image of Moses' mother giving birth to a baby with physical defects of the sort described here was somehow inappropriate, given the stature and importance of Moses" (https://net.bible.org/#!bible/Numbers+12).

48. Tov, *Textual Criticism* (3rd ed.), 250.

versification and in wording. For verse 8, most modern versions have, "For there are three that testify, the Spirit and the water and the blood, and the three are in agreement" (LEB; compare NRSV, NASB, NIV, ESV). However, the KJV first of all combines verses 6 and 7 (as divided in the other versions) into verse 6; then, for verse 7, the KJV reads: "For there are three that bear record in heaven, the Father, the Word, and the Holy Ghost: and these three are one," wording not found in the others at all. In verse 8, the KJV has "And there are three that bear witness in earth, the Spirit, and the water, and the blood: and these three agree in one." This is close to verse 8 in the more modern versions. This affirmation of the Trinity, called the Comma Johanneum (Latin for "Johannine Clause"), has a long history of controversy. The Trinitarian clause, which is not present in any Greek witnesses prior to the fourteenth century, seems to have come from a fourth-century Latin homily and to have been transmitted in some of the Latin tradition. It eventually made its way into the **Textus Receptus** (TR), an early printed Greek edition based on the Byzantine tradition, which in turn became the **base text** for the KJV.[49]

2.2 THE GOAL OF TEXTUAL CRITICISM

The main goal of earlier textual critics was to establish the original reading of the biblical text. The terminology of "original" text is now seen as problematic because textual critics have recognized the complexity of the writing and "publication" process in ancient times.[50] However, the goal of establishing the **Ausgangstext** (the earliest form of the text from which all extant copies descend) is feasible for the New Testament since we have an abundance of manuscripts copied shortly after the **autographs** themselves were written.[51] The primary complication for NT textual critics is

---

49. See more extended discussions of the Comma Johanneum in Metzger, *Textual Commentary*, 647–49; Bruce M. Metzger and Bart D. Ehrman, *The Text of the New Testament: Its Transmission, Corruption, and Restoration*, 4th ed. (New York: Oxford University Press, 2005), 146–48, 162, 182n23, 219; Kurt Aland and Barbara Aland, *The Text of the New Testament: An Introduction to the Critical Editions and to the Theory and Practice of Modern Textual Criticism*, 2nd ed. (Grand Rapids: Eerdmans, 1995), 249, 311; and at https://net.bible.org/#!bible/1+John+5. See also Daniel L. Akin, *1, 2, 3 John*, NAC 38 (Nashville: Broadman & Holman, 2001), 197–200.

50. See Harry Y. Gamble, *Books and Readers in the Early Church: A History of Early Christian Texts* (New Haven: Yale University Press, 1995).

51. See §1.2.3 Textual Criticism Defined for an explanation of the German term *Ausgangstext*. Also see Wegner, *Student's Guide*, 37–39, for a fuller discussion of the more traditional goal of

deciding between the many copies and variant readings of the NT. Yet, as Wegner notes, "The plethora of New Testament manuscripts is a great benefit when trying to determine the original reading of the New Testament, for it is easier to sift through and evaluate the various extant readings than to emend texts with no evidence."[52]

A further goal of NT textual criticism that is pursued by current textual scholars is the history of the transmission of the text, a study that has valuable implications for students of history, exegesis, and theology.[53]

The situation is more complicated for the Old Testament. Bruce Waltke describes and evaluates five different goals that OT textual critics might have.[54] Most scholars recognize that the OT underwent modifications during the long process of its formation,[55] but the lines between the original author's composition, the editorial work of scribes, and the "simple" copying of final manuscripts are blurry. Unlike the majority of NT textual critics, the OT textual critic has to decide exactly which stage of the OT composition or transmission is the goal.

The goal of OT textual criticism as represented in this volume is to reconstruct the text's "final literary product."[56] This final form developed during a complex and irretrievable compositional history. At whatever point it reached its final authoritative status, the text then stood at the beginning of an equally long transmission history. For some books or sections of the OT, there were apparently several valid "final forms" of the text. Such is the case with the book of Jeremiah, which is significantly longer and arranged differently in the Hebrew of the Masoretic Text from

---

establishing the "original text."

52. Wegner, *Student's Guide*, 41.

53. For more on this, see David C. Parker, *An Introduction to the New Testament Manuscripts and Their Texts* (Cambridge: Cambridge University Press, 2008), 181–89.

54. Bruce K. Waltke, "Aims of Old Testament Textual Criticism," *WTJ* 51 (1989): 92–108. Wegner provides a chart of the "perceived goals of Old Testament textual criticism" that includes a sixth goal (*Student's Guide*, 31).

55. Wegner (*Student's Guide*, 30) cites three examples for which "even the most conservative scholars must allow for some modification of the original texts": (1) the reference to "Dan" in Gen 14:14; (2) the account of Moses' death in Deut 34; (3) the phrase "and within yet 65 years Ephraim will be shattered from being a people" in Isa 7:8.

56. Tov, *Textual Criticism* (3rd ed.), 165.

in the Hebrew *Vorlage* that stands behind the Septuagint.[57] Thus, rather than deciding which version of Jeremiah is "right," textual critics should try to determine the final form from which the Septuagint developed and the final form from which the Masoretic Text (and thus, the English Bible) developed. This goal is similar to reconstructing the *Ausgangtext* since both focus on finding the text that gave rise to the known textual variants.

2.3 BASIC PRINCIPLES OF TEXTUAL CRITICISM

Textual criticism is not an exact science, but there is a basic process that controls the evaluation of variants. It is necessary to consider **external evidence** and several types of **internal evidence**, regardless of the Testament under consideration. In each type of evidence, a set of principles guides the process, but not all principles apply in every instance. Determining which variant offers the best reading is an art as well as a science.

2.3.1 EXTERNAL EVIDENCE

External evidence involves the quality, quantity, and textual affiliation of the manuscripts that witness to variant readings. This type of evidence is not concerned with the context of a passage, which reading seems to make the most sense, or even how a variant developed (see §2.3.2 Internal Evidence below). It focuses on evidence *external* to the actual reading: In what kinds of manuscripts is a given variant found? There are three general principles for evaluating external evidence.

- **Prefer the reading found in the oldest manuscripts.**
  Generally, older manuscripts are more reliable than later manuscripts because they are closer in time to the original composition and have theoretically had fewer opportunities for errors to develop. However, even our oldest manuscripts are copies, so this principle has limitations. An early manuscript is just as likely to include errors or deliberate changes. At the same time, a late manuscript may be only one or two

---

57. See Tov, *Textual Criticism* (3rd ed.), 165–69, for additional discussion of the goal of reconstructing the "final literary product" of the biblical text. Compare also Waltke, "Aims of Old Testament Textual Criticism," 92–108.

generations of careful copying from a very ancient one and could preserve an early reading.

- **Prefer the reading that has multiple attestation.** If a reading occurs only in an isolated manuscript, there is less likelihood that such a *singular reading* preserves the *Ausgangstext*. Normally you would expect the best and oldest reading to be in more than one or two witnesses. At the same time, the prolific copying of the NT in the Middle Ages resulted in many hundreds of copies of the later Byzantine type of text. Thus, it frequently occurs that the textual weighs the reading of a few older manuscripts against the reading of many later ones. In such cases, the older witnesses tend to be preferred over the many later witnesses.

- **Prefer the reading found in a variety of manuscripts.** A reading that is carried by several textual traditions (e.g. a reading that is carried by both Alexandrian and Byzantine witnesses) is more likely to be the earliest form of the text than one that occurs in a single textual tradition (e.g. only in the Byzantine witnesses) or in a **family** of manuscripts.[58]

2.3.2 INTERNAL EVIDENCE

Internal evidence is concerned with what happened within the text to cause the occurrence of variant readings. Scribes were prone to making certain kinds of mistakes in their manuscripts, and authors exhibit particular styles of writing, preferences in vocabulary, and systems of belief. When textual critics assess variant readings based on knowledge of scribal habits, they are assessing the **transcriptional probability** of a particular reading. When they consider variant readings based on the larger context of a particular author's style and theology, they are assessing the **intrinsic probability** of a given reading.

---

58. A **family** is a group of manuscripts that are so closely related that it is possible to create a *stemma*, or family tree, showing how they all descend from a common *archetype* or ancestor. Family 1 of the Gospels is one such group.

2.3.2.a Transcriptional Probability

Although the scribes of biblical manuscripts were, for the most part, well trained and cautious, they were human, and humans make mistakes. The task of the textual critic is to determine when copyists made mistakes or intentional changes. Each of these changes has been discussed and illustrated above (see §2.1.2 Changes and Errors in Transmission). A simple review is as follows:

Haplography Writing something once instead of twice
Parablepsis "Eye-skipping" that overlooks and eliminates or repeats text
Dittography Writing something twice instead of once
Conflation Combining multiple readings
Glosses Incorporating marginal notes into the text
Metathesis Switching the order of letters or words
Mistaken letters Confusing one letter for a similar-looking letter
Homophony Confusing words that sound alike
Spelling and Grammar Updating or improving the text
Harmonization Bringing similar passages into conformity
Theological Changes Protecting the text from misunderstanding

Thus, transcriptional probability is all about scribal habits. For each variation unit, the question of the textual critic is: *Which change is a scribe or copyist more likely to have made?*

2.3.2.b Intrinsic Probability

Every author has a particular style in their grammar and vocabulary choices, and every biblical book reflects an author's theology. Because scribes made intentional changes at times to smooth grammar or clarify difficult texts, not every reading represents what the original authors wrote. Textual critics try to determine which variants best reflect a given author's style and theology based on the larger context of a chapter or book (i.e., "Which of these two words is Paul more likely to have used in this context?"). However, matters such as style and theology can be highly subjective, so wise textual critics are not dogmatic in their assessments of intrinsic probability.

2.3.2.c Basic Principles

The basic principle behind evaluation of internal evidence is this: **"The reading that best explains the origin of the other readings is probably original."**[59] Several corollaries accompany this principle:

- **Prefer the shorter reading (*lectio brevior*).** Because the earliest OT scribes considered their text sacred, they were usually reluctant to change any part of it intentionally. The earliest NT scribes considered the NT documents of high importance, but not at the level of authority of their Bible, which was the OT. In either case, if copyists did intentionally smooth out a stylistic difficulty or make a passage easier to understand, they were more likely to *add* to the sacred text than to *take away* from it. Thus, a shorter reading is generally considered to be more original than a longer one. However, the scribe of a shorter text may have unintentionally omitted something, so this principle should be applied cautiously.[60]

- **Prefer the more difficult reading (*lectio difficilior*).** Scribes sometimes made changes intentionally to make a difficult text easier to understand. It is unlikely that a scribe would change the text to make it more difficult to read. Because of this, the textual critic generally considers a more difficult reading more likely to be the earliest form. This principle applies to grammatical or stylistic difficulties as well as conceptual or theological difficulties. However, we should be cautious when applying this rule since an accidentally corrupted text could

---

59. Black, *New Testament Textual Criticism*, 35. In addition, see Eldon J. Epp's discussion of the criteria for internal evidence, "Traditional 'Canons' of New Testament Textual Criticism: Their Value, Validity, and Viability—OR Lack Thereof," in *The Textual History of the Greek New Testament: Changing Views in Contemporary Research* (Atlanta: Society of Biblical Literature, 2011), 79–128.

60. Indeed, recent scholarship has challenged the principle of *lectio brevior*. James R. Royse, in his meticulous and detailed *Scribal Habits in Early Greek New Testament Papyri* (Leiden: Brill, 2007), has argued that the scribes of the early papyri were more likely to omit than to add text. This does not, however, establish scribal habits for the entire period of the hand-copying of the NT. For later documents, *lectio brevior* continues to be a valid criterion.

also yield a difficult or nonsense reading that later scribes would have corrected.

- **Prefer the reading that best fits the author.** Variant readings with vocabulary and syntax that seem out of place for a particular author are candidates for scribal alteration. Variants that reflect a different theology than the dominant theology of a passage or book may also be suspect. Generally, the textual critic should consider the variant that best represents the author's broader style and intent.

Textual criticism is both a science and an art. While basic principles guide the process, some conclusions involve a degree of subjectivity. Learning these principles is the starting point for scientific inquiry, but developing competence in the art of textual criticism takes time and practice. As Black notes:

> Of course, greatest caution must be exercised in applying these principles. They are inferences rather than axiomatic rules. Indeed, it is not uncommon for two or more principles to conflict. Hence none of them can be applied in a mechanical or unthinking fashion. If in the end you are still undecided, you should pay special attention to external evidence, as it is less subjective and more reliable.[61]

2.4 LIMITATIONS OF TEXTUAL CRITICISM

Textual criticism serves an important role in the study of the Bible. People who value the Bible as God's Word should be interested in the earliest wording of the text, and textual criticism helps answer this question. But it cannot answer everything we want to know. For example, it may be able to determine that Mark 16:9–20 and the story of the adulterous woman in John 8 are not original to the works of Mark and John, but it cannot say whether these added texts are inspired.[62] It cannot tell us who wrote the

---

61. Black, *New Testament Textual Criticism*, 35.

62. Such questions are pursued in textbooks on exegesis and hermeneutics. Some helpful books include William W. Klein, Craig L. Blomberg, and Robert L. Hubbard, *Introduction to Biblical Interpretation* (Nashville: Thomas Nelson, 2004); and Gordon D. Fee, *Gospel and Spirit: Issues in New Testament Hermeneutics* (Peabody, MA: Hendrickson, 1991). The best way

Pentateuch or the letter to the Hebrews, and it cannot detail the process of how the Bible came together. Textual criticism cannot speak to the historicity of every story or the reason for conflicting accounts. Many of these questions are considered by scholars working in other areas of biblical criticism such as **canonical criticism, form criticism, historical criticism, redaction criticism,** and **source criticism.** But textual criticism must be the starting place for all biblical study because it works to establish the very text of the Bible used for further research.

2.5 RESOURCES FOR FURTHER STUDY

The best resources for textual criticism vary in complexity. Some are designed for beginners, while others are written with the student of Greek or Hebrew in mind. Additionally, some resources deal with textual criticism for the entire Bible, but many focus on only the OT or the NT.

Black, David Alan. *New Testament Textual Criticism: A Concise Guide.* Grand Rapids: Baker, 1994.

> Black calls his guide "a simple and direct introduction" that "packages up ... and delivers" countless workshops he has presented on the topic of textual criticism to pastors and laypeople. He overviews how and which errors occur, details the history of NT textual criticism, and illustrates the process on several NT texts.

Brotzman, Ellis R., and Eric J. Tully. *Old Testament Textual Criticism: A Practical Introduction.* 2nd ed. Grand Rapids: Baker, 2016.

> Brotzman's book has been a standard introduction to OT textual criticism since its publication in 1994. In his endorsement on the back cover of the first edition, Waltke says the book brings together "an introduction to the Hebrew texts and versions, the theory of textual criticism, an introduction to *BHS*, and a sample of its practice." With this second edition, Brotzman has collaborated with Eric J. Tully to update and expand the work to incorporate the latest research on the textual history of the OT.

---

to pursue such issues as inspiration, authorship, or backgrounds is to consult several good commentaries on the book or passage you are investigating.

Comfort, Philip. *Encountering the Manuscripts: An Introduction to New Testament Paleography & Textual Criticism*. Nashville: Broadman & Holman, 2005.

> Comfort's two-pronged study explores the role of scribes in the production of NT manuscripts.

McCarter, P. Kyle, Jr. *Textual Criticism: Recovering the Text of the Hebrew Bible*. Guides to Biblical Scholarship. Old Testament Guides. Philadelphia: Fortress, 1986.

> McCarter's introduction is succinct and filled with examples of OT text-critical issues. Part of a longstanding series of helpful guides to biblical scholarship, McCarter's manual includes a glossary and a bibliography of primary sources, with descriptions of the textual characteristics of each biblical book.

Porter, J. Scott. *Principles of Textual Criticism with Their Application to the Old and New Testaments*. London: Simms and M'intyre, 1848.

> Porter's introduction was the first of its kind in English. Most of his successors (e.g., Warfield, Robertson, Metzger) dealt exclusively with the NT, but Porter handled both Testaments. His book begins with a chapter on the "Object and Necessity of the Science," in which he describes the extent of variation in the biblical manuscripts and the reasons for such variation. He notes that in light of these variations, textual criticism should be "exercised with due diligence, fidelity, and impartiality" (9–13).

Wegner, Paul D. *A Student's Guide to Textual Criticism of the Bible: Its History, Methods and Results*. Downers Grove, IL: InterVarsity, 2006.

> Wegner's introductory book is an excellent resource for a more detailed overview of textual criticism for both Testaments— though, as an Old Testament scholar, he is stronger in his treatment of the OT. He surveys the history of the discipline and its methods and discusses the goals and results of textual criticism. He also describes each kind of transmissional error and includes a chart summarizing the kinds of errors (44–57).

3
—
INTRODUCTION TO OLD TESTAMENT TEXTUAL CRITICISM

3.1 HISTORY AND KEY FIGURES

Some of the earliest students of the Bible recognized that different versions of the sacred text did not always agree with each other. Jewish scholars were aware of variation even within a single version of the Hebrew Bible (or Old Testament), which has many parallel passages that do not align exactly (e.g., compare 2 Sam 22 and Ps 18). How could they decide which version was closer to the original?

Many of the church fathers, who were most comfortable using the Greek translation of the OT, noticed that the Hebrew text sometimes differed from the Greek text. When they encountered such differences, they exercised a kind of **textual criticism** by selecting one version over the other. Eventually such observations developed into the field of textual criticism.

3.1.1 EARLY HISTORY

As a scholarly discipline, textual criticism originated in the third century AD, when church father and Bible scholar **Origen** embarked on a massive project that remains an important reference today. In a six-column compilation known as the **Hexapla**, he wrote the Hebrew text of his day alongside several Greek translations. In the fifth column, Origen transcribed the primary Greek translation of his day and meticulously recorded where and how it differed from the Hebrew. He did not offer reasons for the differences, but his work was foundational for future studies in textual criticism.

Although Origen's Hexapla did not survive to the modern period, a precise seventh-century **Syriac** translation of the fifth column has survived: the **Syro-Hexapla**.

A century after Origen, church father **Jerome** used the Hebrew text of his day alongside some of Origen's work and, with the help of Jewish scholars, created a new Latin translation of the Bible. Jerome's work, combined with that of others, eventually became the official Bible of the Roman Catholic Church, the **Vulgate** (Latin *vulgata*, "common one"). Jerome's work is valuable for textual criticism in that he consulted the best manuscripts he could find in Latin, Greek, and Hebrew; thus, the Vulgate provides evidence of manuscripts that are no longer available.

3.1.2 MIDDLE AGES AND BEYOND

The invention of the printing press in the fifteenth century revolutionized the study of the biblical text. The Gutenberg Bible, an edition of the Latin Vulgate, rolled off the press in the 1450s. By the late 1400s, Jewish printers in Europe were producing sections of the Hebrew Bible (most commonly the Pentateuch), and in 1488, the first full printed edition of the Hebrew Bible was produced in Soncino, Italy.[1] At about the same time, the Renaissance tradition and humanist ideal of "three languages" (*homo trilinguis*)—Hebrew, Greek, and Latin—had taken root,[2] and non-Jewish scholars showed renewed interest in the text of the Hebrew Bible. The printing press made texts available, and the European *Zeitgeist* ("spirit of the day") revived interest in the biblical languages. The result was an age of textual comparison in which scholars discovered different manuscripts, identified variants, and published treatises about both.

The ideal book format for textual comparison was the **polyglot** ("many tongues"), so scholars produced multilingual editions of the Bible in which the Hebrew, Greek, Latin, Aramaic, Syriac, and Arabic versions were aligned in parallel columns. The first polyglot was the **Complutensian Polyglot** (1514–1517). Two additional polyglots appeared before the final

---

1. Emanuel Tov, *Textual Criticism of the Hebrew Bible*, 3rd ed. (Minneapolis: Fortress, 2012), 71.

2. Moshe Goshen-Gottstein, "Editions of the Hebrew Bible—Past and Future," in *Sha'arei Talmon: Studies in the Bible, Qumran, and the Ancient Near East Presented to Shemaryahu Talmon*, ed. M. Fishbane, E. Tov, and W. W. Fields (Winona Lake, IN: Eisenbrauns, 1992), 222.

and most extensive one, the **London Polyglot** (1654–1657). A second type of comparative text was the Rabbinic Bible (the first appeared in 1516–1517, the second in 1525), which placed the Aramaic text alongside the Hebrew; this text also included commentaries in the margins by various medieval Jewish scholars. The **Second Rabbinic Bible**, edited by Jacob ben Hayyim, included notes from the scribal tradition (the **Masorah**) and remained the standard for Jewish scholars until the twentieth century.

By the eighteenth century, scholars were publishing books to aid in text critical studies. In two separate endeavors, Benjamin Kennicott and Giovanni Bernardo de Rossi compiled hundreds of medieval Hebrew Bible manuscripts produced by the **Masoretes** and cited thousands of variants in their collections.[3] Robert Holmes and James Parsons published a similar list of variants found in manuscripts of the **Septuagint** in their edition of the Greek translation.[4]

---

3. According to Tov (*Textual Criticism* [3rd ed.], 37), de Rossi's four-volume collection of variants was meant to supplement Kennicott's earlier two-volume work: Benjamin Kennicott, *Vetus Testamentum Hebraicum cum varus lectionibus*, 2 vols. (Oxford: Clarendon, 1776, 1780); Johannis B. de Rossi, *Variae Lectiones Veteris Testamenti, ex immensa MSS. Editorumq. Codicum Congerie haustae et ad Samar. Textum, ad vetustiss. versiones, ad accuratiores sacrae criticae fontes ac leges examinatae opera ac studio Johannis Bern de Rossi*, 4 vols. (Parma: Ex Regio Typographeo, 1784–1788); de Rossi, *Scholia Critica in V. T. Libros seu supplementa ad varias sacri textus lectiones* (Parma: Ex Regio Typographeo, 1798).

4. Robert Holmes and James Parsons, *Vetus Testamentum Graecum, cum variis lectionibus*, 5 vols. (Oxford: Clarendon, 1798–1823).

3.1.3 MODERN PERIOD (NINETEENTH–TWENTIETH CENTURY)

The increased availability of information about manuscript variation sparked an ongoing quest for the best version of the OT in both the Hebrew and the Greek. Scholars sifted and evaluated variants to determine which best represented the original author's or translator's writing. They then produced a **critical edition** of the OT based on their evaluations. In each critical edition they included a **critical apparatus**, which details points of comparison in the text. There are two types of critical editions. The first type, known as a **diplomatic edition**, is based on a single manuscript. The second type, called an **eclectic edition**, draws from several textual witnesses to reconstruct a hypothetical original text.

In the late nineteenth century, Hebrew scholar Christian D. Ginsburg began collating Masoretic manuscripts. He published *The Massoretico-Critical Text of the Hebrew Bible* in 1894, essentially creating the first critical edition of the Hebrew Bible.[5] In 1897 he published a massive introduction to this Hebrew Bible in which he described all the manuscripts he used in compiling his Hebrew text.[6] Ginsburg considered Jacob ben Hayyim's Second Rabbinic Bible to be an exemplar of the **Masoretic Text** (MT) tradition and used it as the base text for his 1894 edition, as well as for the Hebrew Bible he prepared for the British and Foreign Bible Society in 1908.[7] In 1906, German OT scholar Rudolf Kittel produced another critical edition based on the Second Rabbinic Bible called the ***Biblia Hebraica* (BHK)**. A second edition of *BHK* appeared in 1913.[8] A third revision of *BHK* carried out in the 1930s moved away from the Second Rabbinic Bible and instead used the eleventh-century **Leningrad Codex** as its base text. A fourth revision, ***Biblia Hebraica Stuttgartensia* (BHS)**, did the same (1967–77),

---

5. Christian D. Ginsburg, ed., *Massoretico-Critical Text of the Hebrew Bible* (London: Trinitarian Bible Society, 1894).

6. Christian D. Ginsburg, *Introduction to the Massoretico-Critical Edition of the Hebrew Bible* (London: Trinitarian Bible Society, 1897).

7. Ernst Würthwein, *The Text of the Old Testament: An Introduction to the "Biblia Hebraica,"* 2nd ed., trans. Erroll F. Rhodes (Grand Rapids: Eerdmans, 1995), 39. Compare Ginsburg, *Introduction*, iii.

8. Ginsburg's edition and the first two editions of *BHK* are difficult to classify as either eclectic or diplomatic. It is unclear which Hebrew manuscript(s) are behind their base text, the Second Rabbinic Bible.

and a fifth revision, **Biblia Hebraica Quinta (BHQ)**, is currently in progress.[9] These diplomatic editions (*BHK*[3]; *BHS*, and *BHQ*) all use the Leningrad Codex as their base text. Another diplomatic edition in progress is the Hebrew University Bible Project (HUBP), which uses the **Aleppo Codex** as a base manuscript. A current eclectic edition project is The Hebrew Bible: A Critical Edition (HBCE), formerly the Oxford Hebrew Bible (OHB).[10]

Table 3.1: Printed Editions of the Hebrew Bible			
Editor	**Title**	**Date**	**Textual Basis**
J. ben Hayyim	Second Rabbinic Bible	1525	unknown
C. D. Ginsburg	*The Massoretico-Critical Text of the Hebrew Bible*	1894	Second Rabbinic Bible
R. Kittel	*Biblia Hebraica*	1906, 1913	Second Rabbinic Bible
R. Kittel	*Biblia Hebraica (BHK)*	1929–1973	Leningrad Codex
K. Elliger and W. Rudolph	*Biblia Hebraica Stuttgartensia (BHS)*	1967–1997	Leningrad Codex
A. Schenker	*Biblia Hebraica Quinta (BHQ)*	2004–ongoing	Leningrad Codex
M. H. Goshen-Gottstein et al.	Hebrew University Bible Project	1965–ongoing	Aleppo Codex
Ronald Hendel	The Hebrew Bible: A Critical Edition (HBCE)	2015–ongoing	eclectic

---

9. Seven fascicles of *BHQ* have been published to date: *General Introduction and Megilloth, Ezra and Nehemiah, Deuteronomy, Proverbs*, the *Twelve Minor Prophets, Judges*, and *Genesis* (http://www.scholarly-bibles.com).

10. The first volume of HBCE was published in 2015: Michael V. Fox, *Proverbs: An Eclectic Edition with Introduction and Textual Commentary* (Atlanta: SBL Press, 2015). More information on the project can be found at its website: http://hbceonline.org/.

Critical scholarship on the Septuagint resulted in two main diplomatic editions, the previously mentioned work produced by Holmes and Parsons (1798–1823) and another by Alan Brooke, Norman McLean, and Henry St. John Thackeray (1906–1940).[11] The eclectic edition is the massive in-progress Göttingen Septuagint series (1926–); an abridged edition by Alfred **Rahlfs** has been available since 1935 (the *Septuaginta*).

The proliferation of manuscript evidence initiated a philosophical debate about the original text of the Bible. In the nineteenth century, Paul de Lagarde (1827–1891) theorized that all versions of the OT trace back to a single, hypothetical original text: the **Urtext** (*Ur* means "original" in German).

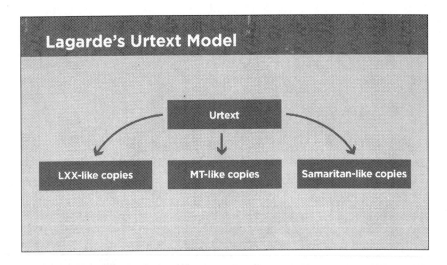

According to de Lagarde, this original text was the **archetype** (or initial ancestor) for what would become the Masoretic Text, the Septuagint, and the **Samaritan Pentateuch** (each is discussed further below). In de Lagarde's view, an original unity—one original text or *Urtext*—became the plurality of texts we know today. Thus, the ultimate goal of textual criticism is to reconstruct the *Urtext* by first reconstructing the earliest version of each textual family. Many scholars agreed with de Lagarde in

11. Alan E. Brooke, Norman McLean, and Henry St. John Thackeray, *The Old Testament in Greek according to the Text of Codex Vaticanus*, 9 vols. (Cambridge: Cambridge University Press, 1906–1940).

theory, though Emanuel Tov admitted, "We do not possess the tools necessary for reconstructing the original biblical text."[12]

In contrast, Paul Kahle (1875–1964) argued that several original corrupted texts eventually merged into a standardized text (the precursor to the MT). In his view, an original plurality became a unity.

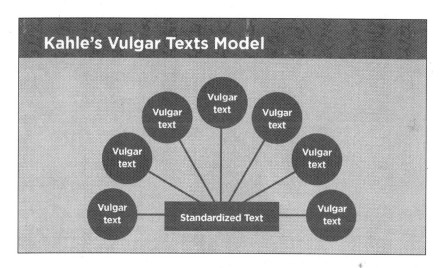

During the twentieth century, William Foxwell Albright and Frank Moore Cross developed a theory that combined the views of de Lagarde and Kahle. They proposed that copies of the original text traveled with Diaspora Jews who left Palestine for Babylon or Egypt during the third–fifth centuries BC, and in each of these locations, the text developed in different ways as it was copied and preserved. This created three "text-types" or "families": Palestinian, Babylonian, and Egyptian. Later, when the MT was standardized and accepted as the authoritative version of the Hebrew Bible, the text essentially returned to a single version.[13] In their view, the original

---

12. Emanuel Tov, *Textual Criticism of the Hebrew Bible*, 2nd rev. ed. (Minneapolis: Fortress, 2001), 183.

13. The idea that the text was intentionally standardized and stabilized over time has been challenged. Tov acknowledges that a standardized text that essentially reflected the MT was in place by the end of the first century AD, but he argues this is more likely the result of "historical coincidence" with the textual tradition that would become MT being "the only text surviving within Judaism from a previous plurality" after the destruction of the temple in AD 70 (*Textual Criticism* [3rd ed.], 175).

unity became a plurality of localized text-types, then became a unified version again in the MT.

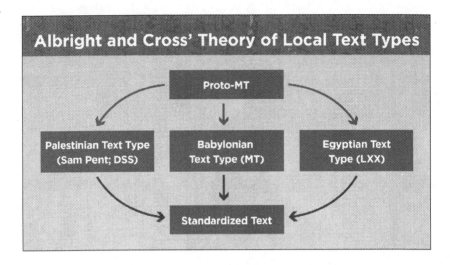

Albright and Cross' theory of regional textual families became difficult to sustain after 1947, when Bedouin shepherds tending their flocks on the northwest side of the Dead Sea inadvertently discovered a trove of documents that electrified the world of biblical scholarship. The shepherds were passing time tossing rocks into the openings of the caves at Qumran when they heard a rock shatter something within a cave.[14] Further explorations of that cave and ten neighboring ones revealed a library of hundreds of scrolls—including two hundred manuscripts of biblical books—dating as far back as the second or third centuries BC. Since all previous manuscript evidence for the OT came from the Middle Ages, the Dead Sea Scrolls moved textual criticism one thousand years closer to the original documents. According to Albright and Cross' theory, the scrolls from the Qumran cave should have been from the Palestinian text family. However, archaeologists discovered multiple text-types among the manuscripts, suggesting a change in location could not explain textual variety.

---

14. James C. VanderKam, *The Dead Sea Scrolls Today* (Grand Rapids: Eerdmans, 1994), 2.

This evidence of textual variety must now be viewed alongside the growing evidence of the antiquity, authority, and stability of the proto-MT.[15] Textual pluriformity existed alongside textual uniformity until the destruction of the Jerusalem temple in AD 70.[16] Different groups within Second Temple Judaism had accepted different, authoritative versions of biblical texts. According to Peter Gentry, this plurality of texts likely resulted from varying scribal tendencies because the textual evidence reveals two basic approaches: (1) scribes who tended to revise and update their text; and (2) scribes who copied their text as precisely as possible.[17] The MT tradition was "internally stable" by the first century BC, if not earlier.[18] Tov argues that the dominance of the MT tradition after AD 70 was the result of "mere coincidence" because the proto-MT "was the only text remaining after the destruction of the Temple," and it was the only text "left in Jewish hands" since the Septuagint "was now in Christian hands" and the Samaritan Pentateuch "was with the Samaritan community."[19]

3.2 TEXTUAL EVIDENCE

The textual evidence for the Hebrew Bible divides into four major categories: (1) the primary Hebrew witness, the Masoretic Text; (2) the primary Greek witness, the Septuagint; (3) manuscripts from the caves at Qumran[20] and elsewhere in the Judean Desert (**Dead Sea Scrolls**); (4) and less significant manuscripts, most of which are in other languages (i.e., the **Peshitta** in Syriac, the Vulgate in Latin, and the **Targums** in **Aramaic**).

---

15. Peter J. Gentry, "The Text of the Old Testament," *JETS* 52.1 (2009): 19–45; compare Tov, *Textual Criticism* (3rd ed.), 186–87.

16. Tov, *Textual Criticism* (3rd ed.), 187.

17. Gentry, "Text of the Old Testament," 33.

18. Tov, *Textual Criticism* (3rd ed.), 179.

19. Tov, *Textual Criticism* (3rd ed.), 179.

20. Note that *BHQ* cites specific scrolls by their standard abbreviation instead of using a general sigla for the Qumran manuscripts, as in *BHS*. For example, the *BHQ* apparatus cites variants from 4QRuth[a] and 4QRuth[b] for Ruth 1:1–2.

Table 3.2: Important Old Testament Witnesses				
BHS Sigla	**BHQ Sigla**	**Title**	**Approximate Date of Oldest Copies**	**Text Type**
𝔔		Qumran manuscripts	2nd century BC– 1st century AD	Hebrew
𝔗	T	Aramaic Targums	1st century BC– 7th century AD	Aramaic
𝔊	G	Septuagint manuscripts	3rd–5th centuries AD	Greek
𝔖	S	Syriac Peshitta	5th–9th centuries AD	Syriac
𝔏	La	Old Latin versions	5th–10th centuries AD	Latin
𝔙	V	Latin Vulgate	5th–8th centuries AD	Latin
𝔐	M	Masoretic manuscripts	9th–11th centuries AD	Hebrew
𝔪	Smr	Samaritan Pentateuch	11th–16th centuries AD	Samaritan Hebrew

3.2.1 Masoretic Text (Hebrew)

The OT was written in Hebrew with the exception of a few chapters and scattered verses in Aramaic (primarily Ezra 4–6 and Dan 2–7). The bulk of Hebrew OT manuscript evidence comes from the **Masoretes**—scribal families who preserved the OT text from AD 500–1000. Several manuscripts represent the Masoretic tradition, including the **Leningrad Codex**, the **Aleppo Codex**, and a codex from Cairo. Before we consider each of these manuscripts, we must understand the work of the Masoretes.

3.2.1.a Masoretic Traditions

The name "Masoretes" derives from the word "**Masorah**," which refers to the collection of "traditions and rules, passed down in Judaism for generations, which regulate all aspects of the copying and use of Bible

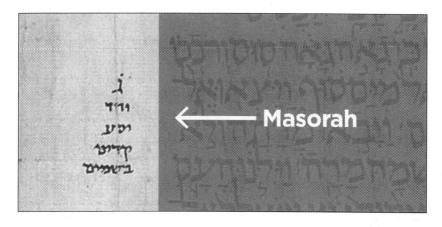

manuscripts."[21] The Masoretes created and preserved "an overall system
to ensure the accurate understanding of the Old Testament text and its
correct transmission to subsequent generations."[22] This system involved
three components that accompanied the consonantal text of the OT: (1) a set
of symbols to represent the vowel sounds (or the "reading tradition") that
had been transmitted orally for centuries; (2) a system of symbols (called
"accents") to mark stressed syllables and identify clauses to aid in reading
and understanding; (3) a set of specialized notes (the Masorah) about various components of the text.[23] These specialized notes included comments
in the side margins ("Masorah *parva*," or "small Masorah"), which detailed
statistics about word usage and textual corrections (*kethiv-qere*), and notes
at the top and bottom ("Masorah *magna*," or "large Masorah") that were a
more extensive version of the Masorah *parva*. Some OT books or sections
conclude with "specialized information about the number of words in the
book (or section), the middle word of the book, the middle consonant, and

21. Page H. Kelley, Daniel S. Mynatt, and Timothy G. Crawford, *The Masorah of "Biblia
Hebraica Stuttgartensia"* (Grand Rapids: Eerdmans, 1998), 1. The meaning of the word *masorah* is
uncertain, though most scholars think it relates to the Hebrew word מסר (*masar*), meaning "to
hand over" or "to transmit." For further discussion, see Kelley, Mynatt, and Crawford, *Masorah*,
2; and A. Dotan, "Masorah," *Encyclopedia Judaica* (New York: Macmillan, 1971), 14:1418–19.

22. Ellis R. Brotzman, *Old Testament Textual Criticism: A Practical Introduction* (Grand
Rapids: Baker, 1994), 50.

23. Ellis R. Brotzman and Eric J. Tully, *Old Testament Textual Criticism: A Practical
Introduction*, 2nd ed. (Grand Rapids: Baker, 2016), 51–56.

so forth."[24] The data of the Masorah provided quality control to prevent any additions to or subtractions from the text. The accents and vowels preserved the correct reading and intonation of the text.

Three centers of Masoretic scribal activity existed in antiquity: Palestine, Babylon, and Tiberias (also in Palestine). The Tiberian group ultimately dominated and is the best-known tradition today. Among the Tiberian Masoretes, two scribal families were dominant: the ben Asher family and the **ben Naphtali** family. Most of the differences between their traditions concern details of vowels and accents, but none is of particular interest to textual critics. The most important Masoretic manuscripts reflect the tradition of the ben Asher family (i.e., the Leningrad Codex, Aleppo Codex, and Cairo Codex of the Prophets).

3.2.1.a.1 Vocalization and Accents

The Hebrew text is only consonantal, which would not have been problematic for native speakers of ancient Hebrew. However, Hebrew usage underwent a major shift during the sixth century, when the Jewish nation went into exile in Babylon and never fully returned to Palestine. As their familiarity with widespread commercial languages of the day (Aramaic and eventually Greek) flourished, their fluency in spoken and written Hebrew diminished.

Unpointed versus Pointed Hebrew

ⴗⴷⴽ ⵝⴷⴸⴽ ⴼⴹⴼ ⴺⵉ	*Paleo Hebrew (Pre-Exilic)*
זה ספר תולדת אדם	*Unpointed Hebrew (Post-Exilic)*
זֶה סֵפֶר תּוֹלְדֹת אָדָם	*Pointed Hebrew (Medieval)*

---

24. Brotzman and Tully, *Old Testament Textual Criticism*, 55.

Scribes had been adding **matres lectionis** to clarify certain vowels and to aid in reading as early as the ninth or eighth century BC (see §2.1.2.d.1 Spelling and Grammar).[25] With the rise of **Diaspora** living and the decline of Hebrew fluency, more *matres lectionis* appeared in the text. But *matres lectionis* could not account for all the vowel sounds, and they were subject to misinterpretation. Over time, the Masoretes developed a system of symbols to represent the vowel sounds behind the pronunciation of the consonantal text. Since the text had a long history of oral tradition, the Masoretes recorded the reading tradition. Most scholars believe that the Masoretes worked to preserve the text of Scripture by maintaining traditions about its pronunciation and wording.[26] The vowels (called "pointing") do not carry the same authority as the consonantal text.

3.2.1.a.2 Kethiv and Qere

In preserving the reading tradition of the Hebrew text, the Masoretes sometimes encountered words or verses they considered "unsatisfactory on grammatical, esthetic, or doctrinal grounds."[27] Their reverence for the text prohibited them from changing it, so they copied all the consonants as they had received them—that is, what was written (כְּתִיב, **kethiv**, "written"), they preserved intact. However, for questionable words in the text, they wrote alternative consonants in the manuscript margins—that is, they adjusted what was read (קְרֵי, **qere**, "read"). This practice is known as "*kethiv-qere*." Thus, when readers see a marked word in the text,[28] they must look in the margin for which consonants to read with the vowels in the text.[29]

An example of a *kethiv-qere* is present in 2 Samuel 23:13, where some of David's warriors assembled in a cave. Most English translations say that "three of the thirty" men came to him, and many include a footnote

---

25. Brotzman and Tully, *Old Testament Textual Criticism*, 24; Tov, *Textual Criticism*, 209.

26. Kelley, Mynatt, and Crawford, *Masorah*, 2.

27. Würthwein, *Text of the Old Testament*, 16.

28. In *BHS* and *BHQ*, a tiny circle hovers over a *kethiv* in the text. The consonants of the *qere* are in the margin above the Hebrew letter *qof* (ק).

29. This accounts for many of the thousands of instances of *qere* and *kethiv*. For further discussion of other kinds of textual corrections, see Ernst Würthwein and Alexander Achilles Fischer, *The Text of the Old Testament: An Introduction to the "Biblia Hebraica,"* 3rd ed., trans. Erroll F. Rhodes (Grand Rapids, Eerdmans, 2014), 19–24.

indicating that some Hebrew manuscripts say "thirty of the thirty." In the Hebrew consonantal text, the letters are שלשים (sh-l-sh-y-m), which form the word "thirty" and should have vowels indicating the pronunciation shĕlōshîm. However, the vowels with the consonantal text (kethiv) read שְׁלֹשִׁים (shĕlōshām), which is not a Hebrew word. The consonants of the qere, שלשה (sh-l-sh-h), are in the margin. The reader is to combine the vowels of the kethiv with the consonants of the qere to read שְׁלֹשָׁה (shĕlōshâ), which means "three."

Some kethiv-qere examples were so widespread that the scribes did not include the alternative set of consonants in the margins. Instead, they used the alternative vowels on the original consonants in the text itself, and readers knew how to read the word when they encountered it. The most well-known of these is the Tetragrammaton, or the divine name of God, Yahweh. Jews would not pronounce this name because it is sacred. Instead, when they encountered the written (kethiv) four letters of the Tetragrammaton in the text, יהוה (YHWH), they would read (qere) "Adonai" (אֲדֹנָי). When the Masoretes pointed the letters יהוה (YHWH) in the text, they used the vowels from the reading "Adonai": יְהֹוָה (Yehovah).[30] This reading is known as a **qere perpetuum** ("perpetual reading") instead of a kethiv-qere because readers know that *every* occurrence of יהוה (YHWH) is to be read "Adonai"; the Masoretes did not need to write the alternate consonants in the margin.

Some text-critical issues relate to instances of kethiv-qere since scholars are unsure what prompted many of the qere readings. They may have originally been scribal corrections, or they may have represented variant readings. According to Tov, most scholars think the truth lies somewhere in between: "Scribes at first wrote marginal corrections, but later this type of notation was also used for denoting variants, which in due course became

---

30. The A and ai of "Adonai" adjust to the e and a of Yehovah for phonetic reasons. They are essentially the same vowels, pronounced slightly differently because of the consonants. In English, consider how the sound of a changes slightly in the words "father" and "farther" because of the consonant r. This qere perpetuum explains the English word "Jehovah," a Latinized version of the Hebrew consonants of the Tetragrammaton with the vowels of the qere perpetuum, Adonai.

obligatory."[31] Textual critics try to determine whether and when a given *qere* may indicate a variant reading, and then whether the *qere* or the *kethiv* is the more original reading.

3.2.1.a.3 Other Notations and Corrections

The Masoretes made at least two additional kinds of changes or corrections in the text of the Hebrew Bible. Neither is particularly significant for textual criticism. The first were the *tiqqune sopherim*, which we discussed in chapter 2 (see §2.1.2.d.3 Theological Changes). These adjustments to the text were attempts to correct statements that appeared irreverent.[32] A second kind of change was the *itture sopherim*, "omissions of the scribes." Page Kelley, Daniel Mynatt, and Timothy Crawford identify five places in which the scribes said they omitted a conjunction (ו, *waw*, "and") because, presumably, the conjunctions "had accidentally crept into the text."[33] Beyond this description, it is unclear what rules scribes followed when determining whether to omit something or to write a correction in the margin (i.e., a *kethiv-qere*).[34]

3.2.1.b Masoretic Manuscripts

The Leningrad Codex is the most influential Masoretic (𝔐) manuscript in studies of the Hebrew Bible. The Aleppo Codex is also significant. Lesser manuscripts came from the Jewish community in Egypt—most notably the Cairo Codex of the Prophets (see Table 2.1: Important Hebrew Manuscripts in §2.1.1.a Old Testament Witnesses).

3.2.1.b.1 Leningrad Codex

The **Leningrad Codex**, or Codex Leningradensis (B 19a), is a complete Hebrew manuscript dating to around AD 1009, making it the oldest complete manuscript of the Hebrew Bible available. The manuscript, which is

---

31. Tov, *Textual Criticism* (3rd ed.), 58. Here Tov is summarizing the view of R. Gordis, *The Biblical Text in the Making—A Study of the Kethib-Qere* (Philadelphia: Dropsie College for Hebrew and Cognate Learning, 1937; repr., New York: Ktav, 1971).

32. As noted earlier, the number of corrections in this category are eighteen according to one Masoretic tradition (see Kelley, Mynatt, and Crawford, *Masorah*, 37).

33. Kelley, Mynatt, and Crawford, *Masorah*, 40.

34. Kelley, Mynatt, and Crawford, *Masorah*, 40.

currently preserved in the National Library of Russia in Saint Petersburg (previously Leningrad), represents the **ben Asher tradition** of **vocalization** and **accentuation** and is the base text of the third *Biblia Hebraica* (*BHK*), *Biblia Hebraica Stuttgartensia* (*BHS*), and *Biblia Hebraica Quinta* (*BHQ*).[35] The codex includes 491 pages of heavy white parchment with text, and it also includes sixteen illustrated pages ("carpet pages"). Each page of text has three columns of writing, except for Job, Psalms, and Proverbs, which have two columns. The order of the biblical books in the Leningrad Codex differs slightly from the traditional order in the Hebrew OT (which differs from the order of books in English Bibles): Chronicles is the first book of the Writings in the Leningrad Codex, whereas it is typically last in the Jewish canon.[36]

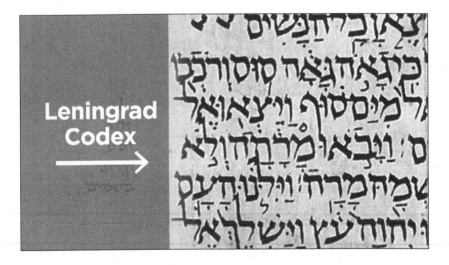

Leningrad Codex
⟶

3.2.1.b.2 Aleppo Codex

The **Aleppo Codex**, which dates to AD 925, was a complete manuscript of the OT until 1948, when about a quarter of its 380 pages were destroyed in anti-Jewish riots in Syria. Seized by crusaders in 1099, the codex was

---

35. Scholars generally believe the Leningrad Codex was corrected toward the ben Asher tradition rather than being originally produced by the ben Asher family.

36. The Jewish canon is divided into three sections: the Law, the Prophets, and the Writings. In most English Bibles today, books from the Writings, such as Ruth or Chronicles, have been moved into historical sequence. While *BHS* is based on the Leningrad Codex, it nonetheless places Chronicles in its traditional place—as the final book in the Hebrew Bible—and begins the Writings with Psalms.

later returned to a Jewish community that took it to Cairo, Egypt.[37] From there it ended up in Aleppo, Syria, where the Jewish community preserved it until the 1948 riots. The surviving pages of the codex have been in Jerusalem since 1960,[38] but debate continues over its missing pages and what really happened to the codex between 1947 and the present.[39] Many medieval scholars, including **Maimonides**,[40] considered the manuscript, which Aaron Ben Asher vocalized and accented, to be a model codex. Its closeness to the ben Asher tradition makes the Aleppo Codex "superior to all other Tiberian [manuscripts] known to us."[41] The Aleppo Codex is the base text for the critical edition of the OT that the Hebrew University is producing (Hebrew University Bible Project [HUBP]).

3.2.1.b.3 Cairo Codex of the Prophets

The fall of Jerusalem to Babylon in 587 BC inaugurated the Diaspora—a time in which many Jews lived outside the land of Israel. Egypt became a center of biblical scholarship as a flourishing community of Diaspora Jews developed there. Late in the nineteenth century AD, archaeologists discovered thousands of manuscript fragments in the old storage area of an Egyptian synagogue (a "**genizah**," where "worn or faulty manuscripts were kept hidden until they could be disposed of formally ... to avoid misusing or profaning a manuscript containing the holy name of God").[42] These fragments include valuable manuscript evidence.

The most significant manuscript from the Jewish community in Egypt is the **Cairo Codex of the Prophets** (C). Also known as Codex Cairensis, the Cairo Codex of the Prophets contains the Former Prophets and Latter Prophets. It is a well-preserved ben Asher manuscript that claims to have been written and pointed by Moses ben Asher in AD 895. Originally housed in Jerusalem, the manuscript belonged to a sect of Jews known as

---

37. Paul D. Wegner, *A Student's Guide to Textual Criticism of the Bible: Its History, Methods and Results* (Downers Grove, IL: InterVarsity, 2006), 158.

38. A. A. MacRae, "Text and Manuscripts (OT)," *ZEB* 5:799.

39. Ronen Bergman, "The Aleppo Codex Mystery," *New York Times*, July 25, 2012, http://www.nytimes.com/2012/07/29/magazine/the-aleppo-codex-mystery.html.

40. Tov, *Textual Criticism* (3rd ed.), 45.

41. Israel Yeivin, *Introduction to the Tiberian Masorah*, trans. and ed. E. J. Revell (Missoula, MT: Scholars Press, 1980), 17.

42. Würthwein, *Text of the Old Testament*, 11.

the **Karaites**. Crusaders seized the manuscript in 1099, but it was later restored to the Karaites and eventually ended up in Cairo, Egypt. Its importance to textual criticism is threefold: (1) it is the oldest dated codex of the Hebrew Bible;[43] (2) it contains all of the Prophets and Historical Books; and (3) it provides evidence for the ben Asher scribal tradition. In his article on "Text and Manuscripts (OT)," A. A. MacRae includes a section on the Cairo Genizah. While the Cairo Codex of the Prophets was not found in the genizah, MacRae's article provides more information about other manuscript evidence from Egypt.[44]

3.2.1.c Modern Critical Editions of the Hebrew Bible

To produce a critical edition of the Bible, scholars sort through textual variants to determine the best representation of what the original author or translator wrote. As we mentioned earlier, there are two approaches to creating a critical edition. The first approach is to use a single manuscript as a base text and then adjust it when variants from other manuscripts provide more convincing readings. This is a **diplomatic edition**. An accompanying **critical apparatus** details when notable variants occur, which manuscripts attest to them, and when a **textual emendation** might be appropriate. The second approach is to use all available manuscript evidence to create the best hypothetically original text. This is called an **eclectic edition**. Eclectic editions also include a critical apparatus that identifies sources and variants.[45] Today there are several critical editions available, although some of them are works in progress.

3.2.1.c.1 Biblia Hebraica—Kittel (BHK)

Several editions of Kittel's *Biblia Hebraica* were published between 1906 and the mid-1970s. In the first two editions (1906, 1913), Kittel and a team of OT scholars reproduced the Second Rabbinic Bible, which appears to have been a composite of late medieval manuscripts.[46] Published in Leipzig, Germany, Kittel's work reflected the standards of textual criticism at the

---

43. Würthwein, *Text of the Old Testament*, 11.

44. MacRae, "Text and Manuscripts (OT)," 798.

45. Some scholars use the term "critical edition" to refer only to eclectic editions. However, its broader use in textual criticism includes diplomatic editions as well.

46. Tov, *Textual Criticism* (3rd ed.), 72.

turn of the twentieth century. However, many scholars criticized the work for its apparatus, in which the editors presented "a selection of variants and conjectures for emending the text"[47] but gave insufficient evidence for such emendations.[48]

The third edition (*BHK³*), published in Stuttgart, Germany, between 1929 and 1937, is considered the first modern critical edition because it used a single manuscript as its base text—the Leningrad Codex. The revised version featured a substantially expanded critical apparatus: "a first apparatus include[ed] 'less important' evidence and a second apparatus contain[ed] 'more important' data."[49] The apparatus also included the Masorah *parva*. After the discovery of the Dead Sea Scrolls, scholars compiled a third apparatus with evidence from the scrolls, first included in the seventh edition of *BHK³*, published in 1951.[50]

3.2.1.c.2 Biblia Hebraica Stuttgartensia (*BHS*)

During the 1960s and 1970s, a fourth major revision to *Biblia Hebraica* was undertaken. This revision continued to use the Leningrad Codex as its base text. Edited by Karl Elliger and Wilhelm Rudolph, *Biblia Hebraica Stuttgartensia* (*BHS*) features a reworked critical apparatus, more evidence from the Dead Sea Scrolls, and evidence from the **Cairo Genizah**, although "without precise indication of the sources."[51] The edition also includes the Masorah *magna*, which *BHK* did not. Published in Stuttgart by the German Bible Society (Deutsche Bibelgesellschaft), *BHS* is the most current complete critical edition available.

3.2.1.c.3 Biblia Hebraica Quinta (*BHQ*)

Like its predecessor, *Biblia Hebraica Quinta* (*BHQ*) continues to use the Leningrad Codex as its base text, although the majority of scholars believe the now-available Aleppo Codex is a superior (albeit incomplete)

---

47. A. Schenker, "General Introduction," *Biblia Hebraica Quinta, Fascicle 18: General Introduction and Megilloth* (Stuttgart: Deutsche Bibelgesellschaft, 2004).

48. Wegner, *Student's Guide*, 100–101.

49. Tov, *Textual Criticism* (3rd ed.), 351.

50. German Bible Society, "Rudolf Kittel's Biblia Hebraica (BHK)," http://www.academic-bible.com/home/scholarly-editions/hebrew-bible/bhk/.

51. Tov, *Textual Criticism* (3rd ed.), 352.

manuscript. The editors of *BHQ* also decided to continue the *Biblia Hebraica* tradition of making a diplomatic edition rather than an eclectic edition, in part because the *Biblia Hebraica* series has focused on serving biblical scholars who are not specialists in textual criticism.[52] *BHQ* features the Masorah and a completely new critical apparatus, in which the editors only include variants "judged to be text-critically significant" and "to be potentially significant for translation or exegesis."[53] Furthermore, the editors will typically indicate the strength of the evidence on a given variant.

3.2.1.c.4 Hebrew University Bible Project (HUBP)

All of the *Biblia Hebraica* editions (*BHK, BHS, BHQ*) are diplomatic editions based on the Leningrad Codex. Another diplomatic edition in process is the **Hebrew University Bible Project (HUBP)**, which uses the Aleppo Codex as a base text. Scholars consider the Aleppo Codex to be the best Masoretic manuscript available, although it is incomplete. Besides using a different base text, the HUBP also features a different format for the critical apparatus. Instead of a single apparatus, the HUBP has four apparatuses divided according to the nature of the textual witnesses: ancient translations compose the first apparatus (e.g., Septuagint, Peshitta, Vulgate); evidence from the Dead Sea Scrolls and rabbinic literature falls in the second; and medieval manuscript evidence divides between the last two apparatuses based on the nature of the variants. In contrast to the critical apparatus of *Biblia Hebraica*, where the editors recommend preferred readings (instead of leaving readers responsible for determining the value of one reading over another), the apparatus of the HUBP purports to "present nothing but the facts."[54]

---

52. Schenker ("General Introduction") details three specific reasons for creating another diplomatic text instead of an eclectic text.

53. Schenker, "General Introduction."

54. Moshe Goshen-Gottstein, *The Book of Isaiah: Sample Edition with Introduction* (Jerusalem: Magnes, 1965).

3.2.1.c.5 The Hebrew Bible: A Critical Edition (HBCE)

A current eclectic-edition project is The Hebrew Bible: A Critical Edition (HBCE), formerly known as the Oxford Hebrew Bible (OHB).[55] Rather than working from a single base text, the textual critics weigh the manuscript evidence and select which readings best represent what the original author or editor wrote. They then combine these selections to create the text of the HBCE. The editor-in-chief of the project says it "requires its editors to exercise their full critical judgment concerning the variant readings and textual problems of the Hebrew Bible."[56] Because of this different approach, Ronald Hendel, the general editor of HBCE, considers the project a complement to the diplomatic editions of the HUBP and *BHQ*.[57] The first volume was released in 2015.[58] The project's website, http://hbceonline.org/, explains the project, including its theory and method. Hendel has also published two journal articles discussing the project.[59]

3.2.1.d English Translations of the Masoretic Text

The Masoretic Text is the base text for virtually all modern English translations of the OT. Most Bibles specify the translation committee's approach to translation and the textual basis of their translation in the introductory material. The majority of translations of the OT use *BHS*, though no such uniformity exists for translations of the NT because the nature of its manuscript evidence differs significantly from that of the OT. Some commentators produce their own translations, which they include in commentaries and that vary from the base text of the Masoretic Text. In such cases, the commentator typically explains the difference. The following English versions are representative of those that use the Masoretic Text as represented by *BHS* as the source text for their translation: the Revised Standard Version (RSV), the New Revised Standard Version (NRSV), the

---

55. "The Hebrew Bible: A Critical Edition," http://hbceonline.org/. The project's old website was http://ohb.berkeley.edu. In 2014, the project's name was changed to "The Hebrew Bible: A Critical Edition" when it was acquired by SBL Press.

56. Ronald Hendel, "The Oxford Hebrew Bible: Prologue to a New Critical Edition," *VT* 58 (2008): 325.

57. Hendel, "Oxford Hebrew Bible: Prologue," 325.

58. Fox, *Proverbs: An Eclectic Edition*.

59. Hendel, "Oxford Hebrew Bible: Prologue," 324–51; R. Hendel, "The Oxford Hebrew Bible: Its Aims and a Response to Criticisms," *Hebrew Bible and Ancient Israel* 2.1 (2013): 63–99.

English Standard Version (ESV), the New American Standard Bible (NASB), the New International Version (NIV), and the Lexham English Bible (LEB).

3.2.2 SEPTUAGINT (GREEK)

The first complete translation of the Hebrew Bible was the Greek **Septuagint** (LXX), which dates to the third and second centuries BC. Jews in Alexandria, Egypt, began translating the books of the Hebrew **Torah** in the third century BC. They then translated the Prophets and the Writings, followed by the **deuterocanonical** books (though some of these may have been originally written in Greek).

The **pseudepigraphal** *Letter of Aristeas* claims to describe the translation project. Aristeas, who claims to be an official of the royal court and eyewitness, wrote the letter to tell his brother, Philocrates, about the mission. He explains that the Egyptian king Ptolemy II (285–247 BC) was amassing a library of all the books in the world, and his librarian thought "that the lawbooks of the Jews [were] worth translation and inclusion in [his] royal library."[60] According to the writing, seventy-two Jewish delegates from Palestine completed their translation of the Pentateuch in seventy days. On hearing the translation, members of the Jewish community resoundingly approved it and pronounced a curse on anyone who changed the translation since it was "so excellent and sacred and accurate."[61] The name Septuagint, from the Latin word for "seventy" (*septuaginta*), derives from the number of translators in this story.

---

60. R. J. H. Shutt, "Letter of Aristeas," *OTP*, 2:12.
61. Shutt, "Letter of Aristeas," 121.

Virtually all scholars agree that the *Letter of Aristeas* is not a historical document but an apologetic treatise designed "to demonstrate the supremacy of the Jewish people—the Jewish priesthood, the Jewish law, the Jewish philosophy, and the Jewish Bible."[62] Scholars have proposed a number of other theories for the Septuagint's origins, but its development continues to be debated.

The singular name "Septuagint" gives the misleading impression that there is one authoritative Greek translation of the OT. This is not the case. To complicate matters further, the term "Septuagint" is used in at least three different ways. First, it can refer to the particular Greek translation of just the Torah (or Pentateuch) for the Alexandrian Jews (as described in the *Letter of Aristeas*). It can also refer to a particular Greek translation that lay behind the later recensions of Origen and others. In more popular usage, it encompasses whatever Greek translation of the entire OT is available.

Of the ancient translations, the Septuagint (𝕾) is generally considered the most valuable for textual criticism.[63] This translation lies the closest to the time of OT authorship, even predating some of the Hebrew manuscript tradition. Thus, its variants *may* reflect Hebrew readings that are earlier than those behind the Masoretic Text. And unlike many other textual witnesses, it includes the entire OT, as well as the deuterocanonical books of the Catholic and Orthodox Bibles.

3.2.2.a Old Greek

Multiple revisions of the Septuagint were produced in the first several centuries after its translation. This proliferation of revisions or recensions makes it difficult to determine which edition scholars mean when they refer to the "Septuagint" (see the discussion above about the various possible meanings for the word "Septuagint"). Because of this, scholars coined the term **"Old Greek"** (OG) to refer to the original Greek translation, which is to be distinguished from "the collection of sacred Greek writings" widely known as the Septuagint. They also gave separate names to the recensions of the Old Greek.

---

62. Shutt, "Letter of Aristeas," 85.
63. Gentry, "Text of the Old Testament," 26–27.

A **recension** of the Old Greek produced between the first century BC and the first century AD is particularly significant because it influenced three major recensions of the second century AD: Aquila, Symmachus, and Theodotion (see below). This particular recension regularly translates the Hebrew word גַּם (gam; "also, as well") with the Greek phrase καί γε (kai ge; "even, at least"). Because of this pattern, it is named the **Kaige recension**. Many scholars consider the Kaige recension to be an attempt to conform the Greek translation to the Hebrew tradition that would develop into the Masoretic Text (and the so called **proto-Masoretic Text**).[64]

3.2.2.b Aquila, Symmachus, Theodotion

The Christian church of the first and second centuries widely adopted the Septuagint and used it in theological debates with Jews. Because of the Christians' affinity for the Greek text, Jews came to regard it with suspicion. During the second century AD, three new versions of the Greek Bible were produced. These three rival texts—translated by Aquila, Symmachus, and Theodotion—each had a unique relationship to their source text, the Septuagint.

Aquila, a second-century Jewish translator, produced the earliest "rival" to the Septuagint.[65] His work was an extremely literal Greek translation of the Hebrew text. Because he attempted "to represent accurately every word, particle, and even morphological constituent,"[66] his work is particularly valuable for textual criticism. Aquila's translation was the third column of Origen's **Hexapla**.

The late-second and early-third century scholar **Symmachus** produced a fresh Greek translation, in which he rendered obscure or technical Hebrew into idiomatic Greek. While this made his translation easily coherent, it makes it less valuable for textual criticism because scholars cannot be sure what Hebrew lies behind many of his Greek expressions. Symmachus' background is uncertain, though many scholars think he was Jewish. Origen included Symmachus' translation as the fourth column of

---

64. Wegner, *Student's Guide*, 200–201.

65. Brotzman and Tully, *Old Testament Textual Criticism*, 68.

66. Tov, *Textual Criticism* (3rd ed.), 144.

his Hexapla, and **Jerome** used Symmachus' work when he produced the Latin **Vulgate**.

Theodotion was a first- or second-century AD Ephesian translator of the Hebrew Bible into Greek.[67] He also revised some existing Greek manuscripts of the OT to align better with his Hebrew text, which closely resembled the eventual Masoretic Text. Various quotations from Theodotion's material appear earlier than the historical Theodotion, prompting some scholars to hypothesize that his work reflects an earlier and unknown translator.[68] This hypothetical work is sometimes connected with the Kaige recension, which is then called "kaige-Theodotion" or "**proto-Theodotion**." A century after Theodotion, Origen attributed the sixth column of his Hexapla to Theodotion, though much of the material was not from Theodotion's Greek translation.[69]

3.2.2.c Origen and the Hexapla

The early church father **Origen** (c. AD 185–253) was both a theologian and a biblical scholar. His significant contribution to textual criticism was the **Hexapla**, a comparison of the Hebrew text with several Greek versions (see §3.1.1 Early History). At that time, most Christians used the Septuagint as their biblical text.[70] When Christian scholars debated issues with Jewish scholars, the Jewish scholars appealed to the Hebrew text, which was largely inaccessible to Christians. Origen's goal in creating the Hexapla was "to equip Christians for their discussion with Jews who made their appeal to the original text."[71]

Origen arranged the different versions side by side in a six-column format. The first column had the unvocalized Hebrew text of his day, and in the second column, he transliterated the Hebrew into Greek letters so that

---

67. Traditionally Theodotion has been dated to the second century. Gentry dates Theodotion to the early first century, earlier than either Symmachus or Aquila (Gentry, "Text of the Old Testament," 39; see also Gentry, "1.3.1.2 Pre-Hexaplaric Translations, Hexapla, Post-Hexaplaric Translations," in *Textual History of the Bible*, vol. 1A, ed. Armin Lange [Leiden: Brill, 2016], 211–34).

68. Tim McLay, "Theodotion," *EDB* 1297.

69. Leonard J. Greenspoon, "Theodotion," *AYBD* 6:447–48.

70. The Septuagint was originally translated by Jews, but, as noted above, when it was adopted by the Christians in the early centuries AD, the Jewish community began to view it with suspicion (Brotzman and Tully, *Old Testament Textual Criticism*, 68).

71. Würthwein, *Text of the Old Testament*, 57.

non-Hebrew readers could pronounce the Hebrew text. In the third and fourth columns, he copied the Greek recensions of Aquila and Symmachus, respectively. The sixth column was primarily the Greek recension credited to Theodotion.

Table 3.3: The Hexapla

First Column	Second Column	Third Column	Fourth Column	Fifth Column	Sixth Column
Hebrew text	Hebrew text transcribed into the Greek alphabet	Aquila	Symmachus	A version of the LXX supplemented with other manuscript readings and compared to the Hebrew.	Kaige-Theodotion

The fifth column is the most valuable for textual critics. In it, Origen transcribed the primary Greek version of the day and marked throughout how it differed from the Hebrew. He used a system of symbols (**sigla**) to indicate the insertions and deletions of the Hebrew text. An obelus (÷) marked the beginning of a Greek section missing from the Hebrew, while an asterisk (※) marked the beginning of a Hebrew section that was missing from the Greek. He marked the end of the added or missing sections with a metobelus (⸓). Where the Septuagint of his day lacked material found in the Hebrew text, Origen added the missing material based on one of his other Greek texts.

Origen's original work was never reproduced entirely, and it disappeared in the seventh century. However, before the Hexapla vanished, the Italian bishop Paul of Tella (near Milan) translated the fifth column, with all Origen's scribal notations, into Syriac. His **Syro-Hexapla** became the primary source for Origen's work.[72] Unfortunately, versions of Origen's fifth

---

72. Other manuscripts include portions of the Hexapla (see Wegner, *Student's Guide*, 194; Würthwein and Fischer, *Text of the Old Testament*, 110–14).

column *without* his system of notes also survived, creating a new, much expanded and corrupted Greek version of the OT that combined readings from multiple recensions into one. Materials that include portions of this new version are called "hexaplaric."

3.2.2.d Daughter Translations of the Septuagint

As the early church spread to people groups who were unable to read the Septuagint, translations of the Greek text—called daughter translations or secondary translations—began to appear in many languages across the Near East. From these daughter translations came tertiary translations— translations twice removed from the Greek text. Not every translation was of equal quality, and most are not of much value for textual criticism of the Hebrew OT since they are related to it only indirectly. However, these daughter translations do contribute to a greater understanding of the Septuagint's history and development.

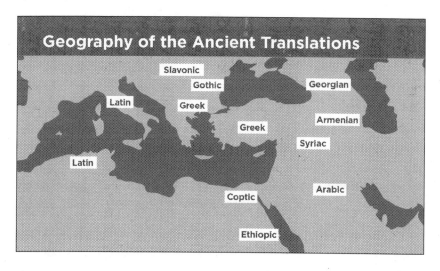

Although these daughter translations typically do not provide strong variants for the Hebrew OT, we discuss several of them here because critical apparatuses and commentators refer to them.

Coptic (𐤊). Coptic was the language of Egyptian Christians. The word can serve as an umbrella term for versions in three different **Coptic** dialects:

Sahidic, Bohairic, and Akhmimic. These versions are especially valuable for Septuagint studies because we have several complete Coptic manuscripts that date prior to the fifth century AD.[73]

Armenian (Arm). Armenia was a region north of Mesopotamia where Christianity may have spread as early as the first century. The Armenian translation was an early daughter translation of the Septuagint, though it shows some influence from the Syriac Peshitta.[74]

Ethiopic (𝔸). Christianity reached Ethiopia in the fourth century AD, but an Ethiopic translation did not appear until some centuries later.[75] The oldest available copy dates to the thirteenth century; it corresponds substantially with a fourth-century codex of the Septuagint (Codex Vaticanus).[76]

Arabic (𝔸). The conquest of Islam made Arabic a widely spoken language. The apparatus symbol A does not represent a unified Arabic text but rather a variety of translations from Greek, Syriac, Coptic, and Latin versions.[77] Medieval Jewish scholar Saadia Gaon produced a translation based on the Hebrew text.[78]

Old Latin (𝔏). Unlike the Vulgate, which Jerome translated from the Hebrew, the **Old Latin** (or *Vetus Latina*) is a daughter translation of the Septuagint. The Greek text that served as a base for the Old Latin predates the second-century recensions of Symmachus, Aquila, and Theodotion, and the third-century work of Origen. The Old Latin is a valuable window to the Old Greek because it "preserved many important Greek readings, sometimes as their only witness."[79] However, like the term "Septuagint,"

73. Würthwein and Fischer, *Text of the Old Testament*, 148–49.
74. Wegner, *Student's Guide*, 280–81.
75. Würthwein and Fischer, *Text of the Old Testament*, 150.
76. Wegner, *Student's Guide*, 282.
77. Wegner, *Student's Guide*, 286.
78. Würthwein and Fischer, *Text of the Old Testament*, 150–51.
79. Tov, *Textual Criticism* (3rd ed.), 133–34.

the expression "Old Latin" is imprecise and can refer to an array of Latin texts rather than a single manuscript.[80]

3.2.2.e Modern Critical Editions of the Septuagint

Three modern critical editions of the Septuagint are noteworthy. The editions by Swete and **Rahlfs** contain the complete Septuagint. The Göttingen edition, begun in the early twentieth century, is still in progress. Rahlfs' *Septuaginta* and the Göttingen volumes are eclectic editions, while Swete's Greek Old Testament is a diplomatic edition.

3.2.2.e.1 Swete

English biblical scholar Henry Barclay Swete published a Greek text of the Old Testament from 1887–1894. He completed his Greek New Testament (GNT) text in 1906, and revisions continued until 1909. Swete used Codex Vaticanus (B) as the base text for his critical edition, but he also consulted other key manuscripts, including Codex Alexandrinus (A) and Codex Sinaiticus (א). He intended to create "a text which might serve as a satisfactory standard of comparison, accompanied by textual notes which would enable the student at a glance to compare with his text the results to be gleaned from sources of information already securely within our reach."[81] Swete's diplomatic edition, which is now in the public domain, became a standard edition and is a widely used resource for students of the Septuagint.

3.2.2.e.2 Rahlfs

Alfred Rahlfs was a German theologian and biblical scholar. With a team of scholars in Göttingen, Germany, Rahlfs created an eclectic edition of the Septuagint primarily based on Codex Vaticanus, Codex Sinaiticus, Codex Alexandrinus, and the work of Origen and others.[82] Rahlfs' 1935 edition includes a brief critical apparatus. Since it is the only complete critical edition in print, it is the most practical edition of the Septuagint for general

---

80. Würthwein and Fischer, *Text of the Old Testament*, 145–46.

81. Henry Barclay Swete, *The Old Testament in Greek: According to the Septuagint* (Cambridge: Cambridge University Press, 1909), xi.

82. Julio Trebolle Barrera, *The Jewish Bible and the Christian Bible: An Introduction to the History of the Bible*, trans. Wilfred G. E. Watson (Leiden: Brill, 1998), 304–5.

study.[83] In 2006, Septuagint scholar Robert Hanhart revised the text and apparatus.[84]

3.2.2.e.3 Göttingen

The Göttingen Septuagint series, the *Septuaginta: Vetus Testamentum Graecum*, began with the work of Alfred Rahlfs in the 1920s. While Rahlfs was working on the "pocket edition" of the Greek OT,[85] he was also director of Septuagint studies at the Göttingen Academy of Sciences and Humanities, which was engaged in the *Septuaginta-Unternehmen* ("Septuagint Project")—a massive translation project whose goal was to produce a complete and thorough critical edition Greek text.[86] Rahlfs completed the volume on Psalms in 1931, and the project continues to this day.

Published by Vandenhoeck & Ruprecht, the Göttingen series represents the most precise critical edition of the Greek text and "the standard text of the books for which is it available."[87] Each volume includes a detailed critical apparatus with manuscript evidence from numerous manuscripts and ancient sources, such as the writings of Philo, Josephus, and the church fathers. The text divides this evidence into groups "so that readers can find their way through the maze of manifold variants."[88]

3.2.2.f English Translations of the Septuagint

Three English translations of the Septuagint are relevant to the study of textual criticism. The first is the nineteenth-century work of Lancelot Charles Lee Brenton. The second is a translation produced by The International Organization for Septuagint and Cognate Studies (IOSCS)

---

83. Jennifer M. Dines, *The Septuagint* (London: T&T Clark, 2004), xv–xvi.

84. Alfred Rahlfs and Robert Hanhart, eds., *Septuaginta*, rev. ed. (Stuttgart: Deutsche Bibelgesellschaft, 2006).

85. German Bible Society, "The Septuaginta-Edition from A. Rahlfs and its history," http://www.academic-bible.com/en/home/scholarly-editions/septuagint/history-of-the-lxx.

86. Gottingen Academy of Sciences and Humanities, "Septuaginta-Unternehmen: History," http://adw-goe.de/en/research/research-projects-within-the-academies-programme/septuaginta-unternehmen/history.

87. Karen Jobes and Moisés Silva, *Invitation to the Septuagint*, 2nd ed. (Grand Rapids: Baker Academic, 2015), 366.

88. Tov, *Textual Criticism* (3rd ed.), 135.

that based its work on the NRSV. The third and most recent translation, the *Lexham English Septuagint*, used Swete's Greek text.

3.2.2.f.1 Brenton's Translation

Lancelot C. L. Brenton's English translation of the Septuagint was first published in 1844 in London. This first version did not include the Apocrypha, but an edition including the deuterocanonical books appeared in 1851.[89] Based for the most part on a single manuscript (Codex Vaticanus), the translation is now outdated and often inaccurate.[90] However, since it is in the public domain, it is the only complete version that is easily available.

3.2.2.f.2 New English Translation of the Septuagint (NETS)

Advances in Greek language study and increased availability of manuscript evidence led The International Organization for Septuagint and Cognate Studies (IOSCS) to produce *A New English Translation of the Septuagint* (NETS).[91] The editors of NETS aimed to "create both 'a faithful translation of the LXX' and 'a tool for synoptic use with the NRSV for the study of the Greek and Hebrew Bible texts.' "[92] The translators consulted Greek editions (i.e., the Göttingen Septuagint and Rahlfs), but their starting text was the NRSV, which they compared to the Greek and then revised as necessary. Published by Oxford University Press, the translation was completed in 2007 (and revised in 2009) and is available digitally and in print.[93] The project's website includes additional information about the translation and its availability (http://ccat.sas.upenn.edu/nets/).

3.2.2.f.3 The Lexham English Septuagint

A team of scholars affiliated with the Faithlife Corporation produced a new translation of the Septuagint for use in Logos Bible Software. The

---

89. Lancelot C. L. Brenton, *The Septuagint with Apocrypha: Greek and English* (Peabody, MA: Hendrickson, 1986).

90. Dines, *Septuagint*, xvi.

91. Albert Pietersma and Benjamin G. Wright, eds., *A New English Translation of the Septuagint* (New York: Oxford University Press, 2007).

92. Dines, *Septuagint*, 153 (citing A. Pietersma, "A New English Translation of the Septuagint," in *X Congress Volume of the IOSCS, 1998*, ed. B. A. Taylor [Atlanta: Society of Biblical Literature, 2001], 217).

93. Jobes and Silva, *Invitation*, 365.

Lexham English Septuagint (LES) includes the deuterocanonical texts and is based on Swete's 1909 edition of the Greek text, *The Old Testament in Greek according to the Septuagint*.[94] The editors sought to produce a relatively literal translation; they translated idiomatic Greek phrases to communicate their meaning but recorded the literal phrasing in footnotes. The text is meant to be used alongside the original Greek text.

3.2.3 DEAD SEA SCROLLS

The discovery of the **Dead Sea Scrolls** (DSS) in 1947 revolutionized the field of OT textual criticism. While most of the six hundred to eight hundred manuscripts discovered were fragmentary, approximately two hundred of these manuscripts were biblical books, with every OT book represented except Esther and Nehemiah.[95] Dating from 250 BC–AD 135, the DSS provide manuscript evidence that lies one thousand years closer to the original OT writings than any of the great Masoretic codices such as the Aleppo Codex or the Leningrad Codex. Most of the scrolls were found in the vicinity of Khirbet Qumran near the Dead Sea, but a number of other manuscripts were discovered in the same region that date to the same era as the Qumran texts. Scrolls were discovered at Masada, Wadi Murabba'at, and Nahal Hever. These other discoveries added another twenty-five biblical manuscripts to the two hundred or so biblical manuscripts found at Qumran.[96] This entire corpus of manuscript discoveries is often discussed under the broad category of Dead Sea Scrolls, or the discoveries are referred to as the texts from the Judean desert.[97]

3.2.3.a Significance for Textual Criticism

By providing manuscript material dated closer to the time of authorship, the scrolls significantly affected textual criticism. First, they helped clarify and relativize the value of other manuscript evidence. Before the

---

94. Rick Brannan, Ken M. Penner, Israel Loken, Michael Aubrey, and Isaiah Hoogendyk, eds., *The Lexham English Septuagint* (Bellingham, WA: Lexham Press, 2012).

95. Nehemiah may have been part of an Ezra scroll.

96. Tov, *Textual Criticism* (3rd ed.), 95.

97. The official publication for these scrolls is the series Discoveries in the Judaean Desert, published by Oxford University Press. A list of the published volumes is available online: http://orion.mscc.huji.ac.il/resources/djd.shtml.

discovery of the scrolls, the medieval Masoretic manuscripts were the earliest Hebrew sources available.[98] In comparative study, textual critics also used ancient translations (and daughter translations), many of which predate the Masoretic manuscripts. Tov notes that from the seventeenth century forward, critics tended to give equal attention to all manuscript evidence, regardless of its language or date. Over time, scholars realized that not all sources have equal value for textual criticism. The DSS helped clarify which sources have greater merit. By substantiating variants found among the Masoretic manuscripts, the Septuagint, and the Samaritan Pentateuch, the scrolls proved that these witnesses were valuable evidence for textual criticism.[99]

The Dead Sea Scrolls also provide evidence of textual diversity in ancient times. As noted above (see §3.1.3 Modern Period), this textual diversity presented a significant challenge to the previous theories on the transmission and development of the OT text. Scholars differ in their evaluations, but most agree that the Dead Sea Scrolls provide evidence that aligns with several different textual groupings. Tov now classifies the textual evidence from the DSS into four categories based on "textual character."[100] The categories are (1) the 𝔐-like texts, including the **proto-Masoretic Text**, referring to Hebrew texts that align with the Masoretic Text;[101] (2) the Hebrew source of the Septuagint; (3) the Samaritan Pentateuch;[102] and the (4) "non-aligned texts," which describes texts that do not consistently line up with any of the other categories.[103] Tov presents his classification based on forty-six texts of the Pentateuch and seventy-five texts

---

98. The Nash Papyrus dates to the first or second century BC but contains only a liturgical version of the Decalogue (Tov, *Textual Criticism* [3rd ed.], 111–12).

99. Tov, *Textual Criticism* (3rd ed.), 107–11.

100. Tov, *Textual Criticism* (3rd ed.), 107. Previously Tov's classification included five text-types: proto-MT, the Hebrew text behind the LXX, the pre-Samaritan texts, Qumran scribal practice texts, and so-called non-aligned texts (Tov, *Textual Criticism* [2nd. ed.], 114–17). It appears that the texts from the "Qumran scribal practice" category have been redistributed into the other four.

101. Tov (*Textual Criticism* [3rd ed.], 31) uses the label "𝔐-like" to distinguish a textual grouping with affinities to MT but not as close as those classified as proto-MT. These texts are similar to the Leningrad Codex (as representative of MT) except for "several differences in small details and orthography."

102. Tov calls these "pre-Samaritan texts." See Tov, *Textual Criticism* (3rd ed.), 90–93, for further discussion.

103. Tov, *Textual Criticism* (3rd ed.), 107–10.

from the rest of the Hebrew Bible, using only texts that were "sufficiently extensive for analysis." The results show that the 𝕸-like texts make up the largest grouping from the DSS biblical texts. Tov's percentages are organized below in Table 3.4.[104]

Table 3.4: Text Types in the Dead Sea Scrolls		
	46 Pentateuch	**75 Other**
𝕸-like / Proto-Masoretic Texts	22 (48%)	33 (44%)
Hebrew *Vorlage* of Septuagint	1 (2%)	5 (7%)
Pre-Samaritan Pentateuch Texts	5 (11%)	NA
Non-Aligned Texts	18 (35%)	37 (49%)

Gentry is critical of this way of presenting the data because it oversimplifies the relationships among textual witnesses and gives the impression there is less uniformity than is actually the case. The category of "non-aligned" texts is especially unhelpful, and the large number of texts placed in that grouping demonstrates the inadequacy of the categorization. Instead, Gentry says, "Each variation must be thoroughly analyzed and scrutinized for its worth in determining textual relationship." He points to a variation in Jeremiah where 2QJer and the Septuagint show "evidence for a common ancestor somewhere in the history of these two witnesses, in spite of the fact that the fragment from Qumran does not agree with the LXX in the arrangement of the chapters."[105] In other words, even if 2QJer is not classified among the texts reflecting the Hebrew parent text of the Septuagint, for this particular variation unit, 2QJer and the LXX reflect the same initial text or archetype. The point is that the textual evidence does not reveal quite as much variation as the percentages in the category of "non-aligned" texts seems to imply. Rather, when the evidence from the biblical scrolls from Qumran is viewed in context with that from the other biblical scrolls found in the Judean desert, the picture emerges of "a central stream dominated by the proto-Masoretic texts."[106]

---

104. The numbers and percentages in Table 3.4 come from Tov, *Textual Criticism* (3rd ed.), 108.

105. Gentry, "Text of the Old Testament," 34–35.

106. Gentry, "Text of the Old Testament," 37.

Another way in which the Dead Sea Scrolls have dramatically affected textual criticism is by supplying readings that were previously unknown in the available manuscript evidence. The editors of *The Dead Sea Scrolls Bible* explain one of the most significant examples—an entire paragraph supplied by a manuscript including 1 Samuel 11 (in 4QSamᵃ):

> An entire paragraph, missing from all our Bibles for two thousand years, has now been restored in the New Revised Standard Version. Its existence had already been footnoted in the New American Bible in 1970. This paragraph graphically describes the atrocities of King Nahash of the Ammonites. 4QSamᵃ is the oldest extant witness to this text. The historian Josephus, writing in the second half of the first century CE, recounts the same details at the same point in his account of the history of the Jewish people, *Jewish Antiquities*. This demonstrates that the story was also in the Greek Bible that he was using.[107]

3.2.3.b Dead Sea Scrolls Identification System

Qumran is located near the Dead Sea, which is in the Judean desert. Scholars use all three place names in discussions of the scrolls.[108] Each scroll has a distinct label composed of some or all of the following elements: the location where the scroll was found, an abbreviated description of its contents, and a superscript letter distinguishing it from similar manuscripts. For example, the Great Isaiah Scroll has the label "1QIsaᵃ": It was found in Cave 1 at Qumran (1Q), it is a manuscript of Isaiah, and it is the first (ᵃ) of two found in Cave 1 (the other is 1QIsaᵇ). The scroll "4QJerᵇ" was found in Cave 4 at Qumran (4Q), and it is the second (ᵇ) of five Jeremiah (Jer) manuscripts found in Cave 4. The additional manuscripts found in caves elsewhere in the Judean desert are identified in essentially the same way: "MasPsᵃ" is the first (ᵃ) of two manuscripts of Psalms (Ps) found at Masada (Mas). When commentators refer to manuscript evidence from the Dead Sea Scrolls, they typically use this identification system.

---

107. Martin Abegg, Jr., Peter Flint, and Eugene Ulrich, *The Dead Sea Scrolls Bible: The Oldest Known Bible Translated for the First Time into English* (New York: HarperOne, 1999), 213–14.

108. Qumran scrolls; Dead Sea Scrolls; scrolls from the Judean desert; etc.

3.2.4 OTHER WITNESSES

The most significant witnesses to the Hebrew Bible are the Masoretic Text, the Septuagint, and the scrolls from the Dead Sea. However, several other manuscript traditions provide valuable evidence of variants. One such tradition is in Hebrew—the Samaritan Pentateuch. Three others are translations from the Hebrew: the Syriac Peshitta, the Aramaic Targums, and the Latin Vulgate.

3.2.4.a Samaritan Pentateuch

The **Samaritan Pentateuch** (ㅆ) is a tradition of Hebrew manuscripts of the Pentateuch associated with the Samaritans, who lived in the territory of the northern kingdom of Israel. The origin of this group is uncertain, though a small community is still in existence today. The Samaritans claim to be direct descendants of the tribes of Ephraim and Manasseh, who survived the Assyrian invasion of Israel in 722 BC and were not among those deported to Assyria. According to the Samaritans, the community split from the mainstream religion of Israel centuries before the Assyrian conquest in response to what they perceived as the illegitimate priesthood and worship site associated with Eli and the sanctuary at Shiloh. The Samaritans believe they represent orthodox Judaism. Their sacred text contains only the Pentateuch, which came from "the Era of Divine Favor"— the time before the schism.[109] In their view, the rest of the Hebrew Bible dates to after the schism, the "Era of Disfavor."[110]

The Deuteronomistic History (Joshua–2 Kings) offers a vastly different explanation of Samaritan origins. Second Kings 17 recounts the demise of the northern kingdom and describes how Assyrian captives "from Babylonia, from Cush, from Arva, from Hamah, and Sepharvaim" (2 Kgs 17:24) were relocated into Israel, where they intermarried with Israelites who had not been deported. "Pure" Israelites viewed the descendants of these intermarriages with contempt and considered their own religious practice to be orthodox. Jews have "argued that the veneer of Israelite

---

109. Robert T. Anderson, "Samaritans," *AYBD* 5:941.
110. Anderson, "Samaritans," 941.

religion displayed by the Samaritans is the result of instruction by an Israelite priest repatriated from Assyria" (see 2 Kgs 17:25-28).[111]

Tov notes that most scholars believe neither of these accounts of the Samaritans' origins and date the community's beginnings to a much later period, though there is no consensus.[112] Ultimately, the history of the Samaritans and the situation leading to the "Samaritan schism" is unclear.

The Samaritans worship at Mount Gerizim, not Jerusalem (compare the story of the Samaritan woman at the well in John 4:20), and they follow their own version of the Torah, which they copy in an archaic Hebrew script. The Samaritan version of the Torah has variant readings that often harmonize similar readings or support the Samaritans' ideological position. For example, each allusion to Israel's future centralized worship site (i.e., Jerusalem) in Deuteronomy has been adjusted in the Samaritan Pentateuch to allude to (or explicitly mention) Mount Gerizim instead.

The Samaritan Pentateuch is significant for textual criticism in that it is a "witness to a form of the text that once enjoyed widespread use as shown by its agreements with the Qumran texts, the Septuagint, the New Testament, and some Jewish texts that escaped revision by official Judaism."[113]

3.2.4.b Peshitta

The Syriac translation of the OT is the **Peshitta** (ܣ), which means the "simple" or the "plain" version.[114] However, in what sense the Peshitta is "simple" is unclear. Ernst Würthwein comments, "It is not certain in what sense [the name] was intended, whether to indicate it as the common (vulgaris) version, or one lacking in paraphrase, or perhaps to distinguish it as 'simple' in contrast to the annotated Syro-Hexaplar text."[115] The origin of the Peshitta is also uncertain, particularly the date of its production and whether it was translated for a Jewish or Christian audience.[116]

---

111. Anderson, "Samaritans," 941.

112. Tov, *Textual Criticism* (3rd ed.), 77.

113. Würthwein, *Text of the Old Testament*, 46.

114. Würthwein, *Text of the Old Testament*, 85.

115. Würthwein, *Text of the Old Testament*, 85.

116. Würthwein and Fischer cover aspects of this debate (*Text of the Old Testament*, 136-37). See also M. P. Weitzman, *The Syriac Version of the Old Testament* (Cambridge: Cambridge University Press, 1999), 258-62. For a recent introduction to the Peshitta, see Sebastian Brock, *The Bible in the Syriac Tradition* (Piscataway, NJ: Gorgias, 2006).

The Hebrew that the Peshitta reflects is closely related to the Masoretic Text, but it aligns well with readings of the Septuagint or the Targums (Aramaic) in several instances. A comparison of the **translation technique** at work in the different books of the Bible suggests that several translators produced the work with techniques that were not uniform.

The Peshitta is significant for OT textual criticism in that "it is a fairly early version of the Old Testament from a separate Jewish tradition."[117] As a textual witness, its value is greater for NT studies because it represents an early translation from original Greek manuscripts.[118]

3.2.4.c Targum

After the Babylonian exile, the Hebrew language was no longer the commonly spoken language of the Jews. Although Jewish intellectuals still understood the language and thus the sacred texts, it became necessary to translate the Hebrew Bible into Aramaic so the larger Jewish community could also understand it. These Aramaic translations were known as **Targums**, from an Aramaic word meaning "to translate" or "to interpret."[119] There are two broad strands of Targumic tradition: the Palestinian Targum and the Babylonian Targum. Targum Neofiti, the largest Palestinian Targum, contains the Pentateuch. In the Babylonian Targum tradition, Targum Onqelos contains the Pentateuch, while Targum Jonathan includes the Prophetic Books.

The translation techniques in the Targums varied. Some were very literal (e.g., Onqelos), while others were quite periphrastic (e.g., Neofiti). This inconsistency limits the Targums' value for textual criticism. However, at times the Targums may reflect an early reading of a text. Also, because the Targums are written in Aramaic, a sister language of Hebrew, they may preserve syntactical or grammatical elements that are lost in more distant languages.

---

117. Wegner, *Student's Guide*, 274.

118. Wegner, *Student's Guide*, 274.

119. For more information on the Targums, see Paul V. M. Flesher and Bruce Chilton, *The Targums: A Critical Introduction* (Waco, TX: Baylor University Press, 2011).

Table 3.5: The Most Important Targums			
Name	**Contents**	**Tradition**	**Approximate Date of Origin**
Onqelos	Pentateuch	Babylonian	2nd–5th centuries
Neofiti I	Pentateuch	Palestinian	3rd–4th centuries
Jonathan	Prophets	Babylonian	4th–5th centuries
Pseudo-Jonathan	Pentateuch	Mixed	7th–8th centuries
Cairo Genizah	Pentateuch	Palestinian	8th–14th centuries

3.2.4.d Vulgate

In the late fourth century AD, Pope Damasus I (366–384) commissioned his secretary **Jerome** (Eusebius Sophronius Hieronymus) to revise the Latin versions of the Bible. The Latin Bible needed revision and standardization because of the many variations in manuscripts now classified as the Old Latin (see §3.2.2.d Daughter Translations of the Septuagint). The abundance of varying Latin translations caused problems in liturgical settings and hampered theological discussions. The church needed a uniform and reliable text.[120]

Jerome began his work in Rome but completed it in a monastery near Bethlehem. He did not revise the existing Latin using the Septuagint, the Bible of the early church, as the pope expected him to. Instead, he learned Hebrew and used Hebrew manuscripts to translate the OT. Jerome's insistence on translating the OT from Hebrew rather than the Septuagint, which many believed to be the inspired text, brought a flood of criticism. Even Saint Augustine opposed his approach, fearing it would divide the Greek and Latin churches.[121] In addition to using the Hebrew text, Jerome also conferred with Jewish scholars, closely adhered to the Greek text, and carefully considered the Latin text, resulting in a translation that was very much in line with tradition.[122]

Known as the **Vulgate**, from the Latin term *vulgata*, meaning "common one," Jerome's text gained popularity over other Latin versions during the

---

120. Würthwein and Fischer, *Text of the Old Testament*, 142.

121. Würthwein, *Text of the Old Testament*, 96.

122. Gentry, "Text of the Old Testament," 25; Würthwein, *Text of the Old Testament*, 96–97.

next several centuries. In 1546 at the Council of Trent, the Roman Catholic Church declared the Vulgate its authentic Bible. The Vulgate is valuable for textual criticism primarily in that it provides evidence for Latin, Greek, and Hebrew manuscripts that are no longer available.

3.2.4.e Modern Critical Editions of Other Witnesses

Critical editions are available for each of the witnesses discussed above (the Samaritan Pentateuch, the Peshitta, Targum, and the Vulgate), but some editions are dated or inaccessible. Fortunately, the witnesses that are the most valuable for textual criticism are both modern and accessible.

3.2.4.e.1 Samaritan Pentateuch

The most recent edition of the Samaritan Pentateuch (ɯ) was published in 2010 by Abraham Tal and Moshe Florentin. Their edition presents the Samaritan and the Masoretic versions side by side.[123] Previously, Abraham Tal's 1994 edition was the main version used for critical study of the Samaritan Pentateuch.[124] Both of these are diplomatic editions based on the text of manuscript Shechem 6, but neither edition includes a critical apparatus of variants from other manuscripts of the Samaritan Pentateuch. Another edition by Avraham and Ratson Sadaqa, published between 1961 and 1965, is out of print.[125] The most accessible edition dates to 1918 (reprinted in 1966) and was edited by A. F. von Gall.[126] Von Gall produced an eclectic edition and included a critical apparatus. Tov calls this five-volume edition "detailed and accurate." The text's two shortcomings are that von Gall often adapted the text to align with the Masoretic Text, and, because of its age, it excludes recently discovered manuscript evidence.[127]

---

123. Abraham Tal and Moshe Florentin, eds., *The Pentateuch: The Samaritan Version and the Masoretic Version* (Tel Aviv: The Haim Rubin Tel Aviv University Press, 2010).

124. Abraham Tal, *The Samaritan Pentateuch, Edited according to MS 6 (C) of the Shekhem Synagogue,* Texts and Studies in the Hebrew Language and Related Subjects 8 (Tel Aviv: Chaim Rosenberg School, 1994).

125. Avraham Sadaqa and Ratson Sadaqa, *Jewish and Samaritan Version of the Pentateuch — With Particular Stress on the Differences between Both Texts* (Tel Aviv: Ruben Mass, 1961–1965).

126. August F. von Gall, *Der hebräische Pentateuch der Samaritaner,* vols. 1–5 (Giessen: Töpelmann, 1914–1918; repr., Berlin, 1966).

127. Tov, *Textual Criticism* (3rd ed.), 78.

Benyamim Tsedaka published an English translation of the Samaritan Pentateuch in 2013.[128]

3.2.4.e.2 Peshitta

The modern critical edition of the Peshitta (𝕾) is a diplomatic edition based on **Codex Ambrosianus** (7a1), which dates to the sixth–seventh centuries AD. A project of the Leiden Peshitta Institute at Leiden University in the Netherlands, the **Leiden Peshitta** includes the entire OT, the NT, and the apocryphal books. In volumes published after 1976, editors emend the text of Codex Ambrosianus if a given reading does not have the support of at least two other manuscripts dating before AD 1000.[129] The critical apparatus identifies only variants in Syriac manuscripts. The entire collection is available in print through Brill and electronically.[130]

3.2.4.e.3 Targum

Many of the Targums (𝕮) are available in critical editions, but the most widely used print edition is *The Bible in Aramaic Based on Old Manuscripts and Printed Texts*, a four-volume set by Alexander Sperber.[131] Critical editions of the Targums are also available electronically via Bible software or through the website of the Comprehensive Aramaic Lexicon project of the Hebrew Union College-Jewish Institute of Religion in Cincinnati.[132]

3.2.4.e.4 Vulgate

The most widely known and used critical edition of the Latin Vulgate is the Stuttgart edition, published by the German Bible Society (Deutsche

---

128. Benyamim Tsedaka and Sharon J. Sullivan, *The Israelite Samaritan Version of the Torah: First English Translation Compared with the Masoretic Version* (Grand Rapids: Eerdmans, 2013).

129. Tov, *Textual Criticism* (3rd ed.), 151–52n256.

130. Peshitta Institute Leiden, *The Old Testament in Syriac according to the Peshitta Version*, 14 vols (Leiden: Brill, 1972–2013); Peshitta Institute, *The Leiden Peshitta*, electronic. ed. (Leiden: Peshitta Institute Leiden, 2008). See http://www.brill.com/publications/peshitta-old-testament-syriac.

131. Alexander Sperber, ed., *The Bible in Aramaic Based on Old Manuscripts and Printed Texts* (Leiden: Brill, 2004).

132. Stephen A. Kaufman, ed., Comprehensive Aramaic Lexicon Project, http://cal1.cn.huc.edu.

Bibelgesellschaft). First printed in 1969, this eclectic text is currently in its fifth edition.[133]

3.3 HOW TO DO OLD TESTAMENT TEXTUAL CRITICISM

Textual criticism is not an exact science, but textual critics do follow a basic process for evaluating textual evidence (see §2.3 Basic Principles of Textual Criticism). Each type of evidence—**external evidence** or **internal evidence**—presents a particular set of issues. How old is this manuscript? Is this reading found elsewhere? Does this reading fit with the author's style and argument?

There are six guiding principles for the evaluation of variants. However, it is important to remember that these principles are not rules, and not every principle applies in every situation.

Table 3.6: Six Principles for Evaluating Variants	
Principles for Evaluating External Evidence	**Principles for Evaluating Internal Evidence**
1. Prefer the reading found in the oldest manuscript.	4. Prefer the shorter reading (*lectio brevior*).
2. Prefer the reading found in the majority of manuscripts.	5. Prefer the more difficult reading (*lectio difficilior*).
3. Prefer the reading found in the largest variety of manuscripts.	6. Prefer the reading that best fits the author.

3.3.1 TOOLS FOR OLD TESTAMENT TEXTUAL CRITICISM

Textual critics need three basic tools to evaluate variants in the biblical text: the biblical text itself, a critical apparatus, and a dictionary (or lexicon) of Biblical Hebrew. Another useful tool for textual study is the footnotes included in certain English versions, which alert readers to important

---

133. Robertus Weber and Roger Gryson, *Biblia Sacra iuxta Vulgatam versionem*, 2nd ed. (Stuttgart: Deutsche Bibelgesellschaft, 1975); Weber and Gryson, *Biblia Sacra Vulgata*, 5th rev. ed. (Stuttgart: Deutsche Bibelgesellschaft, 2007).

textual issues. We have already discussed most of these basic tools, so we will treat them only briefly in this section.

3.3.1.a Critical Texts

The starting place for text-critical study is the biblical text itself. If possible, when you're working through a particular passage, work in the original languages of the text and ancient versions (Hebrew, Aramaic, Greek, Syriac, Latin). If you do not know the original languages, use an English translation that is formally equivalent and carefully observe any marginal notes provided by the translators. Whether you are working in the original languages or in English, read a technical commentary alongside the passage; the commentator will address many text-critical issues. The critical editions available for the Hebrew Bible, the Septuagint, and other important OT witnesses have been discussed at length earlier in the chapter (see §3.2.1.c Modern Critical Editions of the Hebrew Bible; §3.2.2.e Modern Critical Editions of the Septuagint; and §3.2.4.e Modern Critical Editions of Other Witnesses).

3.3.1.b Critical Apparatuses

In part, a critical edition of the text is considered critical because it includes a critical apparatus in which the volume's editors identify variant readings and their sources. Each of the critical editions of the Hebrew Bible noted earlier includes a critical apparatus.

3.3.1.c Lexica

If you are working in the original languages, a good dictionary—or lexicon—is a useful tool for clarifying what Hebrew words mean and how they are used throughout the OT. You can then compare how the same words are used elsewhere and how translations treat the same word in other contexts. Such comparison may help you understand a translator's style or preference for certain words. The standard lexica for biblical Hebrew are "Brown-Driver-Briggs" (BDB) and the *Hebrew and Aramaic Lexicon of the Old Testament* (*HALOT*).[134] In Logos Bible Software, BDB is coded to Strong's

---

134. Francis Brown, Samuel R. Driver, and Charles A. Briggs, *A Hebrew and English Lexicon of the Old Testament* (Oxford: Clarendon, 1906); Ludwig Koehler, Walter Baumgartner, and

Concordance, so it may be more useful for you than *HALOT* if you have not studied Hebrew.[135]

3.3.1.d Translator's Notes

Many English translations, particularly those that classify themselves as study Bibles, include notes that are relevant for textual criticism. They alert the reader that there may be an issue with something in the text, or they may highlight a point of textual interest. In the OT, translators use three primary notes:

Heb/Hebrew: Notes beginning with "Heb" or "Hebrew" specify cases in which translators used an English word or phrase that does not directly correlate with the original language. The note identifies what that original Hebrew wording is.

For example, the word *Sheol* in the OT refers to the place of the dead. It is commonly used in Psalms, where many English translations simply use the name "Sheol." Some translations may use "dead" or "grave" in place of "Sheol," as the footnotes in the NLT indicate (see, e.g., Pss 16:10; 30:3; 31:17).

Or...: This note specifies when translators have chosen a particular English rendering of a word or phrase where other translations were equally possible. Strictly speaking, this is an issue of translation, not textual criticism.

The ESV of Proverbs 15:7 has a note of this kind. The last clause reads, "not so the hearts of fools." A footnote with this verse reads, "Or *the hearts of fools are not steadfast.*" A comparison with the NIV of this clause shows that the translators there preferred the alternate reading: "but the hearts of fools are not upright."

Other Ancient Authorities: This note is the most relevant for seeing how textual criticism affects English translations. English Bibles use this note to inform readers that the translators have selected a particular reading over another as the basis of their translation. Biblical footnotes under this heading alert readers to places where multiple variants are found in the relevant manuscripts.

Johann Jakob Stamm, eds., *The Hebrew and Aramaic Lexicon of the Old Testament*, trans. and ed. under the supervision of M. E. J. Richardson, 5 vols. (Leiden: Brill, 1994-2000).

135. Francis Brown, Samuel R. Driver, and Charles A. Briggs, *Enhanced Brown-Driver-Briggs Hebrew and English Lexicon*, electronic ed. (Oak Harbor, WA: Logos Research Systems, 2000).

We find an example of such a note in Genesis 41:16, where Joseph responds to Pharaoh's request to interpret his dream by saying, "It is not in my power; God will answer concerning the welfare of Pharaoh" (LEB). Some English versions (e.g., the ESV) include a note here pointing out that the Samaritan Pentateuch and Septuagint say something like "Without God it is not possible to give Pharaoh an answer about his welfare." This marginal note might prompt the text critic to investigate which reading is more original.

3.3.2 THE OLD TESTAMENT TEXT CRITICAL PROCESS: STEP BY STEP

Before OT textual critics can prefer a particular reading, they must identify the variants and determine how they developed. The process detailed below will help you in identifying variants so that you can reasonably judge which readings best represent the original text.

The general goal of textual criticism is to restore the most original reading of the biblical text. However, because the compositional process and early transmission of the OT is so uncertain, OT textual critics must further define their goal by deciding which stage of the text's history to aim for (see §2.2 The Goal of Textual Criticism). For the purposes of this chapter, the goal of OT textual criticism is to reconstruct the text's final form or the "final literary product."[136] This refers to the form of the text when the literary composition and editorial arranging was complete, and the text was considered authoritative. At this point, the scribe's task was to meticulously transmit the text—not alter it. According to Tov, "We focus on the written text or edition (or a number of consecutive editions) that contained the finished literary product (or one of its earlier stages) that stood at the beginning of the textual transmission process."[137] In other words, the goal is to reconstruct the text that gave rise to the known variants.[138]

---

136. Tov, *Textual Criticism* (3rd ed.), 165.

137. Tov, *Textual Criticism* (3rd ed.), 165.

138. This goal is *not* the same as reconstructing the *Urtext* or archetype, labels that imply the original text is the goal. Describing his work on a critical edition of the Hebrew text of Proverbs, Michael V. Fox explains his goal as "reconstructing the Masoretic *hyparchetype*," meaning a reconstructed source of variants at some remove from the archetype (M. V. Fox, "Editing Proverbs: The Challenge of the Oxford Hebrew Bible," *JNSL* 32.1 [2006]: 1–22 [5–6]).

3.3.2.a Step 1—Assemble All Variants

Using the critical apparatus in a critical edition of the Hebrew Bible, such as *BHS*, identify the variant readings in the text you are considering. Each critical edition has a key (probably in the book's introduction) explaining the symbols used in the apparatus. Wonneberger's *Understanding BHS* and Scott's *A Simplified Guide to BHS* are especially useful for navigating the apparatus of *BHS*.

Depending on which critical edition and apparatus you are using, there may be additional variants not addressed. You should also check commentators to see whether they mention variant readings.[139] If you are able to check primary sources, you should assemble as many readings as you can from the Septuagint, the Vulgate, the Peshitta, the Dead Sea Scrolls, the Samaritan Pentateuch, and the Masoretic Text. While other witnesses may have variants, they are generally less reliable as sources; typically, specialists consult these witnesses only in certain circumstances.

Next, arrange the collection of readings in a parallel format so you can compare them and identify variants. Then go through each reading and make sure you can account for the form and meaning of every word, as well as the syntax of the reading.

Table 3.7: Aligning the Versions of Lamentations 3:22[140]					
MT	**Peshitta**	**Targum**	**Vulgate**	**Gloss**	**Key**
חסדי	ܚܢ̈ܢܘܗܝ	טיבותא	*misericordiae*	"mercies of"	Plural nouns
יהוה	ܕܡܪܝܐ	דיהוה	*Domini*	"God"	Proper name
כי	ܕ	ארום	*quia*	"because"	Conjunction
לא	ܠܐ	לא	*non*	"not"	Negation
תמנו	ܠܓܡܪ	פסקו	*sumus consumpti*	"we are used up" OR "they are used up"	Plural verbs
כי	ܕ	ארום	*quia*	"because"	Conjunction
לא	ܠܐ	לא	*non*	"not"	Negation

---

139. Commentaries may be pastoral, devotional, or technical. For textual criticism, you should use a technical commentary.

140. Lamentations 3:22-24 is absent from the Septuagint.

כלו	ܐܬܘܒ	אתמניעו	*defecerunt*	"they cease"	Plural verbs
רחמיו	ܘܪ̈ܚܡܘ,	רחמוהי	*miserationes eius*	"his mercies"	Plural nouns

When you come across variants between the translations and any of the Hebrew witnesses, it can be helpful to know what Hebrew the translators had in front of them—that is, their *Vorlage* or parent text. The only way to know this with reasonable confidence is to retrovert the translations back into Hebrew. Doing so will allow you to compare Hebrew to Hebrew in your assessment of variants.

3.3.2.b Step 2—Analyze the Variants

Once you have assembled the readings and retroverted translations back into Hebrew, you will be able to identify the variants between the readings. The next step is to compare the variant readings and determine what kind of variants they are. Some textual critics prefer to treat the Masoretic Text simply as one of several witnesses, while others assign greater value to it and assess other readings in light of it. Brotzman advises, "As a whole, the Masoretic Text is certainly to be valued more highly than the witness derived from the versions. But in any one particular text, the various readings of all witnesses must be considered and a valid decision reached based on internal evidence."[141]

Identify the kind of variant readings and determine what could have caused the variation. Are there differences in entire words or sections? Differences in consonants? Differences that arose from an alternative set of vowels?

Once you have identified the types and causes of variants, discard any that can be explained as scribal mistakes. These include haplography, parablepsis, dittography, metathesis, homophony, or mistaken letters. In order to determine which variant represents a scribal mistake, you must be able to explain how the preferred reading led to the variant.

In the example from Lamentations 3:22, two versions have a first-person plural verb (MT: תָמְנוּ, *tāmĕnû*; Vulgate: *sumus consumpti*; both translate as "we are consumed"), and two versions have a third-person plural

---

141. Brotzman, *Old Testament Textual Criticism*, 127.

verb and make God's "mercies" the subject of the sentence (Peshitta: ܛܠܩܝܢ, ṭalqiyn, "they are being used up"; Targum: פסקו, pěsaqû, "they end"). Many biblical commentators follow the Aramaic variant in this case, accepting the likely Hebrew reading of תַּמּוּ (tammû) as the best reading.[142] The present MT text may be the result of a scribal error—possibly near-dittography or a misspelling. English versions are split between reading the traditional text of MT or following the variant.[143]

At this point, you should be left with variants beyond mechanical mistakes. These might include additions or subtractions to the text in the form of doublets, conflations, glosses, smoothing, harmonization, or clarification. When deciding which reading is preferable, remember that copyists are more likely to add material than delete it, so the shorter reading is typically preferred. Whichever reading can be best explained as the source of the others is the preferred reading.

3.3.2.c Step 3—Draw Conclusions

After you have determined the cause of variants to the best of your ability, you may be left with variants you cannot explain. These might represent differences in literary traditions; if so, they cannot be explained by the scribal process. In this case, it is not your task to pursue the variant any further—the goal of textual criticism is to determine the final form of the text, not the compositional history. Some variants may simply defy explanation.

Now you are ready to conclude which reading is the most original and why. Your reasons for selecting one reading over another should "include as full an explanation as possible for the probable development of the various secondary readings that are 'competing' with the original reading."[144]

3.3.3 EXAMPLES OF TEXT-CRITICAL ISSUES

In the following examples, we will walk you through the three-step process of assembling the variants, analyzing the variants, and drawing conclusions about the reading, as described above (see §3.3.2 The Old Testament Text Critical Process: Step by Step). We will demonstrate how to apply

---

142. Delbert R. Hillers, *Lamentations*, AYBC (New York: Doubleday, 1992), 115.

143. Versions following MT include ASV, HCSB, KJV, NIV. Versions following the Aramaic variant include ESV, JPS, LEB, NASB, NLT, NRSV, RSV.

144. Brotzman and Tully, *Old Testament Textual Criticism*, 139.

this process using the tools introduced earlier (see §3.3.1 Tools for Old Testament Textual Criticism). The goal for our examples is to recover the best reading of the final form of the text.

3.3.3.a Isaiah 40:7–8

1. Assemble All Variant Readings

At the beginning of Isaiah 40:7, *BHS* includes a superscript *a*, indicating there is a textual variant at that point. The corresponding note in the *BHS* apparatus says "v 7 > 𝕲." This indicates that Isaiah 40:7 is omitted (">") in the Septuagint ("𝕲").

When we examine the Septuagint, we will see that most editions have Isaiah 40:7 (see Rahlfs or the **Göttingen Septuagint**). However, it is considerably shorter than the Masoretic Text, consisting of only the phrase ἐξηράνθη ὁ χόρτος, καὶ τὸ ἄνθος ἐξέπεσεν[145] ("The grass is withered, and the flower falls off"). The Septuagint of Isaiah 40:8 is also shorter than that of the Masoretic Text, consisting of only the second half, τὸ δὲ ῥῆμα τοῦ θεοῦ ἡμῶν μένει εἰς τὸν αἰῶνα[146] ("but the word of our God remains forever").

Table 3.8: Variants of Isaiah 40:7–8		
Version	**Text**	**Translation**
MT	‏יָבֵשׁ חָצִיר נָבֵל צִיץ כִּי רוּחַ ‏יהוה נָשְׁבָה בּוֹ אָכֵן חָצִיר הָעָם: ‏יָבֵשׁ חָצִיר נָבֵל צִיץ וּדְבַר־ ‏אֱלֹהֵינוּ יָקוּם לְעוֹלָם:[147]	7 Grass withers; the flower withers when the breath of Yahweh blows on it. Surely the people are grass. 8 Grass withers; the flower withers, but the word of our God will stand forever. (LEB)

---

145. *exēranthē ho chortos, kai to anthos exepesen.*

146. *to de rhēma tou theou hēmōn menei eis ton aiōna.*

147. *yābēš ḥāṣîr nābēl ṣîṣ kî rûaḥ yhwh nāšbâ bw 'āken ḥāṣîr hā'ām. yābēš ḥāṣîr nābēl ṣîṣ ûdĕbar-'ĕlōhênû yāqûm lĕ'ôwlām.*

LXX	⁷ ἐξηράνθη ὁ χόρτος, καὶ τὸ ἄνθος ἐξέπεσεν, ⁸ τὸ δὲ ῥῆμα τοῦ θεοῦ ἡμῶν μένει εἰς τὸν αἰῶνα.[148]	⁷ the grass is withered, and the flower falls off, ⁸ but the word of our God remains forever. (LES)

2. Analyze the Variants

In this case, there are only two possible readings: one reflected by the Masoretic Text and one by the Septuagint. The reading found in the Septuagint is shorter and would fulfill the principle of *lectio difficilior*. However, we could attribute the Septuagint's omission to haplography. Isaiah 40:7 and 40:8 both begin with the Hebrew phrase יָבֵשׁ חָצִיר נָבֵל צִיץ (*yābēš ḥāṣîr nābēl ṣîṣ*). The translator's eye likely skipped from the first occurrence of יָבֵשׁ חָצִיר נָבֵל צִיץ (*yābēš ḥāṣîr nābēl ṣîṣ*) to the second, causing him to miss the intervening text.

This accidental change also appears in the Dead Sea Scrolls. The original scribe of 1QIsaᵃ also skipped from the first occurrence of יָבֵשׁ חָצִיר נָבֵל צִיץ (*yābēš ḥāṣîr nābēl ṣîṣ*) to the second. However, a second scribe noticed the error and added the omitted text.[149]

3. Draw Conclusions

Isaiah 40:7b–8a was likely accidently omitted from the Septuagint. We can easily explain this omission as haplography. All English translations follow the Masoretic Text, and most commentaries include it with little or no comment.[150]

---

148. *exēranthē ho chortos, kai to anthos exepesen. to de rhēma tou theou hēmōn menei eis ton aiōna.*

149. See Abegg et. al., *Dead Sea Scrolls Bible*, 332.

150. See Joseph Blenkinsopp, *Isaiah 40–55: A New Translation with Introduction and Commentary*, AYBC (New York: Doubleday, 2002), 178.

3.3.3.b Ruth 1:14

1. Assemble All Variant Readings

Midway through Ruth 1:14, *BHS* notes that a textual variant is present. The note in the apparatus says, "𝕲 ad καὶ ἐπέστρεψεν εἰς τὸν λαὸν αὐτῆς"—meaning that the Septuagint ("𝕲") adds ("ad") the given phrase, which translates as "and returned to her people" (LES). The apparatus note continues with "frt l וַתָּשָׁב אֶל־עַמָּהּ." Here the editors of *BHS* retroverted the Septuagint's phrase to a possible Hebrew *Vorlage*.[151]

The Peshitta also adds a phrase in Ruth 1:14. After "and Orpah kissed her mother-in-law" (ܠܚܡܬܗ ܥܦܪܐ ܘܢܫܩܬ; *wanešqath Orpah laḥemāth*), the text adds ܘܗܦܟܬ ܘܐܙܠܬ (*wahefkath wa'ezalth*), which translates as "and she turned and departed." The Vulgate also adds the phrase *ac reversa est*, which can be translated as "and returned."

Table 3.9: Variants of Ruth 1:14		
Version	**Text**	**Translation**
MT	וַתִּשַּׁק עָרְפָּה לַחֲמוֹתָהּ וְרוּת דָּבְקָה בָּהּ[152]	And Orpah kissed her mother-in-law, but Ruth clung to her. (ESV)
LXX	καὶ κατεφίλησεν Ορφα τὴν πενθερὰν αὐτῆς καὶ ἐπέστρεψεν εἰς τὸν λαὸν αὐτῆς, Ρουθ δὲ ἠκολούθησεν αὐτῇ[153]	After that Orpah kissed her mother-in-law and returned to her people, but Ruth followed her. (LES)
Peshitta	ܘܗܦܟܬ ܠܚܡܬܗ ܥܦܪܐ ܘܢܫܩܬ ܘܐܙܠܬ. ܒܗ ܕܝܢ ܪܥܘܬ	And Orpah kissed her mother-in-law, and she turned and departed. But Ruth clung to her.
Vulgate	*Orpha osculata socrum est ac reversa Ruth adhesit socrui suae.*	Orpha kissed her mother in law and returned. Ruth clung to her.

---

151. "frt l" means "perhaps read."

152. *watišaq ʿorpāh laḥămōwtāh wěrût dābqāh bāh.*

153. *kai katephilēsen Orpha tēn pentheran autēs kai epestrepsen eis ton laon autēs, Routh de ēkolouthēsen autē.*

2. Analyze the Variants

The variants found in the Septuagint, Peshitta, and Vulgate are all slightly different. However, they seem to share the same function: to clarify that Orpah went back home. The Masoretic Text is somewhat ambiguous when it says, "Orpah kissed her mother-in-law, but Ruth clung to her." We might wonder what became of Orpah after she kissed Naomi. The different versions may have noticed this and attempted to make the text clearer. Therefore, the Septuagint clarified that Orpah "returned to her people." The Peshitta and Vulgate just clarify that she returned or departed.

In this case, the Masoretic Text fulfills the principles of both *lectio brevior* and *lectio difficilior*. However, we could explain the Masoretic Text's omission by parablepsis. The *BHS* apparatus provided a retroverted Hebrew of וַתָּשָׁב אֶל־עַמָּהּ (*watāšāb 'el-'amāh*). If that were part of the original Hebrew, the scribe could have accidentally omitted it if his eye skipped from the ending of לַחֲמוֹתָהּ (*laḥămōwtāh*) to the identical ending of עַמָּהּ (*'amāh*).

3. Draw Conclusions

The Masoretic Text most likely represents the best reading. While a scribe could have accidentally omitted the phrase וַתָּשָׁב אֶל־עַמָּהּ (*watāšāb 'el-'amāh*) because of parablepsis, it is more likely that the additional phrases found in the Septuagint, Peshitta, and Vulgate are attempts to clarify a potentially ambiguous verse.[154] This argument is strengthened in that each of these versions are slightly different. If these versions were following an underlying Hebrew *Vorlage*, they would probably show less variation.

3.3.3.c Proverbs 14:32

1. Assemble All Variant Readings

In *BHS*, there is a variant—marked by a superscript *a*—on the second-to-last word of Proverbs 14:32. The *BHS* apparatus says, "𝕲(𝕾) τῇ ἑαυτοῦ ὁσιότητι, l בְּתוּמּוֹ." This note indicates that the Septuagint ("𝕲"), which is followed by

---

154. Frederic Bush argues that the Hebrew נשק (*nšq*) is *not* ambiguous and has the connotation of "to kiss farewell." See Frederic Bush, *Ruth, Esther*, WBC (Dallas: Word, 1996), 71. The LEB follows this in their translation: "And Orpah kissed her mother-in-law *goodbye*."

the Syriac ("ܣ"), reads τῇ ἑαυτοῦ ὁσιότητι. The editors of *BHS* then provide a possible reading for this with the retroverted Hebrew בְּתֻמּוֹ (*bětûmmô*).

The Biblical Dead Sea Scrolls index in Logos Bible Software shows that Proverbs 14:32 is present in 4QProv[b].[155] This scroll supports the Masoretic Text's reading of במותו (*bmwtw*).

Table 3.10: Variants of Proverbs 14:32

Version	Text	Translation
MT	בְּרָעָתוֹ יִדָּחֶה רָשָׁע וְחֹסֶה בְמוֹתוֹ צַדִּיק[156]	By his evildoing, the wicked will be overthrown, and the righteous will find refuge in his death. (LEB)
LXX	ἐν κακίᾳ αὐτοῦ ἀπωσθήσεται ἀσεβής, ὁ δὲ πεποιθὼς τῇ ἑαυτοῦ ὁσιότητι δίκαιος.[157]	By his evil the ungodly is thrust away, but by his own piety the one who trusts is righteous. (LES)
Retroverted Hebrew	בְּרָעָתוֹ יִדָּחֶה רָשָׁע וְחֹסֶה בתומו צַדִּיק[158]	In his evil, the wicked will be cast down, but the righteous seeks refuge in his integrity.

2. Analyze the Variants

The difference between these two variants is only two letters. The Masoretic Text has בְּמוֹתוֹ (*běmôtô*), which means "in his death," while the Septuagint, when retroverted to Hebrew, has בְּתֻמּוֹ (*bětûmmô*), which means "in his integrity." The difference is the root, which is either מָוֶת (*māwet*), meaning "death," or תֹּם (*tōm*), meaning "purity, integrity."

The variants can be explained two ways. The reading found in the Masoretic Text could be an unintentional error introduced by metathesis of the מ and ת. In this case, the reading of the Septuagint should be preferred. On the other hand, the Septuagint text may be an attempt to clarify or correct the Masoretic Text. The phrase "the righteous will find refuge in his

---

155. Logos Bible Software, *Biblical Dead Sea Scrolls: Bible Reference Index* (Bellingham, WA: Lexham Press, 2011).

156. *běrā ʿātōw yidāḥeh rāšā ʿ wěḥōse běmôtô ṣadîq.*

157. *en kakia autou apōsthēsetai asebēs, ho de pepoithōs tē heautou hosiotēti dikaios.*

158. *běrā ʿātōw yidāḥeh rāšā ʿ wěḥōse bětûmmô ṣadîq.*

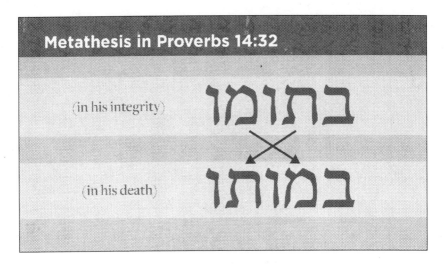

Metathesis in Proverbs 14:32

(in his integrity)   בתומו

(in his death)   במותו

death" reflects the more difficult reading and fulfills the principle of *lectio difficilior*. Furthermore, 4QProv[b] supports the Masoretic Text's reading.

3. Draw Conclusions

Most English translations follow the Masoretic Text.[159] However, some translations, such as the NRSV, NAB, and GNB, follow the Septuagint. Scholars are also split on this issue. Roland Murphy favors the Septuagint's reading, arguing that finding refuge in death would run contrary to the perspectives on death in Proverbs.[160] Duane Garrett agrees and points out that death in Proverbs is the result of evil behavior.[161] Michael V. Fox also believes the Septuagint preserves the more likely reading, noting that the Hebrew "syntax is unnatural" in the MT's reading and that the MT's text is probably best explained as metathesis.[162] Paul Koptak, however, follows the MT, calling the evidence for following the Septuagint "not compelling."[163]

---

159. E.g., the ESV, NASB, NKJV, and NIV.

160. Roland E. Murphy, *Proverbs*, WBC (Dallas: Word, 1998), 102.

161. Duane A. Garrett, *Proverbs, Ecclesiastes, Song of Songs*, NAC (Nashville: Broadman & Holman, 1993), 146–47. As examples he cites Prov 11:19; 14:12; 16:25; 19:16.

162. Michael V. Fox, *Proverbs 10–31*, AYBC (New Haven: Yale University Press, 2009), 586.

163. Paul E. Koptak, *Proverbs*, NIVAC (Grand Rapids: Zondervan, 2003), 382.

He argues that the verse is saying the righteous have a refuge that even death cannot overcome.[164]

But the reading found in the Septuagint makes more sense of the verse's poetic parallelism. The righteous finding refuge "in his integrity" (בְּתֻמּוֹ; bĕtûmmô) would provide a fitting parallel with the wicked being overthrown "by his evildoing" (בְּרָעָתוֹ; bĕrāʿātô). With this reading, Proverbs 14:32 would carry the same meaning as Proverbs 11:6, where the upright are saved by their righteousness.[165] Therefore, it seems most probable that the Septuagint preserves the superior reading for this verse.

3.3.3.d Psalm 145:13

1. Assemble All Variant Readings

The critical apparatus for BHS lists a major variant at the end of Psalm 145:13. In BHS there is a superscript a at the end of the verse. The corresponding entry in the apparatus begins "ins c Ms 𝔊𝔖." This indicates that what follows is inserted ("ins") in some ("c") Hebrew manuscripts ("Ms"), as well as the Septuagint ("𝔊") and Syriac ("𝔖").

According to the apparatus, the inserted phrase is נֶאֱמָן יהוה בְּכָל־דְּבָרָיו וְחָסִיד בְּכָל־מַעֲשָׂיו ("Yahweh is faithful in all his words and loyal in all his deeds").[166] The BHS apparatus provides a retroverted translation of the Greek and Syriac. The specific phrase found in the Septuagint is πιστὸς κύριος ἐν τοῖς λόγοις αὐτοῦ καὶ ὅσιος ἐν πᾶσι τοῖς ἔργοις αὐτοῦ.[167] Most editions (e.g., Rahlfs; Göttingen) list this phrase as Psalm 145:13a. The Peshitta has ܡܗܝܡܢ ܗܘ ܡܪܝܐ ܒܡܠܘܗܝ ܘܙܕܝܩ ܒܟܠܗܘܢ ܥܒܕܘܗܝ.[168] Because of the similarity between the Septuagint and Peshitta in this verse, it is likely that either the translators of these versions were working from a similar Hebrew Vorlage or the translator of the Peshitta was influenced by the reading of

---

164. Dave Bland also favors the MT's reading but interprets the verse to mean the righteous seek God's refuge "even to the point of death"; see Dave Bland, Proverbs, Ecclesiastes, & Song of Songs, College Press NIV Commentary (Joplin, MO: College Press, 2002), 141–42.

165. Fox, Proverbs 10–31, 585–86.

166. ne ʾĕmān yhwh bĕkol-dĕbārāyw wĕḥāsîd bĕkol-maʿăśāyw.

167. pistos kyrios en tois logois autou kai hosios en pasi tois ergois autou; "Faithful is the Lord in his words, and holy in all his works" (LES).

168. məhaymen həw maryaʾ bamluweh wazadīq bakullhon ʿəbādawhy; "The Lord is faithful in all his affairs and righteous in all his deeds."

the Septuagint. Jerome's Vulgate also follows this reading, which could also be due to *Vorlage* or the influence of the Septuagint. These three sources represent only one textual variant. Because the Septuagint is the more relevant text, it will be the focus of this discussion.

The Biblical Dead Sea Scrolls index in Logos Bible Software shows that Psalm 145:13 is represented in 11Q5ᵃ, column XVII, which contains the phrase נאמן אלוהים בדבריו וחסיד בכול מעשי.[169] This mostly matches the added phrase of the Septuagint, but it substitutes אלוהים (ʾlwhym) for יהוה (yhwh) or κύριος (kyrios). The Qumran scroll also includes the refrain ברוך יהוה וברוך שמו לעולם ועד[170] both before and after נאמן אלוהים בדבריו וחסיד בכול מעשיו.[171]

Table 3.11: Variants of Psalm 145:13		
Version	**Text**	**Translation**
MT	מַלְכוּתְךָ מַלְכוּת כָּל־עֹלָמִים וּמֶמְשַׁלְתְּךָ בְּכָל־דּוֹר וָדוֹר[172]	Your kingdom is an everlasting kingdom, and your dominion endures throughout all generations. (LEB)
LXX	ἡ βασιλεία σου βασιλεία πάντων τῶν αἰώνων, καὶ ἡ δεσποτεία σου ἐν πάσῃ γενεᾷ καὶ γενεᾷ. πιστὸς κύριος ἐν τοῖς λόγοις αὐτοῦ καὶ ὅσιος ἐν πᾶσι τοῖς ἔργοις αὐτοῦ.[173]	Your kingdom is the kingdom over all the ages, and your dominion in every generation and generation. Faithful is the Lord in his words, and holy in all his works. (LES)

---

169. *n'mn 'lwhym bdbryw wḥsyd bkwl m'šy.*

170. *brwk yhwh wbrwk šmw l'wlm w'd.*

171. *n'mn 'lwhym bdbryw wḥsyd bkwl m'šy.*

172. *malkûtěkā malkût kol-'ōlāmîm ûmemšeltěkā běkol-dôr wādôr.*

173. *hē basileia sou basileia pantōn tōn aiōnōn, kai hē despoteia sou en pasē genea kai genea. pistos kyrios en tois logois autou kai hosios en pasi tois ergois autou.*

| 11Q5ᵃ | מלכותכה מלכות כול
עולמים וממשֹלתכה בכול
דור ודֹור ברֹוך יהוה וברֹוך
שמֹו לעֹולם זֹעד נאמן
אֵלוהיﬦ בדבריו וחסיד בכול
מעשיו ברוך יהוה זֹברֹוך
שﬦ לעולם זֹעד¹⁷⁴ | Your kingdom is an everlasting kingdom, and your dominion endures throughout all generations. Blessed be the LORD and blessed be his name forever and ever. <u>God</u> is faithful in his words, and gracious in all his deeds. Blessed be the LORD and blessed be his name forever and ever. (DSS Bible) |

2. Analyze the Variants

There are two main readings. The Masoretic Text omits a phrase, while the Septuagint and Dead Sea Scrolls (as well as the Peshitta and Vulgate) include it. Based on the reading of the 11Q5ᵃ, the phrase missing from the MT can be reconstructed as

נֶאֱמָן יהוה בְּכָל־דְּבָרָיו וְחָסִיד בְּכָל־מַעֲשָׂיו¹⁷⁵

The Dead Sea Scrolls also contain two additional variants. First, 11Q5ᵃ includes a repeated refrain not found in any other versions. This refrain is repeated throughout Psalm 145 in 11Q5ᵃ, so its presence in Psalm 145:13 should not be considered a legitimate variant. The added refrain is likely a deliberate change made by whoever complied 11Q5ᵃ. It may indicate that the compiler of 11Q5ᵃ meant this psalm to be recited or sung.¹⁷⁶

The MT's omission of the phrase fits the principle of *lectio brevior*. The text is obviously shorter without the additional phrase. There are no obvious signs that the line was omitted from the MT accidentally. Scribes may have skipped the line due to parablepsis, with the scribe's eye skipping from בְּכָל־ (*bĕkol-*) to בְּכָל־ (*bĕkol-*), but in each line בְּכָל־ (*bĕkol-*) is followed by a phrase that looks significantly different (דֹּור וָדֹור; *dôr wādôr*, and מַעֲשָׂיו; *maʿăśāyw*, respectively).

---

174. *mlkwtkh mlkwt kwl ʿwlmym wmmšltkh bkwl dwr wdr brwk yhwh wbrwk šmw lʿwlm wʿd n ʾmn ʾlwhym bdbryw whsyd bkwl m ʿśyw brwk yhwh wbrwk šmw lʿwlm wʿd.*

175. *ne ʾĕmān yhwh bĕkol-dĕbārāyw wĕḥāsîd bĕkol-ma ʿăśāyw.*

176. See Abegg et al., *Dead Sea Scrolls Bible*, 570.

The literary structure of Psalm 145 provides support for including the additional phrase. The psalm is an acrostic psalm, with each line beginning with a different letter of the Hebrew alphabet. However, there is no line for the letter *nun* (נ) in the MT. Instead, the text skips from *mem* (מ) to *samek* (ס). The added phrase in the Septuagint and Dead Sea Scrolls provides the *nun* line, completing the acrostic.

The Dead Sea Scrolls also differ from the Septuagint with regard to the divine name in the added line. Instead of יהוה—which would match the Septuagint's κύριος—11Q5ᵃ has אלוהים. To determine which divine name more likely reflects an earlier reading, we must examine the rest of the psalm. Outside Psalm 145:1, where the psalmist refers to אֱלֹהַי ('*ĕlôhay*; "my God"), Psalm 145 always uses the divine name יהוה. If the phrase found in the Septuagint and Dead Sea Scrolls were part of the original Hebrew text, it likely would have used יהוה, not אלוהים.

3. Draw Conclusions

The additional line found in the Septuagint—which is supported by the Peshitta, the Vulgate, and the Dead Sea Scrolls—may reflect the final text. The line may have been accidently omitted in the Masoretic Text. Many modern English translations, like the ESV, NRSV, NIV, and NLT, concur with this conclusion and include the additional phrase.[177] A majority of commentaries also favor including the additional phrase.[178]

However, some argue that the MT without the additional line reflects the more original Hebrew. They argue that it is not necessary to include the missing נ-line. Reuven Kimelman, for example, argues that the reading in the Septuagint and Dead Sea Scrolls represents a later attempt to fix the incomplete acrostic pattern. He argues that the missing נ-line is an intentional part of the psalm's message and structure.[179]

The split opinion regarding the inclusion or omission of this phrase in Psalm 145:13 illustrates the difficulty of textual criticism. The decision

---

177. The ESV puts brackets around the added phrase.

178. For example, Hans-Joachim Kraus, *Psalms 60–150*, trans. Hilton C. Oswald, CCS (Minneapolis: Fortress, 1993), 546; Leslie C. Allen, *Psalms 101–150*, rev. ed., WBC (Dallas: Word, 2002), 366.

179. Reuven Kimelman, "Psalm 145: Theme, Structure, and Impact," *JBL* 113 (1994): 49–50. See also Mitchell Dahood, *Psalms III: 101–150*, AYBC (New York: Doubleday, 1970), 335–36.

to include the missing phrase as part of the original Hebrew text is ultimately subjective.

3.3.3.e Deuteronomy 32:43

1. Assemble All Variant Readings

Several variant readings exist in Deuteronomy 32:43. The *BHS* text includes eight different indicators (*a* through *h*). This example focuses on the first half of the verse. For the first indicator (*a*), the *BHS* apparatus suggests the text should perhaps ("frt") read ("l") with ("c") the Qumran texts ("𝔔") and Septuagint ("𝔊"), which have שמים (*šmym*; "heavens") instead of גוים (*gôyim*; "nations").

The second note (*b*), which is more complex, is connected with the Masoretic Text's עַמּוֹ (ʿ*ammô*). The note first points out that manuscripts ("Ms") put אֶת (ʾ*ēt*) before ("pr") this word. It then notes that the Septuagint has ἅμα αὐτῷ (*hama autō*) and suggests that perhaps ("frt") the text should read ("l") עִם עַמּוֹ (ʿ*im* ʿ*ammô*). Finally, it notes that the Qumran texts and Septuagint, along with Hebrews 1:6 ("H 1,6") support the addition ("ad") of והשתחוו לו (כל) אלהים (*whšthww lw* ʾ*lhym*) or ("vel") בני אל (*bny* ʾ*l*). The Septuagint has καὶ προσκυνησάτωσαν αὐτῷ πάντες υἱοὶ θεοῦ,[180] which can be translated "and worship him, sons of God." According to the Biblical Dead Sea Scrolls index in Logos Bible Software, Deuteronomy 32:43 appears in 4QDeut^q. The Hebrew text of that scroll includes the phrase והשתחוו לו כל אלהים (*whšthww lw kl* ʾ*lhym*), which can be translated "and bow down to him, all gods."

The third note (*c*) in the *BHS* apparatus indicates that the Septuagint has a lengthy phrase before ("pr") the כִּי (*kî*): εὐφράνθητε, ἔθνη, μετὰ τοῦ λαοῦ αὐτοῦ, καὶ ἐνισχυσάτωσαν αὐτῷ πάντες ἄγγελοι θεοῦ,[181] which translates as "Delight, O nations, with his people, and prevail with him all angels of God." This phrase is absent from the MT.

When these three variant readings are put together, we see that the Septuagint and 4QDeut^q are much longer than the MT.

---

180. *kai proskynēsatōsan autō pantes huioi theou.*

181. *euphranthēte, ethnē, meta tou laou autou, kai enischysatōsan autō pantes angeloi theou.*

Table 3.12: Variants of Deuteronomy 32:43		
Version	**Text**	**Translation**
MT	הַרְנִינוּ גוֹיִם עַמּ֑וֹ [182]	Call for songs of joy, O nations, *concerning* his people (LEB)
LXX	εὐφράνθητε, οὐρανοί, ἅμα αὐτῷ, καὶ προσκυνησάτωσαν αὐτῷ πάντες υἱοὶ θεοῦ, εὐφράνθητε, ἔθνη, μετὰ τοῦ λαοῦ αὐτοῦ, καὶ ἐνισχυσάτωσαν αὐτῷ πάντες ἄγγελοι θεοῦ [183]	Delight, O heavens, with him and worship him, *you* sons of God. Delight, O nations, with his people and prevail with him, all *you* angels of God (LES)
4QDeut^q	הרנינו שמים עמו והשתחוו לו כל אלהים [184]	Rejoice, O heavens, together with him; and bow down to him all *you* gods (DSS Bible)

2. Analyze the Variants

The Masoretic Text of Deuteronomy 32:43 is much shorter than the versions found in the Septuagint and at Qumran; this would fulfill the principle of *lectio brevior*. However, the presence of additional lines in both the Septuagint and Dead Sea Scrolls makes the additions more credible. Another factor to consider is Hebrews 1:6, where the author presumably quotes Deuteronomy 32:43 when he writes καὶ προσκυνησάτωσαν αὐτῷ πάντες ἄγγελοι θεοῦ. This line is absent in the MT, indicating the author of Hebrews is using the Septuagint or some other version of Deuteronomy that is longer than the MT.

3. Draw Conclusions

The presence of additional lines in both the Septuagint and Dead Sea Scrolls, along with the quotation of this verse in Hebrews, makes it likely that something is missing from the Masoretic Text. Duane Christensen believes a line was omitted in the MT "as a 'nomistic correction' to prevent

---

182. *ḥarnînû gôyim ʿammô.*

183. *euphranthēte, ouranoi, hama autō, kai proskynēsatōsan autō pantes huioi theou, euphranthēte, ethnē, meta tou laou autou, kai enischysatōsan autō pantes angeloi theou.*

184. *hrnynw šmym ʿmw whštḥww lw kl ʾlhym.*

an angelological or polytheistic interpretation."[185] He argues that adding והשתחוו לו כל בני אל (whšthww lw kl bny 'l; "and worship him all you sons of God") improves the balance of the verse. Jeffrey Tigay also argues that the MT is incomplete. He points out that the longer texts of the Septuagint and 4QDeut[q] have better structures, while the shorter MT leaves the first line (הַרְנִינוּ גוֹיִם עַמּוֹ; harnînû gôyim 'ammô) without a parallel.[186]

The English translations differ in their treatment of this verse. While none completely follow the Septuagint, many translations do not follow the MT. Several translations, such as the ESV, NRSV, NAB, and NLT, use "heavens" instead of "nations." These translations also include some form of the second line not found in the MT. The ESV and NRSV have "bow down to/worship him all (you) gods," while the NAB and NLT include "angels" in the second line. Other English translations choose to follow the MT (e.g., LEB, NKJV, NASB, and GNB).

3.3.3.f Summary

The complicated textual issues involved in Deuteronomy 32:43 make it impossible to determine the original Hebrew with certainty.[187] This example demonstrates both the importance and the difficulty of OT textual criticism. Ascertaining the earliest Hebrew text may not always be possible, and it almost always involves subjective decisions. The examples listed here illustrate the types of decisions required in textual criticism. Sometimes, such as in Isaiah 40:7–8, there may be an obvious explanation for a textual variant. For some textual issues, however, there may be valid arguments for following either the Masoretic Text or a variant reading. Some variants, such as the one in Proverbs 14:32, involve only small changes to the text. Others involve adding or deleting entire phrases.

3.4 RESOURCES FOR FURTHER STUDY

Several of the books and articles referenced throughout chapter 3 are listed below. This section also includes several other important resources for OT textual criticism.

---

185. Duane L. Christensen, *Deuteronomy 21:10–34:12*, WBC (Dallas: Word, 2002), 813.

186. Jeffrey H. Tigay, *Deuteronomy* (Philadelphia: Jewish Publication Society, 1996), 516.

187. The above example covered only the first half of the verse. There are several additional variants in the second half.

Abegg, Martin, Jr., Peter Flint, and Eugene Ulrich. *The Dead Sea Scrolls Bible: The Oldest Known Bible Translated for the First Time into English*. New York: HarperOne, 1999.

The above book is an English translation of the biblical manuscripts from Qumran, formatted as a version of the Bible. It includes an introduction that describes how the ancient people viewed sacred texts, the history of the Qumran scrolls, and the method behind the book's compilation.

Barrera, Julio Trebolle. *The Jewish Bible and the Christian Bible: An Introduction to the History of the Bible*. Translated by Wilfred G. E. Watson. Leiden: Brill, 1998.

Barrera's book covers much more than issues of textual criticism. It is an expansive treatment of the Bible's history, including the formation of the canon, the transmission of texts, and the divergence of the two Bibles of Judaism and Christianity.

Brotzman, Ellis R., and Eric J. Tully. *Old Testament Textual Criticism: A Practical Introduction*. 2nd ed. Grand Rapids: Baker, 2016.

Brotzman and Tully have provided both a readable introduction to textual criticism and an introduction to *BHS*, focusing on helping students understand and navigate it. Their table of significant Masoretic manuscripts includes the Leningrad Codex (p. 56). They also describe the general differences between the Leningrad Codex and the Aleppo Codex. In their discussion of Greek versions, Brotzman and Tully address the place of Aquila, Symmachus, and Theodotion's translations in the development of the Greek text.

Fernández Marcos, Natalio. *The Septuagint in Context: Introduction to the Greek Version of the Bible*. Translated by Wilfred G. E. Watson. Leiden: Brill, 2000.

Fernández Marcos's book is a standard in Septuagint studies. It is an advanced introduction best suited for readers preparing for serious work in textual criticism or the Septuagint. He deals comprehensively with the cultural context of the translation and the many theories of its origin. He also considers the Septuagint's role in Jewish and Christian tradition. His treatment of the Septuagint also includes chapters on Aquila, Symmachus, and Theodotion's translations. He surveys ancient evidence for them and considers the characteristics of each translation. He concludes each chapter with an overview of the current research and future direction of scholarship.

Goshen-Gottstein, Moshe. "The Aleppo Codex and the Rise of the Massoretic Bible Text." *Biblical Archaeologist* 42. 3 (1979): 145–63.

Goshen-Gottstein was a leading scholar on the Aleppo Codex. In his 1979 article in *Biblical Archaeologist*, he discusses codices and evaluates the value of the Aleppo Codex. The article is an accessible introduction to the Aleppo Codex and its significance for textual criticism.

Jobes, Karen H., and Moisés Silva. *Invitation to the Septuagint.* 2nd ed. Grand Rapids: Baker Academic, 2015.

Jobes and Silva's highly reviewed introduction to Septuagint studies is now available in a second edition. They detail for the nonspecialist the history of the Greek translation, its transmission and establishment as authoritative, its interpretive value in Judaism and Christianity, and the current state of Septuagint scholarship. It is an excellent and accessible book for beginning and intermediate students.

Kelley, Page H., Daniel S. Mynatt, and Timothy G. Crawford. *The Masorah of "Biblia Hebraica Stuttgartensia": Introduction and Annotated Glossary.* Grand Rapids: Eerdmans, 1998.

Kelley, Mynatt, and Crawford have provided a full-length treatment of the Masorah that is more detailed than the nonspecialist needs, but it is a standard resource for those interested in deeper study of the Masoretes and the Masoretic Text.

Scott, William R. *A Simplified Guide to the BHS.* Berkeley, CA: BIBAL, 1987.

> Scott's concise handbook provides quick reference through the abbreviations, symbols, and Latin words used in *BHS* and its apparatus.

Tov, Emanuel. *Textual Criticism of the Hebrew Bible.* 3rd rev. and exp. ed. Minneapolis: Fortress, 2012.

> Tov's volume is the gold standard in print books on OT textual criticism. He provides extensive descriptions of the major witnesses to the Hebrew Bible's text and gives special attention to textual transmission, literary issues, and the difficulties associated with determining the original shape of the OT. Tov also wrote articles on textual criticism for the *Lexham Bible Dictionary* (*LBD*), which distill the most important theories, developments, and methods of the discipline: "Textual Criticism of the Hebrew Bible, History of Text"; "Textual Criticism of the Hebrew Bible, Methodology."

Ulrich, Eugene. *The Dead Sea Scrolls and the Origins of the Bible.* Grand Rapids: Eerdmans, 1999.

> Ulrich is a world-renowned scholar on the Scrolls. In this book, he details a theory for the development of the text of the OT based on evidence brought to light by the Dead Sea Scrolls. In light of the Qumran evidence, Ulrich advocates "multiple literary editions" in late Second Temple Judaism.

VanderKam, James C. *The Dead Sea Scrolls and the Bible.* Grand Rapids: Eerdmans, 2012.

> In this book, VanderKam provides an up-to-date and thoughtful introduction to the Dead Sea Scrolls and their significance for biblical studies. The first chapter is especially relevant for explaining the implications of the Scrolls for textual criticism.

Waltke, Bruce K. "Textual Criticism of the Old Testament and Its Relation to Exegesis and Theology." *NIDOTTE* 1:51–67.

> Waltke's introductory article is an excellent overview of the topic, particularly with respect to how textual criticism affects

interpretation of the biblical text. He discusses the history of the discipline, the importance of the task for interpretation, and the process of textual criticism.

Weis, R. D. "*Biblia Hebraica Quinta* and the Making of Critical Editions of the Hebrew Bible." *Journal of Biblical Textual Criticism*, 7 (2002). http://rosetta.reltech.org/TC/vol07/Weis2002.html.

Richard Weis, a member of the editorial committee for *BHQ*, gives a detailed look at the approach of the critical edition and compares it to the Hebrew University Bible Project (HUBP).

Wonneberger, Reinhard. *Understanding BHS: A Manual for the Users of "Biblia Hebraica Stuttgartensia."* Translated from the German by Dwight R. Daniels. 2nd rev. ed. Subsidia Biblica 8. Rome: Pontificio Istituto Biblico, 1990.

Wonneberger's manual helps readers navigate the apparatus of the *BHS* text and the Masorah. Available in print and electronically in Logos Bible Software, it defines the terms and sigla of *BHS* and provides examples from the biblical text.

Würthwein, Ernst, and Alexander Achilles Fischer. *The Text of the Old Testament: An Introduction to the "Biblia Hebraica."* Translated by Erroll F. Rhodes. 3rd ed. Grand Rapids: Eerdmans, 2014.

First published in German in 1952, Würthwein's introduction has been a classic in the field of Old Testament textual criticism for decades. Up until the fifth German edition in 1988 (the basis of the second Eerdmans English edition of 1995), Würthwein, who passed away in 1996, kept the text up to date himself. For the latest edition, Alexander Fischer has "completely rewritten" the book to bring it current on the many aspects of OT text criticism and transmission history that have changed since 1988.[188] The book discusses ancient writing practices, each of the major textual witnesses (and many of the lesser ones), and general methods of textual criticism. This resource also includes nearly

---

188. Würthwein and Fischer, *Text of the Old Testament*, xi. We have cited both the 1995 edition of Würthwein and this latest edition since at times we have preferred quoting Würthwein's earlier descriptions of certain positions.

one hundred pages of pictures and descriptions of manuscripts. This book would be an ideal next step for those who want more detailed information on most of the topics covered in this chapter.

4
—

INTRODUCTION TO NEW TESTAMENT TEXTUAL CRITICISM

4.1 HISTORY AND KEY FIGURES

For much of the first century AD, Christians handed down their traditions and teachings verbally. Paul alludes to this practice in 1 Corinthians 15:3: "For I passed on to you as of first importance what I also received" (ESV). However, as Christianity spread throughout the ancient world and the apostles and others penned the documents that eventually became the New Testament, the written word grew in use and authority.

The author of 2 Peter 3:15–16 speaks of Paul's letters and reflects the growing importance of the written word among Christians:

> And regard the patience of our Lord as salvation, just as also our dear brother Paul wrote to you, according to the wisdom that was given to him, as he does also in all his letters, speaking in them about these things, in which there are some things hard to understand, which the ignorant and unstable distort to their own destruction, as they also do the rest of the scriptures. (LEB)

Significantly, this passage indicates that Paul's letters were held in such high regard that they were grouped with "the rest of the scriptures," referring to the Old Testament.

4.1.1 EARLIEST CENTURIES (FIRST–SEVENTH CENTURY AD)

Desiring to share their sacred writings with believers in other regions, the earliest Christians copied and distributed their texts to churches and mission fields throughout the eastern Mediterranean and beyond. This early proliferation of copies took place freely and with few regulations, which caused variation in readings to be introduced into the texts. Such variation would of course then be reproduced in further copies and enter into the manuscript tradition. When modern scholars *collate* the text of the Greek New Testament[1] manuscripts, they find that they separate into groupings based on patterns of variation. These textual groupings are normally called Alexandrian, Western, Byzantine, and Caesarean (see §2.1.1.b New Testament Witnesses). While the titles of these groupings are based on theories about the geography and development of these groupings that are now seen as outdated, the titles remain in use for text critical discussions.

The Alexandrian textual grouping is so named because its most ancient representatives were found in Egypt, where Alexandria was a center of textual studies and manuscript production long before the advent of Christianity. The dry climate in Egypt preserved the oldest extant copies of the New Testament, which were written on papyrus. The textual complexion of the papyri supports the supposition that their early dates and the careful scribal traditions of the region resulted in the preservation of the most reliable manuscripts of the NT. However, the papyri were not discovered until the late 1800s and following, so this textual tradition did not receive attention until modern times. One reason that the text represented by the Alexandrian manuscripts was late on the scene is the tendency of later scribes to preserve the "fullest" text (leading to the Byzantine textual tradition, discussed below).

The Western textual group is associated with locations such as Gaul, Italy, and North Africa, and has only a few Greek representatives. The NT was translated into Latin early in the transmission process, and many of the Latin witnesses align with the Western tradition, so this text was influential in Latin-speaking Europe and the Roman church. Western witnesses are "full of expansions, deletions, harmonizations, and even theological

---

1. From here on, you will regularly see "Greek New Testament" abbreviated as GNT in this chapter.

alterations" that appear to be the result of a tendency to paraphrase rather than sloppy scribal practice.[2]

The fuller readings characteristic of the Byzantine textual tradition (named for its supposed connection to the old Byzantine Empire[3]) began to emerge as early as the third or fourth century. As time went on, it became common for professional scribes to collect and conflate readings, and prolific copying in Byzantine monasteries led to this textual tradition becoming dominant in the East and therefore the Orthodox Church.[4] Most textual scholars consider the Byzantine text to be generally less reliable because of its later date and derivative readings. However, recent scholarship has shed light on the value of this text, as will be seen below.

The fourth textual grouping, often referred to as the so-called Caesarean text, is less certain but still receives consideration in discussions of variants. The members of this grouping do share unique readings, but not consistently. Some evidence links at least Family 1 of the Gospels to the city of Caesarea during the time that **Origen** lived there,[5] but the entire Caesarean group is not linked to any geographical location.

Long before the recognition of these textual streams, some church fathers expressed awareness of differences between the manuscripts that were available to them. This awareness of and commentary on variants was a forerunner to the textual criticism that scholars do today.[6] For example, **Irenaeus** (c. AD 140-202) stated a preference for a particular reading of a verse in Revelation based on its presence in what he considered to be the best available manuscripts.[7] Origen (c. AD 185-253) demonstrated awareness of textual variants in the manuscripts to which he had

---

2. Daniel B. Wallace, "Textual Criticism of the New Testament," *LBD*.

3. Including Greece, Turkey, Bulgaria, Albania, and the former Yugoslavia.

4. Similarly, prolific copying in Latin by Catholic monks led to the dominance of the Latin text in the West.

5. See, for example, Amy S. Anderson, *The Textual Tradition of the Gospels: Family 1 in Matthew* (Leiden: Brill, 2004), 74-83.

6. For a thorough discussion of text-critical awareness and practices by the church fathers, see Amy M. Donaldson, "Explicit References to New Testament Variant Readings among Greek and Latin Church Fathers" (PhD diss., University of Notre Dame, 2009), https://curate.nd.edu/show/571m615k50.

7. Paul D. Wegner, *A Student's Guide to Textual Criticism of the Bible: Its History, Methods and Results* (Downers Grove, IL: InterVarsity, 2006), 208.

access when he produced his commentaries on the Bible.[8] **Jerome** (AD 331–420), who produced at least part of the Latin translation of the Bible (the Vulgate), built on the previous work of Irenaeus and Origen by preferring older manuscripts to new ones and attempting to explain the origin of variants according to scribal practices. However, though individuals during this period recognized the existence of variation in their biblical manuscripts, evaluation of these variants and resultant textual decisions remained unsystematic.

4.1.2 MIDDLE AGES AND LATER (EIGHTH CENTURY TO LATE SEVENTEENTH CENTURY AD)

The Greek New Testament writings became standardized as Constantinople, also known as Byzantium, became the center of transmission. Prolific copying of manuscripts by professionals (mainly monks who worked all day in monastery *scriptoria*, or "writing rooms"), together with the systematic "correction" of their exemplars to bring them into alignment with a fuller version of the text, resulted in the full-blown Byzantine standard ecclesiastical text.

Two significant events altered the history of textual transmission in the fifteenth century: the invention of the printing press (1450) and the resurfacing of numerous Greek minuscules as Christians fled west after the fall of Constantinople (1453). These two events made it possible to print— for the first time in history—a copy of the New Testament writings in the original Greek. The first printed Bible (the Gutenberg Bible) was in Latin, the language of scholarly Europe, but it was not long before the first Greek edition of the NT was produced (but not published), in 1514.[9] In competition, **Erasmus** of Rotterdam, the famous Dutch humanist, produced his own Greek and Latin bilingual NT in 1516 under the patronage of a Swiss

---

8. For a few examples where Origen notices textual variation, see Anderson, *Textual Tradition of the Gospels*, 78–79. Origen also produced the Hexapla, a critical edition of the Hebrew Bible in six versions, four of which were translated into Greek. This magnificent work is discussed in more detail in chapter 3 (see §3.2.2.c).

9. The first printed GNT was produced under Cardinal Francisco Ximenes de Cisneros of Spain as part of a polyglot Bible (in Hebrew, Aramaic, Greek, and Latin). The date of 1514 is misleading, however, since the Bible had to wait until it was sanctioned by Pope Leo X in 1520 and was not circulated until about 1522. Erasmus' Greek and Latin NT printed in 1516 was the first to be offered on the market.

printer. The time pressure meant that Erasmus was only able to locate several late Byzantine manuscripts for his edition, and these required corrections. In fact, when he lacked Greek manuscript evidence for the end of Revelation, Erasmus translated the Latin text from the Vulgate *back* into Greek, creating several otherwise unknown readings. In following years, he issued several amended editions of his NT, with the fifth and final edition printed in 1535.

Erasmus' GNT became the basis for the **Textus Receptus** (TR), meaning "the text received by all."[10] The Textus Receptus, edited repeatedly by various scholars, became the standard Greek text for the next several centuries. Erasmus' text was also the basis for two additional developments in Bible production: Martin Luther used it to translate the NT into German (1522), and William Tyndale drew on Erasmus' work for his English translation of the Bible (1526). Tyndale's translation, in turn, became the foundation for the King James Version (1611).

4.1.3 MODERN ERA (LATE SEVENTEENTH CENTURY TO THE PRESENT)

Though Erasmus' GNT was a landmark contribution to the study of the Greek text of the New Testament, his work had limited value for establishing the earliest form of the text since he had access to only a few late manuscripts. Many earlier NT manuscripts have come to light in the centuries following the publication of the Textus Receptus. The modern era has been a time of collecting and studying thousands of manuscripts, noting their commonalities and variations.

Several people contributed to the study of the Greek text of the NT after Erasmus, including Brian Walton (1600-1661)[11] and John Mill (1645-1707); the latter collected all the evidence from every Greek manuscript known to him as well as evidence from the versions and early fathers. Johann Albrecht Bengel (1687-1752) was a towering figure who advanced the field

---

10. The name "Textus Receptus" was first used in the preface of the 1633 Elzevir edition of the GNT. Numerous editions based on Erasmus' GNT were printed between 1535 and 1678.

11. Walton, who edited a polyglot Bible, was the first to systematically assemble variant readings. See Bruce M. Metzger and Bart D. Ehrman, *The Text of the New Testament: Its Transmission, Corruption, and Restoration*, 4th ed. (New York: Oxford University Press, 2005), 153-54, for more details.

of textual criticism by extensive study of all available witnesses.[12] Building on the work of Mill, Bengel's achievements were characterized by three features: (1) in his apparatuses, he provided positive and negative evidence for variants; (2) he formulated critical principles for assessing manuscripts, including the principle that "the difficult is to be preferred to the easy reading"; and (3) he was the first to classify manuscripts into types according to their text.[13] In the further developing field of textual studies, J. J. Wettstein (1693–1754) stands out. In addition to his own extensive studies, which resulted in a critical edition, he helped standardize the symbols used to represent different manuscripts in critical apparatuses.[14]

The most influential scholar of the modern period was Johann Jakob **Griesbach** (1745–1812), professor of New Testament at the University of Jena in Germany. Griesbach devoted much of his career to collecting NT manuscripts and assessing their value. His research proved foundational to virtually all later work in two respects: (1) Griesbach identified three "types" of texts (Alexandrian, Western, and Byzantine); and (2) he established fifteen "canons" (meaning "principles" or "guidelines") of textual criticism, many of which are still in use. Griesbach's work "laid the foundation for all subsequent textual criticism."[15]

Two monumental contributions date to the mid-nineteenth century. First, unsatisfied with the late sources used for the Textus Receptus, German philologist Karl Lachmann (1793–1851) published the first GNT based exclusively on text-critical principles with the goal of reproducing the text of the late fourth century. This meant a complete break from the Textus Receptus and no small amount of controversy. Second, Constantin von **Tischendorf** (1815–1874), a German Protestant theologian, published a series of critical editions of the GNT throughout his life. The most important of these is the eighth edition, published in two volumes (1869–1872) and containing a detailed apparatus still used by scholars today. In his text-critical decisions for the readings of the eighth edition, Tischendorf

---

12. Eldon Jay Epp, "Textual Criticism (New Testament)," *AYBD* 6:428.

13. J. K. Elliott and Ian Moir, *Manuscripts and the Text of the New Testament: An Introduction for English Readers* (London: T&T Clark, 2003), 80.

14. For more details see Metzger and Ehrman, *Text of the New Testament*, 160–61.

15. Eldon Jay Epp and Gordon D. Fee, *Studies in the Theory and Method of New Testament Textual Criticism* (Grand Rapids: Eerdmans, 1993), 11.

is sometimes accused of placing too much weight on the witness of **Codex Sinaiticus**. He discovered this important manuscript at Saint Catherine's Monastery on the Sinai Peninsula,[16] and he discovered many other manuscripts as well.

If Griesbach's work laid the foundation for future text-critical work, then the endeavors of Brooke F. Westcott (1825–1901) and Fenton J. A. Hort (1828–1892) constructed the discipline's framework by establishing its methodology. **Westcott and Hort**, both professors at Cambridge, spent some twenty-eight years working with early manuscripts, after which they published a new edition of the GNT under a title that matched their ambition: *The New Testament in the Original Greek* (1881).[17] They completely rejected the Textus Receptus as a representative of the earliest form of the NT text, demonstrating that its manuscripts were relatively late in comparison to those used in their own research. Westcott and Hort's GNT soon became the standard in the field.

Several developments have furthered the discipline of New Testament textual criticism since the late nineteenth century. The discovery of the papyri—including important ones such as P46, P66, and P75—provided scholars with new evidence to confirm or refine Westcott and Hort's findings. Scholars have also benefited from further work on citations of the NT found in the early church fathers.[18]

Westcott and Hort's volume has since been surpassed by the publication of several critical editions of the Greek NT. Among these are the *Novum Testamentum Graece* (normally called the **Nestle-Aland** and abbreviated NA, presently in its twenty-eighth edition), published by the Deutsche Bibelgesellschaft,[19] and *The Greek New Testament*, presently in its fifth edition (referred to as the UBS edition due to its association with the United

---

16. The story of Tischendorf's discovery of Codex Sinaiticus is detailed in numerous sources. For a recent overview of this codex intended for a general audience, see David C. Parker, *Codex Sinaiticus: The Story of the World's Oldest Bible* (Peabody, MA: Hendrickson, 2010).

17. Wegner, *Student's Guide*, 215; Metzger and Ehrman, *Text of the New Testament*, 174–81; Brooke F. Westcott and F. J. A. Hort, eds., *The New Testament in the Original Greek*, American ed. (New York: Harper & Brothers, 1881), also available online at http://archive.org/details/newtestamentinoro1west.

18. E.g., Epp and Fee, *Studies in the Theory and Method*, 299–359.

19. Barbara Aland, Kurt Aland, et al., eds., *Novum Testamentum Graece*, 28th ed. (Stuttgart: Deutsche Bibelgesellschaft, 2012). The Nestle-Aland text and other contemporary critical editions of the Greek NT are discussed further in §4.2.4 Modern Critical Editions.

Bible Societies).[20] Several specialized Greek New Testaments have also appeared in recent years, including *The Greek New Testament: SBL Edition* (SBLGNT), produced by the Society of Biblical Literature and edited by Michael Holmes, who started with the Greek text of Westcott and Hort and modified it in consultation with the texts of Samuel Tregelles and Robinson-Pierpont as well as the New International Version.[21] Tyndale House in Cambridge, England, has produced a GNT that is based mainly on manuscripts dating to the fifth century or earlier and incorporates formatting and spelling of the earliest manuscripts—*The Greek New Testament, Produced at Tyndale House, Cambridge* (THGNT).[22]

In the early twentieth century several scholars made key contributions to the field of NT textual criticism. Caspar René Gregory (1846–1917), an American-born German scholar, introduced a numerical system for classifying manuscripts, now called the Gregory-Aland (GA) number. Hermann von Soden (1852–1914) made lasting contributions to the theory of textual history. He produced a multivolume critical edition of the NT that is so massive and with such a complex manuscript classification and numbering system that few people ever master it.[23]

Important contributions to NT textual criticism were made by Bruce Metzger (1914–2007), who wrote prolifically about the discipline and a variety of related topics as well. Among his publications is a well-known trilogy of books on the text, versions, and canon of the NT. Metzger also participated on the editorial committee of the United Bible Societies GNT, for which he produced a textual commentary that enlightens users as to

---

20. Barbara Aland, Kurt Aland, et al., eds., *The Greek New Testament*, 5th rev. ed. (Stuttgart: Deutsche Bibelgesellschaft, 2014). The Greek texts of NA28 and UBS5 are identical. The projects share an editorial committee, and both texts are published by the Deutsche Bibelgesellschaft. The primary difference between the two is that NA28 is designed for text-critical research while UBS5 is designed to meet the needs of Bible translators.

21. Michael W. Holmes, ed., *The Greek New Testament: SBL Edition* (Atlanta: Society of Biblical Literature; Bellingham, WA: Logos Bible Software, 2010).

22. Dirk Jongkind and Peter J. Williams, eds., *The Greek New Testament, Produced at Tyndale House, Cambridge* (Wheaton, IL: Crossway, 2017).

23. Hermann von Soden, *Die Schriften Des Neuen Testaments in Ihrer Ältesten Erreichbaren Textgestalt Hergestellt Auf Grund Ihrer Textgeschichte*, 4 vols. (Göttingen: Vandenhoeck & Ruprecht, 1911–1919). It can be viewed at http://www.csntm.org/printedbook.

the reasoning (and occasional disagreements) of the committee in making its textual decisions.[24]

Kurt Aland (1915–1994) was one of the most important figures for NT textual criticism midcentury. He served as principal editor of several editions of the two major Greek critical versions of the NT used by scholars—*Novum Testamentum Graece* and *The Greek New Testament*, mentioned above. Aland founded the *Institut für Neutestamentliche Textforschung* (INTF) in Münster, Germany, in 1959. The INTF, now led by Holger Strutwolf, has been producing essential text-critical works for sixty years. These include the *Kurzgefasste Liste der griechischen Handschriften des Neuen Testaments*, which is the official list of all extant Greek NT manuscripts.[25] Aland also initiated work on the *Editio Critica Maior* (ECM), a major critical edition of each book of the NT that provides a new basis for the text of the NA and UBS GNTs.[26]

The discipline of NT textual criticism appeared to go into decline after the middle of the twentieth century. Few young scholars were entering the field, and biblical scholarship seemed to assume that the discipline had accomplished all that was necessary or possible. Eldon J. Epp lamented that the field of textual criticism had reached an "interlude" in several essays published in the 1970s and 1980s.[27] Just twenty-five years later, however,

---

24. Bruce M. Metzger, *The Text of the New Testament: Its Transmission, Corruption, and Restoration*, 3rd enlarged ed. (New York: Oxford University Press, 1992); Metzger, *The Early Versions of the New Testament: Their Origin, Transmission, and Limitations* (Oxford: Clarendon Press, 1977); Metzger, *The Canon of the New Testament: Its Origin, Development, and Significance* (Oxford: Clarendon, 1987); Metzger, *A Textual Commentary on the Greek New Testament*, 2nd ed. (Stuttgart: Deutsche Bibelgesellschaft , 1994). The first edition of this commentary is also worth having because it discusses variation units no longer included in the second edition and because it provides a history of the changes made by the editorial committee between UBS3 and UBS4. See Bruce M. Metzger, *A Textual Commentary on the Greek New Testament* (London: United Bible Societies, 1971).

25. The INTF is also responsible for the ANTF (*Arbeiten zur Neutestamentlichen Textforschung*) Series, which publishes research and studies on textual criticism and textual history of the Greek New Testament. An overview of the series can be seen at https://www.degruyter.com/view/serial/16070.

26. A *major critical edition* supplies as much information about as many variation units as possible, with most NT books requiring one or more volumes each. A *hand edition*, like the NA28, provides as much information about the entire NT as can fit in a small volume that is easily used and transported.

27. The essays have been published in several forms. See, for example, Eldon J. Epp, "The Twentieth Century Interlude in New Testament Textual Criticism," *JBL* 93.3 (1974): 386–414, an essay that was also published on pp. 83–123 of *Studies in the Theory and Method of New Testament*

Larry W. Hurtado, a student of Epp, reassessed the situation at the First Birmingham Colloquium on the Textual Criticism of the New Testament,[28] and found much ground for optimism. Indeed, in recent decades, the discipline of NT textual criticism has seen a fresh blossoming, with vigorous research being produced by a steadily increasing number of younger scholars, including women and members of ethnic minorities. Perhaps the new life in the field is best reflected in the recently published second edition of *The Text of the New Testament in Contemporary Research*, which contains twenty-four essays detailing significant advances in every major area of the discipline.[29]

The ongoing efforts of The Center for the Study of New Testament Manuscripts (CSNTM) provide one important contribution to the field of NT textual criticism. Led by Daniel B. Wallace, executive director of CSNTM and senior research professor of New Testament Studies at Dallas Theological Seminary, the CSNTM is a nonprofit organization dedicated to digital preservation of ancient manuscripts of the NT writings. The CSNTM travels to universities, libraries, museums, and other institutions where ancient documents are preserved and makes color digital images of every page. In the process, they have discovered several previously unknown Greek NT manuscripts. Most current online images of the ancient manuscripts (such as those at INTF) are derived from microfilm photography performed a century or more ago. Over time, high quality digital images made by the CSNTM and others will become available to every scholar who has internet access. To date, CSNTM has taken over five hundred thousand images, which amounts to about 20 percent of Greek NT manuscript pages. Using state-of-the-art equipment and highly trained people, the

---

Textual Criticism, ed. Eldon J. Epp and Gordon D. Fee (Grand Rapids: Eerdmans, 1993) and on pp. 59–100 in Eldon J. Epp, *Perspectives on New Testament Textual Criticism: Collected Essays, 1962–2004* (Leiden: Brill, 2005). See also, Eldon J. Epp, "New Testament Textual Criticism: Requiem for a Discipline," in *Perspectives on New Testament Textual Criticism*, 175–84.

28. His paper was published two years later as Larry W. Hurtado, "Beyond the Interlude? Developments and Directions in New Testament Textual Criticism," in *Studies in the Early Text of the Gospels and Acts: The Papers of the First Birmingham Colloquium on the Textual Criticism of the New Testament*, ed. David G. K. Taylor (University of Birmingham Press, 1999), 26–48.

29. Bart D. Ehrman and Michael W. Holmes, eds., *The Text of the New Testament in Contemporary Research: Essays on the Status Quaestionis*, 2nd rev. ed. (Leiden: Brill, 2013).

CSNTM makes these images available to the general population through their website.[30]

Now that electronic editing of ancient texts has become not only possible but mandatory, much effort is being invested in the goal of transcribing the complete text of NT manuscripts into electronic form. The INTF maintains the New Testament Virtual Manuscript Room (NTVMR),[31] the most complete source of digital images of NT manuscripts. The NTVMR also provides online tools that make it possible for textual scholars all over the world to assist in the transcription effort as well as make use of the results in their own research. The Institute for Textual Scholarship and Electronic Editing (ITSEE) at the University of Birmingham, England, led by David Parker, and now Hugh Houghton, is collaborating with the INTF on the *Editio Critica Maior*.

One of the most significant developments in NT textual criticism in recent decades is the Coherence-Based Genealogical Method (CBGM). The CBGM was introduced by Gerd Mink in the 1980s and continues to be refined by the INTF.[32] The goal of this method is to explain the flow of texts by examining the level of coherence between textual witnesses. Scholars using the CBGM create stemmata[33] for each variation unit. These are then combined by computer software to create a textual-flow diagram for that reading, showing how the text of the surviving manuscripts may be related, first in the individual reading and then across the entire writing. The aim is to determine the **Ausgangstext**, or starting point, of each reading. This method has led to the rejection by many textual scholars of the classification of manuscripts into text types (e.g., Alexandrian, Western). One result of the application of the CBGM is the preference for certain variants attested in the Byzantine tradition, even though these witnesses have often not been considered as important in more traditional text-critical methods.

---

30. http://www.csntm.org.

31. http://ntvmr.uni-muenster.de/home.

32. http://egora.uni-muenster.de/intf/index_en.shtml.

33. "Stemmata" is the plural of **stemma**, which is something like a family tree. This can be done with a group of manuscripts such as Family 1, but in the case of the CBGM, a stemma attempts to explain the relationship between the readings of a particular variation unit. This is often called a "local stemma."

The full impact of the CBGM on the field of textual criticism is yet to be seen since the method is relatively new. One of the most prominent uses of the method has been its influence on the text of the NA28 and UBS5. The first instance occurred when the NA28 was published in 2012, containing over thirty changes to the Greek text of the Catholic Epistles in light of ECM decisions.[34] Future use of the CBGM to assess the text of the NT will determine the method's overall value and contribution to the field of textual criticism.[35]

4.2 TEXTUAL EVIDENCE

The witnesses to the oldest text of the New Testament can be categorized into three main groups: (1) the actual Greek manuscripts that contain parts of the NT writings; (2) early translations of the NT into languages such as Latin, Syriac, Coptic, and others; and (3) citations of the NT found in the writings of the early church fathers. Collectively, these groups contain most of the evidence that textual critics use to determine the best readings for a given word or passage.[36]

4.2.1 GREEK MANUSCRIPTS

When Erasmus worked on his Greek NT in the early sixteenth century, he had about seven manuscripts at his disposal. Today, scholars working on the text of the NT have data from more than fifty-five hundred manuscripts. To categorize and simplify the sheer number of witnesses, scholars divided them into groups and introduced a cataloging system to identify the individual manuscripts. The three major groups of Greek manuscripts are papyri, majuscules, and minuscules. We will also describe a fourth group of witnesses to the Greek text—the lectionaries used by churches for liturgical readings of Scripture.

---

34. It is expected that the next editions of the NA and UBS (expected in 2021 and 2022) will in particular make use of the recently published ECM text of Acts and the forthcoming text of Mark. See the bibliography under "Critical Editions" for publication details of the ECM volumes.

35. On this topic, see Tommy Wasserman and Peter Gurry, *A New Approach to Textual Criticism: An Introduction to the Coherence-Based Genealogical Method* (Atlanta: SBL Press, 2017).

36. Another early source of NT citations is found on *ostraca*, pieces of broken pottery that were used as a writing surface. Brice C. Jones has recently argued for the usefulness of amulets (in the case of NT citations, these were typically scraps of papyrus with a NT passage, worn or kept for superstitious reasons) as a source of readings (see Brice C. Jones, *New Testament Texts on Greek Amulets from Late Antiquity* [London: Bloomsbury, 2016]).

4.2.1.a Papyri

The first and earliest manuscripts of the New Testament were written on **papyrus**. At the time of the publication of the NA28, 127 NT papyri had been listed. The papyri are typically designated by the capital letter P and a number (e.g., P66).[37] Many of these manuscripts are fragmentary, but collectively they contain a considerable portion of the NT. Most papyri date to the third to fifth centuries, but some are later. Others are as early as the second century (e.g., P52). Because these documents were created early in the history of Christianity, many papyri appear to have been copied by nonprofessional scribes and, as a result, may demonstrate some inconsistency in quality of copying, with errors and changes being fairly common. At the same time, they are closest in time to the writing of the NT and thus extremely valuable for establishing the text.

Because the papyri were discovered and studied after the original "text-type" designations were developed, most textual scholars resist assigning them to these rigid categories. For that reason, the descriptions below will also avoid such assignments. Some of the best-known and most-often-cited papyri are described here, while descriptions of others can be found in the standard texts.[38]

P45

P45 is one of a number of significant manuscripts in the Chester Beatty collection in Dublin, Ireland, and dates to the third century.[39] Only thirty

---

37. Some resources (such as the apparatus in NA) use a capital Gothic P to designate the papyri. The manuscript number may also be set in superscript—e.g., 𝔓⁶⁶. See http://www.csntm.org/manuscript to view examples of NT papyri.

38. For example, see Aland and Aland, *Text of the New Testament*, 83–102; Metzger and Ehrman, *Text of the New Testament*, 53–61; Philip W. Comfort, *Early Manuscripts and Modern Translations of the New Testament* (Grand Rapids: Baker Books, 1990), 3–71; Bruce M. Metzger, *Manuscripts of the Greek Bible: An Introduction to Greek Paleography* (New York: Oxford University Press, 1981), 62–69; and refer to the index in David C. Parker, *An Introduction to the New Testament Manuscripts and Their Texts* (Cambridge: Cambridge University Press, 2008), 355.

39. The dates provided for manuscripts listed here are those given in NA28. In recent years a lively debate has developed concerning the dating of NT manuscripts and papyri in particular. Some scholars have argued for earlier dates and/or narrower date ranges while others have more cautiously claimed later dates and/or broader date ranges. On this topic, see Orsini and Clarysee, "Early New Testament Manuscripts and Their Dates," 443–74; Brent Nongbri, "Grenfell and Hunt on the Dates of Early Christian Codices: Setting the Record Straight," *Bulletin of the American Society of Papyrologists* 48 (2011): 149–62; Roger S. Bagnall, *Early Christian Books in Egypt* (Princeton: Princeton University Press, 2009); and Philip W.

leaves are extant from a papyrus codex that originally had approximately 220 leaves (110 folios) and contained all four Gospels and Acts. As is the case with many artifacts discovered in the late nineteenth and early twentieth centuries, the *provenance*[40] and other circumstances of the find are uncertain, though some theorize that P45 and eleven other manuscripts purchased by Beatty came from the same site.[41]

P46

Part of P46 was purchased with P45 for the Chester Beatty collection. P46 dates to the early third century[42] and contains portions of all of Paul's letters, except Timothy/Titus, and includes Hebrews. As the earliest extant collection of the Pauline corpus, P46 is perhaps the most important witness to the text of his epistles. The codex originally had 104 leaves, with 86 remaining today. Because antiquities dealers divided it up and sold it in small sections, the reassembled codex ended up in two locations: the special collections library of the University of Michigan and the Chester Beatty collection in Dublin, Ireland.[43]

P52

The earliest papyrus manuscript, P52, contains a small section of John 18 (verses 31–33 on the *recto* and 37–38 on the *verso*)[44] and is roughly the size of a playing card. With writing on both sides, the fragment was likely part of a codex, not a scroll. Dating to the second century, the papyrus could be within fifty to **seventy-five years** of the autograph of John's Gospel; Philip Comfort notes that it may even be earlier, dating to within twenty years

---

Comfort and David P. Barrett, eds., *The Text of the Earliest New Testament Greek Manuscripts* (Wheaton, IL: Tyndale House Publishers, 2001).

40. Provenance is the location where an ancient artifact was found.

41. http://www.csntm.org/manuscript/View/GA_P45.

42. It should be noted that some scholars date P46 to the middle of the second century (see Philip Comfort, *Encountering the Manuscripts: An Introduction to New Testament Paleography & Textual Criticism* [Nashville: Broadman & Holman, 2005], 66–67).

43. http://www.csntm.org/manuscript/View/GA_P46_Mich

44. While "recto" and "verso" may have a different meaning when dealing with papyrus scrolls, typically with NT documents, "recto" refers to the front of a two-sided page, while "verso" refers to the back. Thus, if you have a two-page spread open in front of you, the left side will be the verso, and the right side will be the recto of two separate folios.

of the original.[45] Originally found in Egypt, the papyrus is currently part of the John Rylands University Library in Manchester, England.[46]

P66

This papyrus is one of the earliest and best-preserved New Testament manuscripts. P66 is dated to the early third century and contains seventy-eight leaves.[47] The manuscript contains most of the Gospel of John. Much the opposite of P46, P66 was found nearly intact in 1952 near Dishna, Egypt, with the first folio containing John 1:1 and following fully readable.[48] The manuscript is known for the large number of corrections, possibly by the original scribe. Notably, P66 does not include the *pericope adulterae* (John 7:53–8:11). The bulk of the codex is housed at the Bodmer Library in Cologny, Switzerland.

P75

Discovered in the 1950s, P75 dates to the third century.[49] The codex originally contained about 144 leaves, but only 51 remain.[50] The manuscript contains extensive portions of Luke and John, making it one of the earliest copies of these Gospels. P75 appears to have been carefully and faithfully copied, so that some scholars argue that it is the product of a professional scribe. Its text of Luke and John is close to the text of **Codex Vaticanus**

---

45. Comfort and Barrett, *The Text of the Earliest New Testament Greek Manuscripts*, 365–66. It should be noted, however, that Comfort's view is in the minority.

46. http://www.csntm.org/manuscript/View/GA_P52.

47. A good example of the debate surrounding the dating of the NT papyri can be seen in the recent article by Brent Nongbri, "The Limits of Palaeographic Dating of Literary Papyri: Some Observations on the Date and Provenance of P. Bodmer II (P66)," *Museum Helveticum* 71 (2014): 1–35. Also, see the blog response by veteran textual critic, Larry Hurtado, "The Date of P66 (P. Bodmer II): Nongbri's New Argument," *Larry Hurtado's Blog*, June 3, 2014, https://larry-hurtado.wordpress.com/2014/06/03/the-date-of-p66-p-bodmer-ii-nongbris-new-argument/.

48. https://en.wikipedia.org/wiki/Papyrus_66#/media/File:Papyrus_66_(GA).jpg.

49. Similar to the discussion of Nongbri and Hurtado on P66 above, the following interaction is revealing for the current trends in the dating of the papyri—see Brent Nongbri, "Reconsidering the Place of Papyrus Bodmer XIV-XV (P75) in the Textual Criticism of the New Testament," *JBL* 135.2 (2016): 405–37; and Larry Hurtado, "A Challenge to the Dating of P75," *Larry Hurtado's Blog*, June 22, 2016, https://larryhurtado.wordpress.com/2016/06/22/a-challenge-to-the-dating-of-p75/.

50. Metzger and Ehrman, *Text of the New Testament*, 58–59.

(B 03). P75 was originally part of the Bodmer collection along with P66, but it was donated to the Vatican Library by the Hanna family in 2007.[51]

Table 4.1: Important New Testament Papyri			
Number	Date	Contains	Location
P1	3rd century	Matt 1:1–9, 12–13; 1:14–20, 23	Penn Museum, University of Pennsylvania, Philadelphia
P10	4th century	Rom 1:1–7	Harvard University, Cambridge, MA
P4, P64, P67	3rd century	Portions of Luke and Matthew	Bibliotheque Nationale, Paris; Magdalen College, Oxford; Abadia de Montserrat, Montserrat
P13	3rd–4th century	Portions of Heb 2; 10–12	British Library, London
P18	3rd–4th century	Acts 1:4–7	British Library, London
P29	3rd century	Acts 26:7–8; 26:20	Bodleian Library, Oxford
P38	3rd century	Acts 18:27–19:6; 19:12–16	University of Michigan Library, Ann Arbor
P45	3rd century	30 leaves from the Gospels and Acts	Chester Beatty Library, Dublin; Oesterreichische Nationalbibliothek, Vienna
P46	3rd century	86 leaves from the Pauline Epistles and Hebrews	Chester Beatty Library, Dublin; University of Michigan Library, Ann Arbor
P47	3rd century	Rev 9:10–11:3; 11:5–16; 16:17–17:2	Chester Beatty Library, Dublin
P48	3rd century	Acts 23:11–17; 23:25–29	Biblioteca Medicea Laurenziana, Florence
P52	2nd century	John 18:31–33; 18:37–38	John Rylands University Library, Manchester

---

51. http://digi.vatlib.it/view/MSS_Pap.Hanna.1(Mater.Verbi).

P66	3rd century	78 leaves from John	Institut für Altertumskunde, Köln; Chester Beatty Library, Dublin; Bibliotheca Bodmeriana, Cologny
P72	3rd–4th century	18 leaves from 1–2 Peter and Jude	Bibliotheca Bodmeriana, Cologny; Biblioteca Apostolica, Vatican
P75	3rd century	50 leaves from Luke and John	Biblioteca Apostolica, Vatican
P98	2nd century	Rev 1:13–20	Institut Français d'Archéologie Orientale, Cairo
P104	2nd century	Matt 21:34–37; 21:43–45	Ashmolean Museum, Oxford
P115	3rd–4th century	9 fragments of Revelation	Ashmolean Museum, Oxford
P127	5th century	8 leaves from Acts	Ashmolean Museum, Oxford

4.2.1.b Majuscules

Around three hundred manuscripts compose the second group of New Testament witnesses, the majuscules (sometimes called "uncials"). These manuscripts are written in the same majuscule (capital) letters as the papyri, but the writing material is parchment, which is made from specially treated animal hides. Every **majuscule** has a numeric designation starting with zero, but the best-known manuscripts are more typically discussed using their name and/or letter designation.

Dating between the fourth and tenth centuries AD, most majuscules are later than most papyri, though there is overlap. The bulk of the majuscules are less fragmentary and contain more content than the papyrus witnesses, including several that contain the entire New Testament or even the entire Bible. By the time the majuscules were being produced, Christianity had gained official recognition, so the likelihood is higher that a majuscule

Codex Sinaiticus (Matt 2:6, 12)

manuscript would have been copied by a professional.[52] Two of the most important majuscules are Codex Sinaiticus (א 01) and Codex Vaticanus (B 03), but others deserve attention as well.[53]

4.2.1.b.1 Codex Sinaiticus (א 01)

The oldest complete manuscript of the New Testament is Codex Sinaiticus (א 01), a majuscule that dates to the fourth century.[54] The codex was discovered by Constantin von Tischendorf at Saint Catherine's monastery in the Sinai Peninsula, though the original provenance is unknown. A **colophon** at the end of Esther connects a large number of the Old Testament corrections in Sinaiticus to the scholar and martyr Pamphylus and hints that the manuscript may have been located in Caesarea Maritima during the sixth or seventh century.[55] Sinaiticus is one of the most important New Testament witnesses due to its early date and completeness. Its textual

---

52. J. H. Greenlee, "Texts and Manuscripts (NT)," *ZEB* 5:808.

53. Additional details on the majuscules listed below and descriptions of many others can be found in Aland and Aland, *Text of the New Testament*, 103–28; Metzger and Ehrman, *Text of the New Testament*, 62–86; Comfort, *Early Manuscripts*, 71–73; Metzger, *Manuscripts of the Greek Bible*, 74–101; and refer to the index of Parker, *New Testament Manuscripts*, 355–56.

54. Even though sections of the OT are missing, it is widely thought that Sinaiticus originally contained the entire Bible. It also contains much of the deuterocanonical books (according to the canon of the Septuagint), as well as the *Epistle of Barnabas* and the *Shepherd of Hermas*.

55. J. N. Birdsall, "Codex Sinaiticus," *ZEB* 1:941–42. The bibliography on Sinaiticus is extensive. For a recent overview of this codex intended for a general audience, see David Parker, *Codex Sinaiticus: The Story of the World's Oldest Bible* (Peabody, MA: Hendrickson, 2010).

affiliation is more or less Alexandrian, though Western readings are also present. The New Testament portion of Sinaiticus is housed in the British Library; however, other portions are in Saint Petersburg, Leipzig, and at Saint Catherine's.[56]

4.2.1.b.2 Codex Alexandrinus (A 02)

If you visit the British Library in London, you will find two large codices displayed side by side. One is a volume of Codex Sinaiticus, and the other is a volume of **Codex Alexandrinus** (A 02).[57] In 1627 the patriarch of Constantinople presented the codex to King Charles I of England. Alexandrinus dates to the fifth century and contains both the Old and New Testaments, although it is missing nearly all of Matthew, some of John, and most of 2 Corinthians.[58] Scholars suspect that the codex was produced from several different exemplars and that this is the reason for its uneven textual affiliation. In the Gospels, Alexandrinus is the oldest example of the Byzantine textual grouping, while in the rest of the New Testament, it "ranks along with B and ℵ as representative of the Alexandrian type of text."[59]

4.2.1.b.3 Codex Vaticanus (B 03)

Codex Vaticanus (B 03) is known to have been present in the Vatican Library since at least the fifteenth century, but it was not made generally available for study until a facsimile edition was released in 1889–1890. A fourth-century manuscript of unknown provenance, Vaticanus originally contained both the Old and New Testaments, plus most of the Apocrypha, or deuterocanonical books.[60] Many scholars consider the text of Vaticanus to be the best Greek text of the NT. This attitude is supported by its close agreement with the text of P75 in Luke and John, demonstrating a tradition of careful copying that has preserved the oldest form of the text. Vaticanus

---

56. http://www.codexsinaiticus.org/en/.

57. http://www.bl.uk/manuscripts/Viewer.aspx?ref=royal_ms_1_d_viii_fs001r.

58. The codex contains several of the OT deuterocanonical books, as well as 1 *Clement* and part of 2 *Clement*.

59. Metzger and Ehrman, *Text of the New Testament*, 67. See also Aland and Aland, *Text of the New Testament*, 109.

60. The first forty-six chapters of Genesis have not survived, as well as about thirty of the Psalms and the end of the codex, which would have contained the end of Hebrews, 1 and 2 Timothy, Titus, Philemon, and Revelation.

is considered the leading representative of the Alexandrian textual grouping. The modern critical editions tend to follow the text of Vaticanus closer than any other manuscript.[61]

4.2.1.b.4 Codex Ephraemi Rescriptus (C 04)

Codex Ephraemi Rescriptus (C 04) is the best-known **palimpsest**[62] manuscript of the Bible. The fifth-century codex originally contained text from both the Old and New Testaments, and the parchment was reused in the twelfth century to copy sermons of the fourth-century Syrian church father Ephraem. In the mid-nineteenth century Tischendorf used chemical reagents to assist in painstakingly deciphering the biblical underwriting. His surprisingly accurate transcription was later confirmed (and corrected in places) using modern techniques such as ultraviolet lighting. The text of the New Testament is considered mixed, with readings that agree with both the Alexandrian and the Byzantine traditions. Ephraemi Rescriptus is presently kept in the Bibliothèque Nationale in Paris.[63]

4.2.1.b.5 Codex Bezae (D 05)

Codex Bezae (D 05) dates to the fifth century and contains most of the Gospels, Acts, and a fragment of 3 John. Bezae is named for Theodore Beza, who presented the manuscript to the library at Cambridge University in 1581.[64] There is much about the formatting of Bezae that sets it apart from other major majuscules.[65] First, it is a bilingual: the left page (verso) contains the Greek text while the right page (recto) is the corresponding Latin. Bezae is written in sense-lines,[66] so that the right margin is not straight. The Gospels are arranged in what is called the "Western order:" Matthew, John, Luke, Mark.[67] In addition, the text of Bezae has been much studied because it

---

61. http://digi.vatlib.it/view/MSS_Vat.gr.1209.

62. A **palimpsest** is a document that was erased to make the parchment available for another writing. (Hence the Latin designation *rescriptus*.) It is typically the biblical text that was written over and that must be painstakingly recovered. More than sixty of the NT majuscules are palimpsests.

63. http://gallica.bnf.fr/ark:/12148/btv1b8470433r/f15.image.

64. For this reason it is also sometimes called Codex Cantabrigiensis.

65. https://cudl.lib.cam.ac.uk/view/MS-NN-00002-00041/10.

66. Sense lines are meant to be spoken in one breath and to stand alone as a sensible phrase.

67. This order places the two apostles first, followed by the two who were companions of apostles.

departs from the "normal" New Testament text more than other manuscripts, and is the main Greek representative for the Western textual group. The text of Acts is almost one-tenth longer than the text found in NA28. Some scholars claim that Acts in particular shows an anti-Judaic bias, while others argue that Bezae contains the best representation of the *Ausgangstext* of Acts.[68]

4.2.1.b.6 Codex Washingtonianus (W 032)

Codex Washingtonianus (W 032) dates to the fourth or fifth century.[69] It was purchased in Egypt by Charles L. Freer in 1906 and is kept in the Freer Museum of the Smithsonian Institution in Washington, DC.[70] Like Codex Bezae, Washingtonianus contains the Gospels in the Western order. Metzger and Ehrman report that the text is "curiously variegated" and speculate that it was copied from several exemplars of differing textual affinities.[71] Codex Washingtonianus notably includes a long variant reading near the end of Mark's Gospel that is attested by Jerome.

Table 4.2: Important New Testament Majuscules				
Sigla	Name	Date	Contains Portions of	Location
ℵ 01	Sinaiticus	4th century	Entire NT	British Library, London
A 02	Alexan-drinus	5th century	Entire NT	British Library, London

---

68. See, for example, David C. Parker, *Codex Bezae: An Early Christian Manuscript and Its Text* (Cambridge: Cambridge University Press, 1992); Eldon Jay Epp, *The Theological Tendency of Codex Bezae Cantebrigiensis in Acts* (Cambridge: Cambridge University Press, 2005); and Jenny Read-Heimerdinger, *The Bezan Text of Acts: A Contribution of Discourse Analysis to Textual Criticism* (London: Sheffield Academic Press, 2002).

69. http://www.csntm.org/Manuscript/View/GA_032. Recently, Ulrich Schmid has argued for a seventh century dating—see "Reassessing the Palaeography and Codicology of the Freer Gospel Manuscript," in *The Freer Biblical Manuscripts: Fresh Studies of an American Treasure Trove*, ed. Larry W. Hurtado (Leiden: Brill, 2006), 227–49.

70. Therefore it is also referred to as Codex Freerianus.

71. According to Metzger and Ehrman (*Text of the New Testament*, 80), "in Matthew and Luke 8.13-24.53, the text is of the common Byzantine variety; but in Mark 1.1-5.30, it is Western, resembling the Old Latin; Mark 5.31-16.20 is Caesarean, akin to P45; and Luke 1.1-8.12 and John 5.12-21.25 are Alexandrian."

B 03	Vaticanus	4th century	Entire NT except 1–2 Timothy; Titus; Philemon; Revelation	Biblioteca Apostolica, Vatican
C 04	Ephraemi	5th century	Entire NT except 2 Thessalonians and 2 John	Bibliotheque Nationale, Paris
D 05	Bezae	5th century	Gospels; Acts; 3 John	University Library, Cambridge, UK
Dᴾ 06	Clarom-ontanus	6th century	Pauline Epistles; Hebrews	Bibliotheque Nationale, Paris
Fᴾ 010	Augiensis	9th century	Pauline Epistles; Hebrews	Trinity College, Cambridge, UK
Gᴾ 012	Boerneri-anus	9th century	Pauline Epistles	Sächsische Landesbibliothek, Dresden
L 019	Regius	8th century	Gospels	Bibliotheque Nationale, Paris
W 032	Freeri-anus (or Washing-tonianus)	5th century	Pauline Epistles except Romans; Hebrews	Freer Gallery, Smithsonian Institute
Θ 038	Koridethi (or Coride-thianus)	9th century	Gospels	Institut für Handschriften, Tbilisi
Ψ 044	Athous Laurae	8th–9th century	Mark 9–Acts; Pauline Epistles; Hebrews; General Epistles	Lavra Monastery, Mount Athos

4.2.1.c Minuscules

By far, the largest group of Greek witnesses is the **minuscule** manuscripts, numbering over twenty-eight hundred manuscripts. Written in lower-case letters, minuscules were produced during a time of church expan-sion when dedicated monks spent their days in the monastery *scriptorium*, copying scripture. The prolific copying of this time period led to the high number of minuscules. The minuscules chiefly date between the eleventh and fourteenth centuries, though the entire range goes from the ninth century until well after the invention of the printing press. Most minuscules support the Byzantine textual tradition, also called the **Majority Text**, but there are a good number of important exceptions. Minuscules are identified simply by Arabic numbers.

Because of the large number of minuscules and because many of them represent basically the same textual tradition, scholars have grouped the majority using the symbol of the Gothic "M" (𝔐) in NA and the abbreviation *Byz* in the UBS.[72] At the same time, they have sorted out particular minuscule witnesses that differ significantly from the majority reading. These minuscules are constantly cited in the apparatus of the NA28 and UBS5. A few of the constantly cited minuscules are described below.[73]

4.2.1.c.1 Family 1

Named for Codex 1, this group of Gospel manuscripts is so closely related that they are called a **family**, and scholars have created a **stemma**, something like a family tree, that shows how they are related to each other. The oldest Family 1 members are Codex 1582 and Codex 2193, both of which date to the tenth century. Several scholars are currently working to update Family 1, incorporating newly identified family members and establishing the **archetype** (or common ancestor) for each Gospel.[74] Since they all trace back to that text, it is then possible to cite them in the apparatus as a group under the symbol ƒ¹ instead of individually. Normally, when Codex 1 and Codex 1582 agree in a variation unit, their reading is likely to be the

---

72. In NA28, the Gothic M has been replaced by the designation *Byz*, but only in the Catholic Epistles, where the CBGM was used. For an example of recent scholarship on the Majority Text, see Gregory S. Paulson, "An Investigation of the Byzantine Text of the Johannine Epistles," *Review and Expositor* 114.4 (2017): 580–89.

73. Additional details on the minuscules listed below and descriptions of many others can be found in Aland and Aland, *Text of the New Testament*, 128–58; Metzger and Ehrman, *Text of the New Testament*, 86–92; Metzger, *Manuscripts of the Greek Bible*, 102–39. Also refer to the index of Parker, *New Testament Manuscripts*, 356. Another excellent resource is William Henry Paine Hatch, *Facsimiles and Descriptions of Minuscule Manuscripts of the New Testament* (Cambridge, MA: Harvard University Press, 1951).

74. When dealing with closely related manuscripts, scholars attempt to establish the text of their common ancestor or archetype.

text of the archetype, which is thought to represent the type of text found in Caesarea in the third century.[75]

4.2.1.c.2 Family 13

Named for Codex 13, this closely related group of Gospel manuscripts is also included in the so-called Caesarean textual grouping. Like Family 1, Family 13 has unique shared readings, which allows scholars to create a stemma and establish the text of the archetype so that they are often cited as a group in the GNT apparatus. An oddity of the Family 13 manuscripts is that the *pericope adulterae* (the account of the woman taken in adultery) follows Luke 21:38 instead of John 7:52, but this has been shown to be inadequate as a criterion of membership in the family.[76]

4.2.1.c.3 Codex 33

Codex 33 is one of the earliest extant New Testament minuscules (ninth century), and it contains the entire New Testament except Revelation. In the early nineteenth century, it was given the name "the queen of the cursives," and it is housed in the Bibliothèque Nationale in Paris. Typical of many "Alexandrian" minuscules, Codex 33 shows the influence of the developing Byzantine textual tradition, especially in Acts and the Pauline Epistles.[77] Codex 33 has water damage that has led to some difficulties in deciphering the microfilm images that are available.

4.2.1.c.4 Codex 565

Produced in the ninth century and housed at the Russian National Library in Saint Petersburg, Codex 565 is another of the earliest extant minuscules. It is a deluxe copy of the Gospels, with purple-stained parchment and gold writing and ornamentation.[78] It has quite a few readings that align with the

---

75. See, for example, Anderson, *Textual Tradition of the Gospels*, 146–47; Alison Welsby, *A Textual Study of Family 1 in the Gospel of John* (Berlin: de Gruyter, 2013).

76. See the study by Jac Perrin, *Family 13 in St. John's Gospel: A Computer Assisted Pylogenetic Analysis* (Leiden: Brill, forthcoming). Perrin lists over three hundred unique readings that assist in establishing family membership. He points to Codex 788 as being closest to the archetypal text of the family.

77. Metzger and Ehrman, *Text of the New Testament*, 88.

78. It appears to have been made for royalty and is also called Empress Theodora's Codex. Sadly, as of this writing there has not been a color facsimile made of Codex 565.

Caesarean textual grouping, but it often agrees with the Alexandrian manuscripts and is known for having readings that are otherwise unknown.[79]

4.2.1.c.5 Codex 1739

This tenth-century manuscript contains Acts as well as the Pauline and Catholic Epistles, and it is kept at the Lavra Monastery on Mount Athos.[80] Besides being an excellent example of the Alexandrian textual grouping, Codex 1739 is important for notes made by the scribe, a monk named Ephraim,[81] in the margins, quoting early church fathers (none later than Basil, who was mid-fourth century) and offering variant readings. The careful work of Ephraim, the age of the marginal quotations, and the quality of the biblical text suggest that the 1739 faithfully reproduces a much older exemplar.

Table 4.3: Important New Testament Minuscules			
Number	**Date**	**Contains**	**Location**
33	9th century	Entire NT except Revelation	Bibliotheque Nationale, Paris
81	11th century	Acts; Pauline Epistles; General Epistles	British Library, London; Patriarchate Library, Alexandria
157	12th century	Gospels	Biblioteca Apostolica, Vatican
565	9th century	Gospels	Russian National Library, St. Petersburg
700	11th century	Gospels	British Library, London

---

79. In an extensive study of the text of Mark done by the INTF, 565 was sixth out of all Greek manuscripts for the amount of *Sonderlesarten* (singular readings). See Barbara Aland and Kurt Aland, eds., *Text und Textwert der Griechischen Handschriften des Neuen Testaments*, IV, Die Synoptischen Evangelien 1, Das Markusevangelium, Band 1,1: Handschriftenliste und Vergleichende Beschreibung (Berlin: de Gruyter, 1998), 37.

80. Mount Athos is a peninsula of Greece that is self-governed by the Holy Community of Orthodox monasteries located there. The larger monasteries all have libraries with many ancient books, including scriptures.

81. Ephraim is also the scribe of Codex 1582, one of the leading members of Family 1.

1175	10th century	Acts; Pauline Epistles	Joannu Monastery, Patmos
1241	12th century	Gospels; Acts; Pauline Epistles	St. Catherine's Monastery, Mount Sinai
1424	9th–10th century	Entire NT	Jesuit-Krauss-McCormick Library, Chicago
1739	10th century	Acts; Pauline Epistles; General Epistles	Lavra Monastery, Mount Athos
2053	13th century	Revelation	Biblioteca Regionale Universitaria, Messina
2344	11th century	Acts; Pauline Epistles; General Epistles; Revelation	Bibliotheque Nationale, Paris

4.2.1.d Lectionaries

Numbering well over twenty-three hundred, the **lectionaries** of the early church represent the second-largest group of witnesses to the Greek text of the New Testament after minuscules. Lectionaries are liturgical books that provide the daily or weekly readings for church and devotional use. Lectionaries do not have continuous text but do have lengthy passages, so they are valuable as a witness to the earliest wording. Because they have their own history of transmission and have not been as intensively studied, they tend to be less cited than other sources. Lectionaries are designated by the symbol 𝓁 followed by a numeral (e.g., 𝓁170).[82]

4.2.2 PATRISTIC EVIDENCE

Significant evidence for the earliest text of the New Testament documents also comes from writings of the church fathers, in which they routinely

---

82. Additional details on the lectionaries can be found in Aland and Aland, *Text of the New Testament*, 163–70; Metzger and Ehrman, *Text of the New Testament*, 46–50; and Parker, *New Testament Manuscripts*, 56–57, 99.

quote Scripture.[83] Not only does a father's support of a particular reading provide evidence for the age of that reading, but often it is possible to associate the text a church father was using with his location. For example, Gordon Fee has pointed out that the text used by Origen, who lived and studied in Alexandria, typically agrees with the readings of Alexandrian witnesses. However, after he moved to Caesarea, Origen's citations of Mark 12–15 cease to follow the Alexandrian pattern and become "a witness to the so-called Caesarean MSS."[84] By this we learn that Origen did not quote from memory but opened and cited locally available manuscripts of NT documents, and that he switched from one copy of Mark to another when he lived in Caesarea.[85] In addition, a church father may cite two or more variants that occur in a variation unit, thus demonstrating his awareness of several different readings at that point in time. However, there are a number of difficulties with patristic citations. For one, it is possible that a particular father was not citing from a text that was open before him but from memory, or that he was summarizing or paraphrasing a passage. Finally, one must always remain aware that documents written by a church father also have a history of transmission and that the scribes may have "corrected," harmonized, or made mistakes in copying. Among the church fathers often cited in text-critical work are Origen, Athanasius, Irenaeus, Clement of Alexandria, Justin Martyr, Tertullian, Jerome, and Cyril of Alexandria.[86]

4.2.3 ANCIENT VERSIONS

As Christianity spread through the ancient world, the New Testament was translated into other languages, beginning with Latin, Syriac, and Coptic. These translations witness to the early Greek text that served as

---

83. Metzger and Ehrman note the citations are so extensive "that if all other sources for our knowledge of the text of the New Testament were destroyed, they would be sufficient alone for the reconstruction of practically the entire New Testament" (*Text of the New Testament*, 126).

84. Gordon D. Fee, "The Majority Text and the Original Text of the New Testament," in *Studies in the Theory and Method of New Testament Textual Criticism*, ed. Epp and Fee, 205.

85. See further speculation about Origen's text in Anderson, *Textual Tradition of the Gospels*, 74–83.

86. For additional details on the patristic evidence, see Aland and Aland, *Text of the New Testament*, 171–84; Metzger and Ehrman, *Text of the New Testament*, 126–34; and refer to the index of Parker, *New Testament Manuscripts*, 361–68.

their source text.[87] For example, because Latin translation began as early as the late second century, the Greek source documents would have been from the second century or even earlier, certainly older than nearly all of our extant Greek witnesses. At the same time, as any student of language knows, translations are never a word-for-word representation of the source text, and all languages have features that cannot be transferred into the receptor language. For instance, Latin does not have a definite article, Syriac does not differentiate between the aorist and perfect tenses, and Coptic does not have a passive voice.[88] In such instances, the textual critic will not be able to use the ancient version for direct evidence of a reading. In addition, each version will have had its own history of transmission, with both corrections and mistakes made by scribes producing copies in the new language. Nonetheless, there is much to be gained by a study of the versions, and you will find them cited in the apparatus of the NA28 and UBS5.

Important Latin translations are the "Old Latin"—a translation of the GNT that is considered a representative of the Western textual grouping—and the Vulgate, a revision of the Latin Bible undertaken by Jerome (c. 340–420) in the late fourth century.[89] Among the most significant Syriac manuscripts are two copies of the four Gospels in Old Syriac, possibly dating back to the early third century, and the Peshitta, a fifth-century translation of most of the New Testament. The important Coptic versions, which date between the third and fifth centuries, include the Sahidic and Bohairic dialects and show relationship to the Alexandrian textual grouping.[90] Other early versions used in text-critical work include the Gothic, Georgian, Ethiopic, Armenian, Arabic, and Slavonic.

---

87. For additional details on these ancient versions, see Aland and Aland, *Text of the New Testament*, 185–221; Metzger and Ehrman, *Text of the New Testament*, 95–126; and refer to the index of Parker, *New Testament Manuscripts*, 361–68.

88. Metzger and Ehrman, *Text of the New Testament*, 95.

89. It is uncertain whether Jerome himself revised any of the New Testament beyond the Gospels.

90. Metzger and Ehrman, *Text of the New Testament*, 110–11.

NT Textual Evidence at a Glance

127	**Papyri**
300	**Majuscules**
2800	**Minuscules**
2300	**Lectionaries**

4.2.4 MODERN CRITICAL EDITIONS

A number of critical editions of the Greek New Testament have been produced in modern times.[91] Most editions are *eclectic*, meaning that they do not follow the text of one or two favored manuscripts but instead choose, at each variation unit, which reading is most likely the oldest based on the rules of textual criticism. Even so, the editions diverge in the number of manuscripts used, the prevailing theory of the oldest form of the text, and the weight the editors place on differing text-critical criteria. The groundbreaking edition produced by Westcott and Hort in 1881 used three primary manuscripts, while the *Editio Critica Maior* attempts to consult the entire manuscript tradition. The degree of eclecticism that is appropriate in NT textual criticism is a matter of ongoing scholarly debate.[92]

---

91. For a full and detailed description of the history of critical editions, see Aland and Aland, *Text of the New Testament*, 11–47; Metzger and Ehrman, *Text of the New Testament*, 165–94; and Parker, *New Testament Manuscripts*, 191–223. An essay that brings the discussion of the critical editions to the present time is Eldon Jay Epp, "In the Beginning Was the New Testament Text, but Which Text?" in *Texts and Traditions: Essays in Honour of J. Keith Elliott*, ed. Peter Doble and Jeffrey Kloha (Leiden: Brill, 2014), 35–70.

92. For an excellent collection of essays concerning eclecticism, see David A. Black, ed., *Rethinking New Testament Textual Criticism* (Grand Rapids: Baker, 2002). Particularly the essays by Michael Holmes (pp. 77–100) and J. K. Elliott (pp. 101–24) will be of interest for this topic.

4.2.4.a Westcott and Hort

Though several other scholars pioneered in breaking from the Textus Receptus as representing the "original" text, the publication of *The New Testament in the Original Greek* by nineteenth-century British scholars **Westcott and Hort** was a landmark event in text-critical studies.[93] While Westcott and Hort did not provide a critical apparatus in their GNT, they did publish a second volume that contained the rationale for their textual decisions. The principles that they set out, with some adjustment, are still in use today. Westcott and Hort placed emphasis on transcriptional probability (how the scribe is most likely to have changed the text), followed by intrinsic probability (what the author is most likely to have written). Recognizing that these principles would not always bring the textual scholar to a conclusion about a variation unit, they also asserted that Codex Vaticanus and Codex Sinaiticus were superior representations of the original text, and that agreement between the two must be seen as the most likely reading.[94]

4.2.4.b Nestle-Aland (NA)

The **Nestle-Aland** critical edition (*Novum Testamentum Graece*) has been consequential for more than one hundred years. Begun by Eberhard Nestle in the late 1800s, the project was continued by his son, Erwin, in the early 1900s, and then by Kurt Aland in 1952. Nestle based his original text on three editions of the Greek New Testament: those of Tischendorf, Westcott and Hort, and Bernhard Weiss. His practice was to print the reading chosen by at least two of the three editions. Thus, the early Nestle editions represented the majority consensus of nineteenth-century critical editions[95] and provided from the start an informative and accurate apparatus. Over time the editors switched to a reasoned-eclectic approach with an apparatus that strives to provide as much information as possible in a hand edition. Nestle-Aland, currently in its twenty-eighth edition, is the GNT

---

93. See the discussion above in §4.1.3 Modern Era.

94. A helpful summary of the principles set out by Westcott and Hort can be found in Metzger and Ehrman, *Text of the New Testament*, 174–81. In addition, see Jack Finegan, *Encountering New Testament Manuscripts* (Grand Rapids: Eerdmans, 1974), 64–66; and M. R. Vincent, *A History of the Textual Criticism of the New Testament* (New York: Macmillan, 1899), 145–56.

95. Comfort, *Encountering the Manuscripts*, 100.

of choice for most textual scholars and is the primary text behind most modern English translations.

The NA28 employed a new method for establishing the text, debuting it in the Catholic Letters.[96] This method comes out of the work of the *Editio Critica Maior* (ECM), or major critical edition, of the Catholic Letters, a project of the Institut für Neutestamentliche Textforschung (INTF) at the University of Münster. In order to evaluate the textual witness of the entire manuscript tradition and to detect genealogical connections between readings, the Coherence-Based Genealogical Method (CBGM)[97] was developed and utilized for the Catholic Letters. This led to thirty-three changes from the text of the NA27. Subsequent editions of the Nestle-Aland GNT will incorporate the ECM text of other NT documents as they are completed. There is currently a lively debate among textual scholars concerning the theory and use of the CBGM.[98]

4.2.4.c United Bible Societies (UBS)

The United Bible Societies is the world's largest translator, publisher, and distributor of Bibles.[99] In 1955 a committee was formed to prepare an edition of the GNT designed primarily for Bible translators. They published the first edition in 1966. The apparatus included fewer variation units than the NA, aiming to list only those that would affect translation but providing more complete evidence for each unit. Editorial committee member Bruce Metzger wrote a commentary that describes the reasoning behind the committee's textual decisions.[100] The 26th edition of NA adopted the Greek text used in UBS3, and subsequently both editions have continued to agree in terms of the Greek text (i.e. the UBS4 and NA27 have the same text, as do the UBS5 and the NA28). While the NA and UBS editions use an identical Greek text, the apparatus, punctuation, and other details continue to differ.

---

96. I.e., the seven epistles written to a general (or catholic) church audience: James, 1–2 Peter, 1–3 John, Jude.

97. http://egora.uni-muenster.de/intf/index_en.shtml.

98. For further discussion of the CBGM, see §4.1.3 Modern Era (Late Seventeenth Century to the Present).

99. http://www.unitedbiblesocieties.org.

100. Metzger, *Textual Commentary*. The first edition was published in 1971 and the second edition in 1994. The first edition is still valuable because it demonstrates changes and developments between the UBS editions.

The UBS apparatus still focuses on variants that are significant for translators, while the NA apparatus caters to textual critics and NT specialists.

4.2.4.d The Greek New Testament according to the Majority Text

Since the work of Westcott and Hort, most textual critics have preferred
the papyri and the earlier majuscules, such as Vaticanus and Sinaiticus,
over the later manuscripts that represent the Byzantine textual tendencies. Some conservatives, particularly those involved in the so-called KJV-
only movement, have objected, saying that "God would not have allowed a
corrupt or inferior text to be found in the majority of manuscripts, while
permitting a superior text to be hidden away in a few early manuscripts
somewhere in the sands of Egypt," an assertion that leads to the accusa-
tion that arguments in favor of the Majority Text are "more theological
than textual."[101]

Nevertheless, a small group of scholars persists in building an academic
foundation for the claim that, since the late manuscripts represent the
majority of the evidence (80 to 90 percent),[102] scholars should not consider
them secondary to earlier manuscripts. The Majority Text is seen as "a text
that employs the available evidence of the whole range of surviving manuscripts rather than relying chiefly on the evidence of a few."[103] Majority
Text scholars instead offer historical and transmissional reasons for preferring that text. As a result, two modern critical editions have been produced
based on this approach: *The Greek New Testament according to the Majority
Text*, edited by Zane Hodges and Arthur Farstad; and *The New Testament
in the Original Greek*, edited by Maurice Robinson and William Pierpont.[104]

In a pair of *Bibliotheca Sacra* articles, NT scholar Daniel Wallace discusses the relationship between the Majority Text and the original text of
the GNT.[105] He details and critiques the movement back toward the Majority

---

101. Comfort, *Encountering the Manuscripts*, 98.

102. Zane Clark Hodges and Arthur L. Farstad, *The Greek New Testament according to the
Majority Text*, 2nd ed. (Nashville: Thomas Nelson, 1985), v.

103. Hodges and Farstad, *Greek New Testament*, v.

104. Maurice A. Robinson and William G. Pierpont, *The New Testament in the Original Greek:
Byzantine Textform*, 2nd ed. (Southborough, MA: Chilton Book Publishing, 2005).

105. Daniel B. Wallace, "Some Second Thoughts on the Majority Text," *BSac* 146 (1989):
270–90; Wallace, "The Majority Text and the Original Text: Are They Identical?" *BSac* 148
(1991): 151–69.

Text in a 1994 article in the *Journal of the Evangelical Theological Society*.[106] Regardless of one's position in the debate, the Majority Text (or Byzantine-priority) position provides a thoughtful challenge to other critical editions of the GNT even while recent studies for the *Editio Critica Maior* and the CBGM have taken the Byzantine textual grouping into account as a possible witness to the earliest form of the text.

4.2.4.e Society of Biblical Literature Greek New Testament (SBLGNT)

In 2011 the Society of Biblical Literature (SBL) released a critical edition of the GNT in cooperation with Logos Bible Software. Using Westcott and Hort's GNT as the starting point, editor Michael Holmes first modified that text to match the orthographic standards he had chosen for the edition. He then considered three other texts in comparison to this modified version: Tregelles,[107] Robinson-Pierpont (RP),[108] and the Greek text behind the NIV.[109] Occasionally Holmes found that "a reading not found in any of the four editions commended itself as the most probable."[110] The text of SBLGNT differs from the text of Nestle-Aland in more than 540 places,[111] and the apparatus provides all instances of variation between the four editions, plus the NA, instead of itemizing Greek witnesses. Thus, the SBLGNT critical apparatus complements that of the NA, which details manuscript information for serious text critics, and UBS, which is geared toward translators, and highlights readings that may merit further research. One of the

---

106. Daniel B. Wallace, "The Majority-Text Theory: History, Methods and Critique," *JETS* 37.2 (1994): 184–215. This essay is also published as part of *The Text of the New Testament in Contemporary Research: Essays on the Status Quaestionis*, ed. Bart D. Ehrman and Michael W. Holmes, 2nd ed. (Leiden: Brill, 2013), 711–44.

107. Samuel Prideaux Tregelles, ed., *The Greek New Testament, Edited from Ancient Authorities, with their Various Readings in Full, and the Latin Version of Jerome* (London: Bagster; Stewart, 1857–1879). This edition was seen as offering a "discerning alternative perspective alongside Westcott and Hort" (Holmes, "Introduction," SBLGNT, x; available online at http://sblgnt.com/about/introduction/).

108. As described above, RP is considered a reliable representative of the Byzantine textual tradition.

109. Richard J. Goodrich and Albert L. Lukaszewski, eds., *A Reader's Greek New Testament* (Grand Rapids: Zondervan, 2003). This is the reconstructed text behind the NIV (1973), representing textual choices made by the translation committee and differing from the UBS GNT in 231 places (see Holmes, "Introduction," SBLGNT, x; available online at http://sblgnt.com/about/introduction/).

110. Holmes, "Introduction," SBLGNT, xi.

111. Holmes, SBLGNT.

most significant features of the SBLGNT is that it is available free online, making it accessible to pastors, scholars, and students who may not have easy electronic access to a current critical edition of the GNT.

4.2.4.f The Greek New Testament by Tyndale House (THGNT)

In 2017 a team of scholars at Tyndale House in Cambridge, England, published a critical edition of the Greek New Testament "based on a thorough revision of the great nineteenth-century tradition of Samuel Prideaux Tregelles."[112] The editors have taken as their goal to produce a GNT that is as close as possible to the appearance and content that would have prevailed in the first five centuries of the church. Although they do not use *scriptio continua, nomina sacra*, or majuscule script, they do aim to reproduce the paragraphing and spelling of the ancient documents. Punctuation is restrained, and text-critical sigla are not used in the text. The order of the New Testament books is the four Gospels, Acts, the Catholic Epistles, the Pauline corpus, and Revelation.

The apparatus is more limited than in other editions. Significant variant readings are provided in the form of footnotes with a restricted number of witnesses cited. One rule used by the editors to establish the text is that the variant they choose must be "attested in two or more Greek manuscripts, at least one being from the fifth century or earlier."[113] The editors plan to produce a textual commentary in order to demonstrate the reasoning for their textual choices.

4.3 HOW TO DO NEW TESTAMENT TEXTUAL CRITICISM

In a departure from earlier generations, many pastors and students today bypass mastering the biblical languages and are therefore unable to effectively use tools such as commentaries that discuss textual variants as the basis for exegetical arguments and translation decisions. Even those who learn the languages and use their Greek NT rarely make use of the critical

---

112. Dirk Jongkind and Peter J. Williams, "Preface," in *Greek New Testament, Produced at Tyndale House, Cambridge*, vii.

113. THGNT, 506. They relaxed this rule for the text of Revelation because it has a more limited range of early witnesses.

apparatus, let alone examine the actual manuscripts. This textbook has provided an introduction to text-critical principles to help students gain an initial understanding of what is involved in text-critical decisions. The final section of this chapter is intended to refine those foundational skills and provide you with chances to practice and internalize.

4.3.1 TOOLS FOR NEW TESTAMENT TEXTUAL CRITICISM

To evaluate variants in the Greek text of the New Testament, textual critics need a critical edition of the biblical text with a critical apparatus and a dictionary (or lexicon) of NT Greek. Other useful tools for textual study include the translators' notes included in some English versions[114] and technical commentaries, which can help identify variants and the rationale behind particular readings.

4.3.1.a Using the Critical Apparatus

As you begin to develop your skills in New Testament textual criticism, you will want to own a critical edition of the Greek New Testament. While there will be good reasons to work directly from images of one or more Greek manuscripts, a critical edition provides you with the Greek text that the editors have chosen as well as an apparatus outlining alternative readings found in other textual witnesses. The most widely used critical editions are the NA28 and the UBS5, though the SBLGNT, THGNT, and the majority-text editions are also useful.

It is best to work from the Greek when exploring the textual variation of the New Testament. However, if you do not know Greek or if your grasp is rusty, you can start with your English Bible and study the footnotes that refer to the readings of other ancient witnesses. All of the important variation units should be provided in the footnotes of a good English Bible. After pinpointing places where variation occurs, you can then use various helps such as commentaries to investigate the textual situation.

---

114. It would be wise to have several versions of the literal/formal type and the dynamic/functional equivalence type. Check to see that they have footnotes that provide information such as the ones discussed below in §4.3.1.f. The New English Translation (NET) is particularly useful in this regard because it offers over 58,000 translators' notes from a committee of experts in the biblical languages. For further information, see http://netbible.com/.

As has been discussed elsewhere, the main difference between the NA28 and the UBS5 is that the NA lists more variation units in its apparatus, whereas the UBS tends to list only those that will affect translation decisions, assigning a grade of certainty to each textual decision made by the committee. We will use the NA28 in most of the following discussions, though much of what we will cover applies to the use of other critical apparatuses as well.

Besides its Greek text, the NA28 provides a number of useful tools. You will want to page through the front and back parts of the GNT to see everything that is available. For now, we will focus on the critical apparatus at the bottom of every page.[115] Because scholars pack a lot of manuscript names and details into the apparatus, they employ a system of sigla (symbols) and abbreviations to make the data concise. Some of the most common ones are as follows:[116]

Table 4.6: Common Sigla and Abbreviations in the Critical Apparatus	
°	The single word following the siglum is *omitted* by the witnesses cited.
□ \	The words or sentences between the two sigla are *omitted* by the witnesses cited.
⌐	The word following the siglum is *replaced* with one or more words by the witnesses cited.
⌐ ⌐	The words between the two sigla are *replaced* with other words by the witnesses cited. The replacement can include some of the same words.
⊤	At this position, one or more words have been *inserted* by the witnesses cited.
⌐ ⌐	The words between the two sigla are transposed (same words, but in a different order) by the witnesses cited.

---

115. In a digital edition of the NA28, you can typically access the information from the apparatus by hovering over or clicking on the relevant parts of the Greek text. For information on digital editions, see http://www.nestle-aland.com/en/extra-navigation/digital-editions/.

116. The following list is a brief adaptation of pages 54*–88* in the NA28. Refer to those pages for more details.

txt ("text")	The witnesses cited after this word contain the reading printed above in the text.
*	If the reading in a manuscript has been corrected by a later scribe, an asterisk next to the ID of the manuscript indicates the reading of the first hand (the original scribe).
c	Written superscript next to a witness, "c" indicates that this is the reading of a correction made by the original scribe or, more likely, by a later scribe.
vid ("as it appears")	Written superscript next to a witness, this abbreviation for "ut videtur" indicates that the reading in the manuscript is not clearly legible, so it cannot be cited with complete confidence.

The apparatus of the NA presents the variant readings first, each with its supporting evidence (i.e., which manuscripts contain each variant).[117] Some variation units have only one alternative reading, but for others there will be multiple variants, separated by a broken vertical line.[118] Next, the NA lists the variant that the editorial committee has decided to print in the text, along with its supporting manuscript evidence. Occasionally, only the evidence for an alternative reading is provided.

4.3.1.b Metzger's Textual Commentary

As mentioned earlier, an invaluable tool for understanding the process that the editorial committee of the **UBS Greek New Testament** went through is Bruce Metzger's *A Textual Commentary on the Greek New Testament*. The second edition, designed as a companion to the UBS4, provides a complete explanation of each textual decision made by the editorial committee. Entries where the evidence clearly favors a particular variant are brief, whereas several paragraphs may be devoted to more difficult variants. In some places the committee did not reach complete agreement, and the reasoning of both sides is provided. The commentary is not exhaustive, but it is a valuable tool for translators and exegetes.

---

117. The UBS uses the opposite order, listing evidence for the editors' chosen reading first, followed by evidence for the alternatives.

118. Variants are separated by slash lines in the UBS.

A related resource is *A Textual Guide to the Greek New Testament*, an adaptation of Metzger's *Textual Commentary* written by Roger L. Omanson.[119] This resource is designed as a further assistance for translators who do not have formal training in textual criticism and presents the information in a less technical manner. The guide also includes an introduction to NT textual criticism.

4.3.1.c New Testament Commentaries with Text-Critical Notes

A text-critical analysis of the passage should be the first step in the exegetical process of any good commentary. The commentator should first establish the text, then exegete it in its historical and literary context, and finally provide guidance for interpretation. For an example of how a commentator factors text-critical issues into the interpretation of a passage, consider the following discussion of Ephesians 1:1.

The main textual issue concerning Ephesians 1:1 is whether the phrase "in Ephesus" (ἐν Ἐφέσῳ, *en Ephesō*) was part of the original letter. If you have a look at this variation unit in your GNT, you will see that there is manuscript evidence for both its omission and its inclusion. Commentators must weigh the evidence and arrive at a position (i.e., "establish the text"). When F. F. Bruce addresses the variant in his comments on Ephesians 1:1, he discusses both internal and external evidence.[120] In terms of internal evidence, Bruce observes that "the construction without 'at Ephesus' or any similar phrase is awkward: 'to the saints who are also believers in Christ Jesus' is not a natural form of address."[121] Paul's letters characteristically identify the location of their recipients (compare 1 Cor 1:2; Gal 1:2; 1 Thess 1:1), and the syntax of the Greek phrase in Ephesians 1:1 "prepares the reader for an indication of place."[122] On the other hand, Bruce argues that nothing in the rest of the letter suggests "it was written to the church in a city where

---

119. Roger L. Omanson, *A Textual Guide to the Greek New Testament: An Adaptation of Bruce M. Metzger's Textual Commentary for the Needs of Translators* (Stuttgart: Deutsche Bibelgesellschaft, 2006).

120. F. F. Bruce, *The Epistles to the Colossians, to Philemon, and to the Ephesians*, NICNT (Grand Rapids: Eerdmans, 1984), 249–51. For a more recent survey of the debate, see Frank Thielman, *Ephesians*, Baker Evangelical Commentary on the New Testament (Grand Rapids: Baker Academic, 2010), 12–16.

121. Bruce, *Ephesians*, 250.

122. Bruce, *Ephesians*, 250n9.

Paul had spent the best part of three years," thus calling the addition of ἐν Ἐφέσῳ (en Ephesō) into question.[123]

In terms of external evidence, Bruce asserts that the "weight of documentary evidence indicates that the phrase 'at Ephesus' is not part of the original wording."[124] The oldest and best manuscripts of the letter do not contain the words ἐν Ἐφέσῳ (en Ephesō), including P46, Sinaiticus, Vaticanus, and minuscule 1739. In addition, the manuscripts known to and used by the church fathers appear not to have had ἐν Ἐφέσῳ (en Ephesō).[125] However, the copies that omit ἐν Ἐφέσῳ (en Ephesō) offer no alternative destinations for the letter, which one might expect if Ephesus was not the original destination. Bruce's creative solution—that copies of the letter had included a blank "space left for the insertion of an indication of place"—has been debated, primarily because of the lack of external evidence for such a practice.[126] While Bruce considers ἐν Ἐφέσῳ (en Ephesō) a later insertion that was not part of the original letter, other New Testament scholars such as Clinton Arnold and Frank Thielman have reviewed the same evidence and come to the opposite conclusion.[127] Thielman sees this issue as "one of the most difficult textual problems in the New Testament."[128]

Bruce was attempting to find a solution that accounted for both the external and internal evidence in Ephesians 1:1. The external evidence says the phrase was added later. The internal evidence implies the opening text of the letter should have "an indication of place" at just the point where later manuscripts read ἐν Ἐφέσῳ (en Ephesō). Of course, such a lack is exactly what could have caused a later corrector to add the address. Not all text-critical problems present such a difficult challenge, but Ephesians 1:1 is an example of a variation unit where the commentator must draw on textual criticism in order to establish the text, and that decision will affect the exegesis and interpretation of the entire letter.

---

123. Bruce, *Ephesians*, 250.

124. Bruce, *Ephesians*, 249–50.

125. Bruce, *Ephesians*, 249n4.

126. Bruce, *Ephesians*, 250.

127. Clinton E. Arnold, "Ephesians, Letter to the," *DPL* 238–48, esp. 244; Thielman, *Ephesians*, 15–16.

128. Thielman, *Ephesians*, 12.

4.3.1.d Lexica

If you are working in the Greek text, a good dictionary or lexicon is a useful tool for clarifying what Greek words mean and how they are used throughout the NT. You can then compare how the same words are used elsewhere and how various translations might treat the same word in other contexts. Such comparison may help you understand a translator's style or preference for certain words. The standard lexicon for biblical Greek is *A Greek-English Lexicon of the New Testament and Other Early Christian Literature* (commonly abbreviated BDAG after several generations of editors: Bauer, Danker, Arndt, and Gingrich). Another useful Greek lexicon is *A Greek-English Lexicon* by Liddell and Scott (often referred to as Liddell-Scott or abbreviated LSJ). This lexicon, compiled in the nineteenth century, was updated regularly from 1843–1897; it was supplemented less frequently throughout the twentieth century.[129] Liddell-Scott covers ancient Greek, including the biblical Greek of the NT and the Septuagint. Its scope has made it the standard lexicon for ancient Greek for the last 150 years.[130]

4.3.1.e Translator's Notes

Every English Bible is the product of the complex process of translating the original languages into English that is intelligible and relevant to contemporary readers. Before translators of the NT select the right *English* words to use in translation, they must determine which *Greek* texts to use as the basis for the translation. Translation teams typically rely on established critical texts for their work, but they will also add notes when a text-critical issue is worth highlighting. Translation notes are present in almost every English translation of the Bible.

You will find three primary types of notes in English versions. The first two have to do with translation decisions, and the third one is about text-critical decisions:

---

129. Multiple major updates to the lexicon took place prior to 1940. The abbreviation LSJ derives from the addition of the name of the primary editor in the early twentieth century—Henry Jones (i.e., Liddell-Scott-Jones). The ninth edition of 1940 was the result of the major revisions and supplements completed by Jones and others from 1911–1939. Another major supplement to LSJ appeared in 1996, with 25,000 updates to the roughly 125,000 entries of LSJ.

130. If you purchase an edition of LSJ, it is much preferred to have the unabridged version. However, a completely updated edition is less necessary. Older editions will serve well.

Gk/Greek: Notes beginning with "Gk" or "Greek" indicate that transla-tors chose to use an English word or phrase that does not directly correlate with the Greek wording. For example, the Gospel of Matthew frequently uses the word γεέννη (*geennē*). While a few English versions translate γεέννη phonetically as "Gehenna" (e.g., Young's Literal Translation), most English translations use "hell." To inform the reader of a difference between the English translation and the underlying Greek text, translators will add a note that provides the reader with a transliteration of the Greek term. The ESV translation of Matthew 10:28, for example, has the following note: "Greek: Gehenna."

Or…: This note specifies when translators have chosen a particular English rendering of a word or phrase where other translations were equally possible. An example of this type of note appears in the ESV at Romans 3:9. Paul's question in Romans 3:9 reads, "What then? Are we Jews any better off?" The ESV supplies the word "Jews" as the subject of the verb, whereas in the Greek it is unspecified, though clear from the context. By contrast, the NIV translates the Greek more straightforwardly: "What shall we conclude then? Do we have any advantage?"

Other Ancient Authorities/Some MSS read…: This note is the most relevant for seeing how textual criticism affects English transla-tions. English Bibles use this note to inform readers that the transla-tors have selected a particular variant over another as the basis of their translation. Biblical footnotes under this heading alert readers to places where multiple variants are found in the manuscripts. Several English translations have this sort of note at Ephesians 1:15, the opening verse of Paul's prayer for his readers. He begins: "I have heard of your faith in the Lord Jesus and *your love* toward all the saints." Most English trans-lations of Paul's letter (e.g., LEB, ESB, NRSV, NASB) include the phrase "your love," but note that the expression is missing from some witnesses. For example, the NASB informs the reader that "many ancient mss. do not contain *your love*."

4.3.2 REVIEWING BASIC PRINCIPLES

Because of the sheer number of extant New Testament manuscripts and the complexity involved in comparing them, scholars have established principles and methods that assist in the evaluation of a variation unit or of a given witness. While we have already introduced the basic concepts of external evidence and internal evidence (see §2.3 Basic Principles of Textual Criticism), we will discuss them in more detail here.

4.3.2.a External Evidence

Textual critics first examine the external evidence, which is *information about the actual manuscripts*. They must consider three key issues. Textual critics must first consider the relative date of the witnesses to a variant reading. Generally, scholars consider the earlier manuscripts to be more likely to have preserved the oldest form of the text. This principle has exceptions, however; sometimes a later manuscript preserves an early tradition. Second, textual critics consider the textual affiliation of the witnesses. A reading attested by manuscripts from several textual groupings is more likely to represent the earliest text than one found in only one textual tradition. Third, text critics need to keep in mind that the quality of some witnesses varies according to the books (or groups of books) within the NT. For example, Codex Alexandrinus (A 02) is the oldest example of Byzantine textual affiliation in the Gospels, but it is a good Alexandrian witness for the rest of the NT, and it is also considered one of the most important manuscripts for the Revelation.

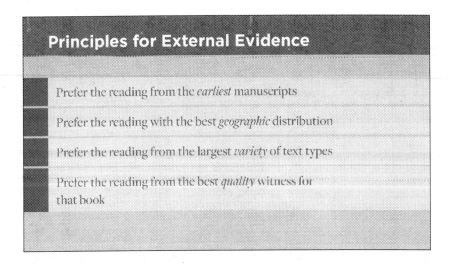

Principles for External Evidence

Prefer the reading from the *earliest* manuscripts

Prefer the reading with the best *geographic* distribution

Prefer the reading from the largest *variety* of text types

Prefer the reading from the best *quality* witness for that book

4.3.2.b Internal Evidence

The second set of data that textual critics examine is internal evidence, which concerns *the content of the witnesses*. Internal data falls into two categories: intrinsic probability and transcriptional probability.

When scholars examine **intrinsic probability**, they ask which variant reading better fits with the author's style and vocabulary. For example, if a word or grammatical construction in a witness is otherwise unknown for that author, then it might not be the authorial reading. For instance, intrinsic probability must be considered in 1 Corinthians 2:1, where the external evidence is fairly evenly divided. The textual critic must search the surrounding text and consider usage elsewhere in Paul's writings in order to decide whether Paul is more likely to have written "mystery of God" or "testimony of God." The main rule of intrinsic probability is to prefer the reading that best fits the author's style and vocabulary.

Considerations of **transcriptional probability** are normally given more weight than intrinsic probability. **Transcriptional evidence** is related to the practices of the scribes and editors of the manuscripts. The question is what a scribe is more likely to have done. For some variants, a case can be made that the scribe may have made a mechanical mistake such as haplography, parablepsis, dittography, metathesis, homophony, or

Principles for Internal Evidence

Prefer the reading that *best fits* the author's style and vocabulary

Prefer the *shorter* reading

Prefer the *more difficult* reading

Prefer the *less theologically harmonized* reading

Prefer the *less polished* reading

mistaken letters. Other variants have been caused by a deliberate action of the scribe. These might include additions to or subtractions from the text in the form of conflations, glosses, smoothing, harmonization, or clarification.[131] Luke 23:38 provides an example of probable harmonization or assimilation to another biblical passage. The phrase "it was written in Hebrew, in Latin, in Greek" was almost certainly added in some manuscripts in order to harmonize the verse with John 19:20.

The following guidelines (sometimes called "canons") summarize the basic principles that govern how text critics weigh transcriptional evidence:

Table 4.4: Guidelines for Evaluating Transcriptional Probability	
Guideline	**Explanation**
Prefer the shorter reading (*lectio brevior*).	Scribes tended to add, not delete.
Prefer the more difficult reading (*lectio difficilior*).	Scribes tended to fix a potentially problematic reading, not make it more complicated.
Prefer the less polished reading.	Scribes tended to smooth out awkward syntax and to correct grammar.
Prefer the reading that is less likely to be a theologically motivated alteration.	Scribes tended to amplify theological points or to harmonize readings with other NT passages.

Although application of these guidelines for internal evidence varies depending on who uses them, they are designed to help scholars work toward a single, ultimate goal: *to identify the reading that best explains how the other readings arose.* If you can explain how one variant led to the occurrence of the other variants, that variant is the most probable *Ausgangstext*.[132]

---

131. All of these types of accidental and intentional variation are described in §2.1.2 Changes and Errors and listed with brief definitions in §2.3.2 Internal Evidence.

132. Remember that the *Ausgangstext* is the earliest form of the text that gave rise to the readings found in others (see §1.2.3 Textual Criticism Defined to review the definition).

4.3.3 THE NEW TESTAMENT TEXT-CRITICAL PROCESS: STEP BY STEP

New Testament textual critics incorporate the principles described above into a three-stage process that involves gathering data about variants and then analyzing the data to make a judgment about the reading of a particular passage.

4.3.3.a Identify the Variation Unit and Review the Witnesses

Variation units will be marked in the text of your Greek NT (e.g., Nestle-Aland uses *sigla* and UBS uses footnotes).[133] First, identify where variation occurs in the verse or passage that you are considering. Find the same identifying marks where that verse is listed in the apparatus. We will start with a simple variation by way of example.

In John 3:32 the NA28 looks like this:

32 ᵀὃ ἑώρακεν καὶ ἤκουσεν °τοῦτο μαρτυρεῖ, καὶ τὴν μαρτυρίαν αὐτοῦ οὐδεὶς λαμβάνει.[134]

The first variant in verse 32 comes immediately. Note the small "T" shape (ᵀ) in front of ὃ ἑώρακεν (*ho heōraken*). This mark is always used to clue the reader in about an insertion of text, so now we know that one or more manuscripts insert a word at this place. Next, look in the apparatus for verse 32, where you can see the following:

32 ᵀ καὶ A K Γ Δ Θ f¹³ 700. 892. 1241. 1424 𝔐 lat sy^s.p.h ¦ *txt* 𝔓⁶⁶.⁷⁵ ℵ B D L Wˢ Ψ 083. 086 f¹ 33. 565. 579 it syᶜ

Notice the "T" shape (ᵀ) immediately after the verse number, signifying that the following information applies to the same mark in the verse above. The first information given is that A K Γ Δ Θ f¹³ 700 892 1241 1424 𝔐 lat sy^s.p.h have the word καὶ (*kai*, "and") at the beginning of the verse. Most

---

133. It will be important for you to become acquainted with the sigla used in the NA apparatus. Table 4.6 has a list of common sigla, but they are explained in more detail in the introduction of your edition of NA. For the NA28, the explanation of the sigla and abbreviations are on pages 54*–88*. You should not try to memorize them all, but you should get in the habit of looking them up as you work through variation units. Over time, you will find you have memorized the most common ones.

134. *ho heōraken kai ēkousen touto martyrei, kai tēn martyrian autou oudeis lambanei.*

of the manuscripts in this list are representatives of the Byzantine and/or Caesarean textual groupings. Remember that the 𝔐 stands for the great majority of Byzantine minuscules (see §4.2.1.c. Minuscules). We can see that the Latin Vulgate plus some Old Latin as well as three Syriac versions also have their respective translations for καὶ here.[135]

Those witnesses that do not have καὶ are in the second list on the other side of the broken vertical line, where the variant is designated as *txt,* meaning the reading given in the text, which is the omission of καὶ. The manuscripts that do not include καὶ are P66 P75 א B D L Wˢ Ψ 083 086 f¹ 33 579 it syᶜ. There are fewer witnesses in this list, but they are the oldest ones, especially the two papyri, and they represent a mix of textual groupings: Alexandrian, Western, and Caesarean, plus much of the Old Latin and one Syriac version.

4.3.3.b Analyze the Evidence

Our analysis typically begins with the question of external evidence. Here with John 3:32 one would quickly come to the conclusion that the strongest external evidence is for the omission of καὶ. The oldest and best manuscripts omit, and the omission is shared by witnesses from several textual groupings.

Moving to internal evidence, the question to be asked is what might have caused καὶ to either be added or omitted. Presence or absence of καὶ is not likely to be an issue of intrinsic probability (though one could examine John's Gospel for how frequently καὶ is used to connect related sentences). Transcriptional probability is more relevant to this variation unit. When scribes copied this text, would they have been more likely to have added or omitted the conjunction? While it is possible that a scribe could have accidentally omitted καὶ, it seems more likely that a scribe would have added the conjunction to make the text flow better.

---

135. Again, the abbreviations for the witnesses mentioned in the apparatus are found in the introduction to NA.

4.3.3.c Draw Conclusions

This is the stage at which the textual critic will look at the evidence, make a choice, and *establish the text* for this variation unit. In John 3:32, the transcriptional probability leans in the favor of a later insertion of καὶ, and the external evidence clinches that tendency because of the strength of the evidence that καὶ was not in the oldest form of the text.

4.3.4 EXAMPLES OF TEXT-CRITICAL ISSUES

The following are five examples of passages requiring text-critical decisions in order to establish the text. You will learn best by first working through the variation units on your own, following the steps outlined above. After you have done your own work, come back to the book, and we will walk you through each text step by step.

4.3.4.a Mark 1:2

1. Identify the Variation Unit and Review the Witnesses

Mark 1:2 begins with the phrase καθὼς γέγραπται ἐν (*kathōs gegraptai en*, "Just as it has been written in"). The critical apparatuses of Nestle-Aland and UBS5 indicate there is a variant reading for the words that follow. NA28 alerts you to the variant with the sigla ⌐ ⌐,[136] which means that some witnesses replace the words between the two marks—τῷ Ἠσαΐᾳ τῷ προφήτῃ (*tō Ēsaia tō prophētē*, "Isaiah the prophet")—with another reading. The two possibilities for what follows καθὼς γέγραπται ἐν (*kathōs gegraptai en*) are (1) the reading that the two critical editions have in their texts (τῷ Ἠσαΐᾳ τῷ προφήτῃ, *tō Ēsaia tō prophētē*, "in Isaiah the prophet"), and (2) the reading that they have in the apparatus (τοῖς προφήταις, *tois prophētais*, "in the prophets"). The text critic's decision about this variation unit will affect the translation as follows:

---

136. UBS5 indicates there is a variant by means of a footnote after τῷ Ἠσαΐᾳ τῷ προφήτῃ (*tō Ēsaia tō prophētē*).

Table 4.7: Variants of Mark 1:2	
NA28 and UBS5	**Hodges/Farstad Majority Text**
Καθὼς γέγραπται ἐν τῷ Ἡσαΐᾳ τῷ προφήτῃ· Ἰδοὺ ἀποστέλλω τὸν ἄγγελόν μου πρὸ προσώπου σου, ὃς κατασκευάσει τὴν ὁδόν σου.[137]	Ὡς γέγραπται ἐν τοῖς προφήταις, Ἰδού, ἐγὼ ἀποστέλλω τὸν ἄγγελόν μου πρὸ προσώπου σου, Ὃς κατασκευάσει τὴν ὁδόν σου ἔμπροσθέν σου.[138]
NASB	**KJV**
As it is written in Isaiah the prophet, "Behold, I send my messenger before your face, who will prepare your way."	As it is written in the prophets, Behold, I send my messenger before thy face, which shall prepare thy way before thee.

There are actually three variants in this unit.[139] NA28 presents the first one as follows:

2-4 D Θ f¹ 700. *l*844. *l*2211; Ir Or^pt Epiph

In this first variant, the numbers 2-4 tell you that the listed witnesses have a wording variation in relationship to the four words written above in the text. The first word (τῷ, *tō*) is missing, but words 2 through 4 are present and in the same order. That is, in these few witnesses it reads Ἡσαΐᾳ τῷ προφήτῃ (*Ēsaia tō prophētē*). There is no difference in translation since the missing article is not translated in English anyway. The witnesses that support this reading are two majuscules, several minuscules, two lectionaries, and several church fathers. Or^pt means that part of Origen's citations do not have the article. The textual affinities tend towards both Western and Caesarean.

The second variant in NA28 comes after a broken vertical line:

τοις προφηταις A K P W Γ f¹³ 28. 579. 1424. 2542 𝔐 vg^ms sy^h (bo^mss); Ir^lat

---

137. *Kathōs gegraptai en tō Ēsaia tō prophētē, Idou apostellō ton angelon mou pro prosōpou sou, hos kataskeuasei tēn hodon sou.*

138. *Hōs gegraptai en tois prophētais, Idou, egō apostellō ton angelon mou pro prosōpou sou, Hos kataskeuasei tēn hodon sou emprosthen sou.*

139. UBS5 presents a fourth variant (ἐν Ἡσαΐᾳ καὶ ἐν τοῖς προφήταις; *en Ēsaia kai en tois prophētais*), but it is an uncertain reading in one Latin manuscript and is clearly a conflation.

The reading "in the prophets" is found in a large number of manuscripts, as indicated by 𝔐. Several majuscules and minuscules [40] that tend toward a more Byzantine or Caesarean textual affiliation are also listed, as well as one Vulgate manuscript, the Harclean Syriac, and the Latin translation of Irenaeus. The Bohairic is in parentheses because it tends to support this reading but has some sort of difference (not given).

Finally, after another broken vertical line, the witnesses for the variant that the editors have chosen and used above in the text are listed:

txt ℵ B L Δ 33. 565. 892. 1241 sy[p.hmg] co; Or[pt]

The abbreviation *txt* (for "text") indicates that these witnesses have the variant that the editors think is the *Ausgangstext*. Here we find Sinaiticus, Vaticanus, two more majuscules, several good minuscules, the Syriac Peshitta, and a marginal reading in the Harclean, the Coptic, and part of Origen. The textual tendency of this group is Alexandrian.

2. Analyze the Evidence

External Evidence. One might think of *lectio brevior* as a text-critical guideline to apply to this textual decision. However, the longer reading is found in earlier and higher-quality witnesses. The first variant is part of the evidence for the third variant since it is basically the same reading with only an article missing. Thus, the evidence for "Isaiah the prophet" is found in witnesses that support Western, Caesarean, and Alexandrian textual streams.

Internal Evidence. Now we come to the crux of the matter. Should we lean on intrinsic probability? Mark has quoted not only Isaiah 40:3 but also Malachi 3:1[141] in the text that follows our variation unit. Would Mark have mistakenly identified the entire OT quote as "from Isaiah"? Based on the citing habits of ancient times, it is indeed possible that Mark would have lumped both quotes under Isaiah. It is also possible

---

140. Minuscules such as these are constantly cited in the apparatus because they differ significantly from the Byzantine grouping. Some of them are even considered good representatives of the Alexandrian grouping. You should, over time, learn to recognize their GA numbers.

141. With possible reference to Exod 23:20 as well.

that he was simply passing on an oral tradition credited to Isaiah without checking it. Remember, Mark would not have had a personal "Bible," and he may not have had any access at all to copies of OT books in order to check his quotes.

Transcriptional probability now enters the picture. If Mark attributed the entire quotation to Isaiah, it is easy to see why later scribes would have changed the wording from τῷ Ἡσαΐᾳ τῷ προφήτῃ (tō Ēsaia tō prophētē) to τοῖς προφήταις (tois prophētais). It is much more difficult to imagine a later scribe changing τοῖς προφήταις to τῷ Ἡσαΐᾳ τῷ προφήτῃ.

3. Draw Conclusions

Given the strength of the manuscript evidence for τῷ Ἡσαΐᾳ τῷ προφήτῃ (tō Ēsaia tō prophētē) plus the transcriptional probability, it appears that the more difficult reading (lectio difficilior) is most likely the Ausgangstext. It is likely that one or more scribes noticed that the quotation from the Hebrew Bible was from both Isaiah and Malachi and attempted to better represent the actual situation by replacing the Ausgangstext "in Isaiah the prophet" with "in the prophets." Most of the newer English Bible translations follow the reading of the older manuscripts and translate "in Isaiah the prophet" (see ESV, NASB, NIV, LEB, NRSV).

4.3.4.b 1 Thessalonians 2:7

1. Identify the Variation Unit and Review the Witnesses

In 1 Thessalonians 2:7, a difference in one letter provides two distinct readings: "we became infants" (ἐγενήθημεν νήπιοι, egenēthēmen nēpioi) versus "we became gentle" (ἐγενήθημεν ἤπιοι, egenēthēmen ēpioi). NA28 identifies this variation unit with the siglum ⌐, which means that the following word is different in some manuscripts. The editors of the NA have chosen the variant νήπιοι (nēpioi, "infants"). Many English translations follow the NA choice (compare NET, NLT, LEB). However, several English versions instead use ἤπιοι (ēpioi, "gentle ones"; compare ESV, NASB, KJV, NIV), which is also the preferred reading of the SBLGNT.

Table 4.8: Variants of 1 Thessalonians 2:7	
SBLGNT	**Nestle-Aland**
ἀλλὰ ἐγενήθημεν ἤπιοι ἐν μέσῳ ὑμῶν, ὡς ἐὰν τροφὸς θάλπῃ τὰ ἑαυτῆς τέκνα.[142]	ἀλλὰ ἐγενήθημεν νήπιοι ἐν μέσῳ ὑμῶν, ὡς ἐὰν τροφὸς θάλπῃ τὰ ἑαυτῆς τέκνα,[143]
NASB	**LEB**
But we proved to be gentle among you, as a nursing mother tenderly cares for her own children.	yet we became infants in your midst, like a nursing mother cherishes her own children.

The NA28 presents the variation unit as follows:

ηπιοι ℵ^c A C² D² K L P Ψ^c 0278. 33. 81. 104^c. 326*. 365. 630. 1241. 1505. 1739. 1881. 𝔐 vgst (sy) sa^{mss}; Cl

You will notice that scribes have struggled with this reading. The superscript "c" (for corrector), "2" (for second corrector), or "*" (for first hand) tell us that Sinaiticus, Ephraemi Rescriptus, Claromontanus,[144] and three others named above have had corrections made in one direction or the other.[145]

Although 1739 tends to align with the Alexandrian grouping, most of the witnesses here are more likely to represent the Byzantine tradition. The abbreviation vgst tells us that the *Stuttgartiensis* edition of the Vulgate chose this reading. The Syriac supports it with a difference (not given), and some Sahidic manuscripts and the church father Clement also agree.

Next, the witnesses for the reading that the editors have used in the main text are listed:

txt 𝔓⁶⁵ ℵ* B C* D* F G I Ψ* 104*. 326^c it vg^{cl.ww} sa^{ms} bo

---

142. *alla egenēthēmen ēpioi en mesō hymōn, hōs ean trophos thalpē ta heautēs tekna.*

143. *alla egenēthēmen nēpioi en mesō hymōn, hōs ean trophos thalpē ta heautēs tekna.*

144. Remember that Bezae (D 05) only contains the Gospels and Acts. D in the Paulines refers to Claromontanus (06, sometimes designated D^P).

145. The text used/preferred by a corrector can be discerned by making a study of all changes made to a manuscript. In some cases, research has been done on the textual affiliation of a particular corrector (those of Sinaiticus, for example). The corrector of Claromontanus might be assumed to be non-Western, and most corrections in minuscules are towards the majority text. But further study is needed before leaning on such assumptions as an indication of textual affiliation of a corrector.

The reading chosen by the editors is supported by P65, a third-century collection of the Pauline letters and the oldest witness in this passage, as well as Sinaiticus, Vaticanus, Ephraemi Rescriptus, Claromontanus, and several other majuscules and minuscules. Most of the Old Latin, several Vulgate editions, one Sahidic manuscript, and the Bohairic also have this reading. This group of witnesses includes the oldest witness and has members from both the Alexandrian and the Western traditions.[146]

2. Analyze the Evidence

External Evidence. The reading ἐγενήθημεν νήπιοι (*egenēthēmen nēpioi*, "we became infants") has somewhat stronger manuscript support, with an early papyrus plus the first-hand reading of Sinaiticus, Vaticanus, and several others. The reading ἐγενήθημεν ἤπιοι (*egenēthēmen ēpioi*, "we became gentle") appears in the majority of manuscripts, including several correctors and others that lack the age, quality, and broad textual witness of the first group. Thus, the external evidence favors ἐγενήθημεν νήπιοι (*egenēthēmen nēpioi*).

    Internal Evidence. The only difference between these two expressions is the Greek letter *nu* (ν, *n*) at the beginning of the second word, νήπιοι (*nēpioi*) versus ἤπιοι (*ēpioi*). The transcriptional probability could be explained one of two ways. It could reflect dittography—that is, ἐγενήθημεν ἤπιοι (*egenēthēmen ēpioi*) was the *Ausgangstext*, and a copyist accidentally duplicated the *nu* from the end of the preceding word to create ἐγενήθημεν νήπιοι (*egenēthēmen nēpioi*).[147] Alternatively, one could argue that the latter reading is older and, through haplography, a later scribe skipped over the *nu* at the beginning of νήπιοι (*nēpioi*) because they saw the *nu* at the end of ἐγενήθημεν (*egenēthēmen*) and thought they had already written the start of νήπιοι (*nēpioi*).

    The intrinsic probability can be seen to provide slightly stronger support for ἐγενήθημεν ἤπιοι (*egenēthēmen ēpioi*, "we were gentle"). Paul uses

---

146. F and G in the Paulines often support Claromontanus and the Old Latin as representatives of a Western type of text.

147. Remember that the earliest copies of the NT were made in *scriptio continua*, so that the words ran together and line breaks could occur anywhere in a word. Remember also that the earliest copies of the NT did not have accenting and breathing marks that could have provided guidance here.

ἤπιοι (ēpioi, "gentle") only one other time in his writings (2 Tim 2:24), but he uses νήπιοι (nēpioi, "infants") several times. However, Paul's use of νήπιοι (nēpioi) usually has negative connotations or refers to spiritual immaturity (see 1 Cor 13:11; Eph 4:14). He never uses the word to refer to himself, as he would be doing in 1 Thessalonians 2:7. Furthermore, the word would have positive connotations in 1 Thessalonians 2:7 since Paul is speaking of the kind way he has dealt with the Thessalonian believers.

3. Draw Conclusions

Ultimately, the evidence in this case does not lead to a clear conclusion. NA28 and English translations like the NET, NLT, LEB make their text-critical decision primarily on the basis of external evidence, while the SBLGNT and the ESV, NASB, KJV, and NIV weigh the intrinsic probability more heavily in their decision. Every good English translation should have a footnote at 1 Thessalonians 2:7 to let the reader know that there is an alternative reading.

4.3.4.c Luke 4:4

1. Identify the Variation Unit and Review the Witnesses

NA28 indicates a variation unit at the end of Luke 4:4 as follows: οὐκ ἐπ' ἄρτῳ μόνῳ ζήσεται ὁ ἄνθρωπος [T] (ouk ep' artō monō zēsetai ho anthrōpos, "Man shall not live by bread alone"). In the apparatus we find the following entry:

> p) αλλ επι (εν D 0102. 892) παντι ρηματι (+ εκπορευομενω δια στοματος 1424) θεου A D K Γ Δ Θ Ψ 0102 f[1.13] 33. 565. 579. 700. 892. 1424. 2542. l844. l2211 𝔐 latt sy[p.h] bo[pt]

We learn from the apparatus that quite a few witnesses have added the phrase "but by every word of God." The abbreviation p) right after the siglum tells us that the editors think the cause of this variant is found in the wording of a parallel passage. If you go to the beginning of Luke 4 in NA, you will see a note indicating that this **pericope**[148] occurs in Matthew

---

148. A pericope is a segment of text taken as a unit—e.g., a parable or a healing narrative. When working with the Synoptic Gospels (Mark, Matthew, and Luke), it is important to compare whether and how each of them records the same pericope.

4:1–11 as well. In addition, NA28 has noted a connection between Luke 4:4 and Deuteronomy 8.3, which reads "… that He might make you understand that man does not live by bread alone, but man lives by everything that proceeds out of the mouth of God" (NASB). Matthew's record of this saying of Jesus is closer to the verse from Deuteronomy: "Man shall not live on bread alone, but on every word that proceeds out of the mouth of God" (Matt 4:4 NASB).

This variant is found in many witnesses, including representatives of Western, Caesarean, and Byzantine groupings. You have probably noticed the two times in this variant where witnesses are given in parentheses. These are manuscripts that support the existence of the variant but have slightly different wording, as provided. Support is also found in the entire Latin tradition, the Syriac Peshitta and Harclean, and part of the Bohairic.

txt ℵ B L W 1241 sy[s] sa bo[pt]

The reading chosen by the editors is found in fewer, but older, witnesses, including Sinaiticus and Vaticanus, and supported by the Syriac Sinaiticus, Sahidic, and part of the Bohairic. This group is mainly related to the Alexandrian textual stream.

The two variants result in the following two translations of Luke 4:4:

Table 4.9: Variants of Luke 4:4	
SBLGNT and NA28	**Hodges/Farstad Majority Text**
Γέγραπται ὅτι οὐκ ἐπ' ἄρτῳ μόνῳ ζήσεται ὁ ἄνθρωπος.[149]	Γέγραπται ὅτι Οὐκ ἐπ' ἄρτῳ μόνῳ ζήσεται ἄνθρωπος Ἀλλ' ἐπὶ παντὶ ῥήματι Θεοῦ.[150]
LEB	**KJV**
It is written, "Man will not live on bread alone."	It is written, That man shall not live by bread alone, but by every word of God.

---

149. *Gegraptai hoti Ouk ep' artō monō zēsetai ho anthrōpos.*

150. *Gegraptai hoti Ouk ep' artō monō zēsetai anthrōpos All' epi panti rhēmati Theou.*

2. Analyze the Evidence

External Evidence. It is possible to argue for the longer reading based on the number and broad representation of the supporting witnesses. However, the witnesses that *do not* include the phrase ἀλλ' ἐπὶ παντὶ ῥήματι θεου (*all' epi panti rhēmati theou*) are older and typically considered of higher quality, even though only one textual grouping is represented. Thus, the external evidence seems to favor seeing the additional phrase as a later addition.

Internal Evidence. When transcriptional probability is considered, a straightforward solution presents itself. It is entirely reasonable that a scribe copying Luke may have harmonized the shorter reading to match more closely with Matthew and/or Deuteronomy. It is hard to imagine a scribe deliberately leaving off ἀλλ' ἐπὶ παντὶ ῥήματι θεου (*all' epi panti rhēmati theou*) if it were part of the *Ausgangstext*.

3. Draw Conclusions

We can reasonably conclude that the phrase ἀλλ' ἐπὶ παντὶ ῥήματι θεου (*all' epi panti rhēmati theou*, "but by every word from God") was probably not part of the original writing but has been added because of harmonization. Both the external and internal evidence supports the shorter text.

Secondary Literature. This and the following examples provide an opportunity to demonstrate appropriate use of the secondary literature when establishing the text. Commentaries and other resources should not be consulted until you have worked through the text-critical issues on your own. After doing your own work, however, it can be encouraging to discover confirmation of your decision, or it can be enlightening to learn about factors that you did not think of. Text-critical studies of Luke 4:4 come to a largely unanimous conclusion. In his commentary on Luke, Joseph Fitzmyer concludes that the reading "comes from a scribal harmonization of the Lucan text with Matt 4:4."[151] Alfred Plummer also argues that if the additional text were genuine, its absence from the older manuscripts would be extraordinary.[152] I. Howard Marshall cites the man-

---

151. Joseph A. Fitzmyer, *The Gospel according to Luke I–IX: Introduction, Translation, and Notes*, AYBC (New York: Doubleday, 1970), 515.

152. Alfred Plummer, *A Critical and Exegetical Commentary on the Gospel according to St. Luke*, ICC (Edinburgh: T&T Clark, 1896), 110.

uscript evidence for omitting the phrase, calling it "decisive."[153] Finally, in his *Textual Commentary*, Metzger concludes that the shortest reading must be original because it has early support and its omission from these manuscripts cannot be explained.[154]

4.3.4.d Revelation 1:8

1. Identify the Variation Unit and Review the Witnesses

NA28 lists one significant variant in Revelation 1:8. The editors' text reads Ἐγώ εἰμι τὸ ἄλφα καὶ τὸ ὦ [T], λέγει κύριος ὁ θεός (*Egō eimi to alpha kai to ō, legei kyrios ho theos*, "I am the Alpha and Omega, says the Lord God"). The [T] siglum in the apparatus shows that some manuscripts include additional words—in this case, the phrase ἀρχὴ καὶ τέλος (*archē kai telos*, "the beginning and the end").

Table 4.10: Variants of Revelation 1:8	
SBLGNT and NA28	**Scrivener's Textus Receptus**
Ἐγώ εἰμι τὸ Ἄλφα καὶ τὸ Ὦ[155]	Ἐγώ εἰμι τὸ Α καὶ τὸ Ω, ἀρχὴ καὶ τέλος[156]
LEB	**KJV**
I am the Alpha and the Omega.	I am Alpha and Omega, the beginning and the ending.

The critical apparatus provides the following information about the extra phrase:

(+ η 2329) αρχη και (+ το 2329) τελος [2.*𝕭b] 1854. 2050. 2329. 2351 𝔐[A] lat bo

First, notice that no evidence is provided for *txt*. This means that the witnesses cited in the apparatus are the only manuscripts currently known to have the extra phrase. Codex 2329 is apparently the only witness to have

---

153. I. Howard Marshall, *The Gospel of Luke: A Commentary on the Greek Text*, NIGTC (Exeter, UK: Paternoster, 1978), 171.

154. Metzger, *Textual Commentary*, 113.

155. *Egō eimi to A kai to Ō.*

156. *Egō eimi to A kai to Ō, archē kai telos.*

the articles in front of the nouns, but it otherwise supports the presence of this reading. Sinaiticus' first hand, as well as that of the second corrector plus a number of minuscules, includes the phrase.

The 𝔐 has a somewhat different meaning in the Revelation than it does in the rest of the NT. There are two separate textual traditions for the Majority Text. 𝔐ᴬ "represents the large number of manuscripts with the commentary on Revelation by Andreas of Caesarea."[157] In addition, the Vulgate and part of the Old Latin, as well as the Bohairic, have this reading.

2. Analyze the Evidence

External Evidence. The apparatus indicates that Sinaiticus and the Andreas type of Byzantine text support the reading ἀρχὴ καὶ τέλος (archē kai telos).

Internal Evidence. One might investigate intrinsic probability and notice that when the author of the Revelation uses the phrase ἐγώ εἰμι τὸ ἄλφα καὶ τὸ ὦ (egō eimi to alpha kai to ō), it is followed by ἡ ἀρχὴ καὶ τὸ τέλος (hē archē kai to telos) in 21:6, while in 22:13 the reading occurs again, at the end of a longer phrase: ἐγὼ τὸ ἄλφα καὶ τὸ ὦ, ὁ πρῶτος καὶ ὁ ἔσχατος, ἡ ἀρχὴ καὶ τὸ τέλος (egō to alpha kai to ō, ho prōtos kai ho eschatos, hē archē kai to telos, "I am the Alpha and the Omega, the first and the last, the beginning and the end"). This could indicate that ἀρχὴ καὶ τέλος (archē kai telos) fits the author's normal practice.

However, transcriptional probability is more likely to guide us in the right direction. The phrase ἀρχὴ καὶ τέλος (archē kai telos) could have been added to Revelation 1:8 in an attempt to harmonize it with the later verses. It could possibly also be understood as an explanation of "the alpha and omega," so the guidelines of lectio difficilior and lectio brevior both apply here.

3. Draw Conclusions

While there is significant manuscript evidence for ἀρχὴ καὶ τέλος (archē kai telos) in Revelation 1:8, it is most likely a later addition. We can explain its presence as harmonization to the phrase's appearance later in Revelation.

Secondary Literature. Now, if we turn to the commentaries, we will discover that they support our decision to understand ἀρχὴ καὶ τέλος (archē kai telos) as a later addition. In his commentary on Revelation 1–5, David

---

157. NA28, 66*.

Aune calls the phrase a scribal insertion, arguing that it was "influenced by the use of the phrase in similar contexts in 21:6; 22:13."[158] G. K. Beale also notes that the repetition of "the Alpha and the Omega, the Beginning and the End" in Revelation 21:6 and 22:13 likely influenced the scribe to insert the complete title in 1:8.[159] Metzger supports this opinion, adding that there is no good explanation for the shorter text if the longer text were original.[160]

4.3.4.e Romans 5:2

1. Identify the Variation Unit and Review the Witnesses

The text-critical issue in Romans 5:2 is whether to include the phrase τῇ πίστει (tē pistei, "by faith"). NA28 includes the reading in the text, but surrounds it with brackets, indicating that its inclusion is disputed.[161] The sigla ⌐ ⌐ outside the brackets point out that there is also a second question of wording: If the inclusion is correct, should it be τῇ πίστει (tē pistei) or ἐν τῇ πίστει (en tē pistei)?[162]

Table 4.11: Variants of Romans 5:2	
SBLGNT and NA28	**Codex Vaticanus (B)**
δι' οὗ καὶ τὴν προσαγωγὴν ἐσχήκαμεν τῇ πίστει εἰς τὴν χάριν ταύτην ἐν ᾗ ἑστήκαμεν[163]	δι' οὗ καὶ τὴν προσαγωγὴν ἐσχήκαμεν εἰς τὴν χάριν ταύτην ἐν ᾗ ἑστήκαμεν[164]
LEB	**NRSV**
through whom also we have obtained access by faith into this grace in which we stand	through whom we have obtained access to this grace in which we stand

---

158. David E. Aune, *Revelation 1–5*, WBC (Dallas: Word, 1997), 51.

159. G. K. Beale, *The Book of Revelation: A Commentary on the Greek Text*, NIGTC (Grand Rapids: Eerdmans, 1999), 200.

160. Metzger, *Textual Commentary*, 663.

161. Similarly, the grading system of the UBS5 calls this variation unit a "C," meaning a relatively high degree of uncertainty.

162. The meaning is not changed between these two choices. The phrase τῇ πίστει (tē pistei) is in the dative case, which would be translated in English with a preposition such as "in," "by," or "with." The variant ἐν τῇ πίστει (en tē pistei) provides an explicit preposition, but the preposition ἐν (en) allows the same range of meanings.

163. di' hou kai tēn prosagōgēn eschēkamen [tē pistei] eis tēn charin tautēn en hē hestēkamen.

164. di' hou kai tēn prosagōgēn eschēkamen eis tēn charin tautēn en hē hestēkamen.

For this variation unit in Romans 5:2, the NA critical apparatus reads:

εν τη πιστει ℵ¹ A vg^{mss} ¦ — B D F G 0220 sa; Ambst ¦ *txt* ℵ^{*.c} C K L P 33. 81. 104. 630. 1175. 1241. 1505. 1241. 1505. 1506. 1739. 1881. 2464 𝔐 lat

The first part of the entry indicates the reading ἐν τῇ πίστει (*en tē pistei*) (with the preposition) is found only in Alexandrinus, the first corrector of Sinaiticus, and some Vulgate manuscripts. Considered alone, this variant is unlikely, but it provides additional support for the third variant. The second section of the entry indicates the evidence for the omission of the entire phrase. Very few witnesses omit the phrase, but those that do include Vaticanus, Codex 0220—a third-century parchment leaf of Romans that is almost identical to Vaticanus—and three strong Western witnesses, as well as the Sahidic version and the church father Ambrosiaster.

In addition to the witnesses listed above for the first variant, the presence of τῇ πίστει (*tē pistei*) is supported by the first hand of Sinaiticus and a later corrector of Sinaiticus, the text of Ephraemi Rescriptus, and other manuscripts including minuscule 1739. It is also supported by the Majority Text, the Vulgate, and some of the Old Latin. The combination of the witnesses for the first and third variants means that this reading is found in part of the Alexandrian and most of the Western and Byzantine textual streams.

2. Analyze the Evidence

External Evidence. The first and third variants combined provide a hefty support for the inclusion of *tē pistei*, probably without the preposition *en*.[165] On the other hand, those that omit the phrase are from two textual streams and include several old and high-quality witnesses.

Internal Evidence. If we look first at intrinsic probability, we would be asking about the likelihood that Paul would have written the phrase τῇ πίστει (*tē pistei*). This is, of course, common terminology for Paul. In the preceding chapters of Romans, Paul has argued for justification by faith in Romans 3:28 (πίστει, *pistei*, "by faith"), and uses the exact phrase τῇ πίστει (*tē pistei*, "by faith") twice in Romans 4 (Rom 4:19, 20) and twice later in the book (Rom 11:10; 14:1). In Romans 5:1, a similar phrase, ἐκ πίστεως (*ek pisteōs*,

---

165. If the inclusion of "by faith" is thought to be the *Ausgangstext*, it would be likely that ἐν (*en*) was added by some scribes to smooth out the syntax. The ending of the previous word ἐσχήκαμεν (*eschēkamen*) could be seen as evidence either for or against omission. However, the addition of ἐν would be much more likely than that it was omitted by so many.

literally "out of/from faith"), is usually translated the same as τῇ πίστει (*tē pistei*, "by faith"). Because Paul has been emphasizing justification *by faith*, the inclusion of the term here would fit within his theological framework. Thus, it is reasonable to argue that the phrase fits Paul's usage and the immediate literary context.

Transcriptional probability, on the other hand, would point to the principle of *lectio brevior*, stating that a scribe is more likely to add τῇ πίστει (*tē pistei*) than to omit it. It is also possible that a scribe would add the phrase out of familiarity with Paul's usage. Finally, the meaning of Romans 5:2 is not drastically altered by the presence or absence of τῇ πίστει (*tē pistei*).

Secondary Literature. As one might expect, the secondary literature is divided on this variation unit. Leon Morris argues that since the manuscript evidence against including the phrase is strong, it should probably be considered a scribal insertion.[166] By contrast, Robert Jewett notes that ancient manuscripts strongly support the phrase and argues that it was probably deleted for stylistic reasons.[167] Joseph Fitzmyer says manuscript evidence does not solidly attest to the presence of τῇ πίστει (*tē pistei*) in this verse, but he believes it should be retained since it occurs so frequently in the previous chapters.[168]

3. Draw Conclusions

Ultimately, we cannot be certain whether τῇ πίστει (*tē pistei*) is the *Ausgangstext* or a later scribal addition. The external evidence for the inclusion or exclusion of τῇ πίστι (*tē pistei*) is divided, and the internal evidence makes either option equally likely. A scribe could have omitted the phrase, thinking it was redundant, or a scribe could have inserted it to maintain Paul's emphasis.

---

166. Leon Morris, *The Epistle to the Romans*, PNTC (Grand Rapids: Eerdmans, 1988), 219.

167. Robert Jewett, *Romans: A Commentary*, Hermeneia (Minneapolis: Fortress, 2006), 344, note b.

168. Joseph A. Fitzmyer, *Romans: A New Translation with Introduction and Commentary*, AYBC (New York: Doubleday, 1993), 396.

4.4 RESOURCES FOR FURTHER STUDY

Several of the resources referenced throughout chapter 4 are listed below. This section also describes some of the more important resources you should be familiar with for further study in NT textual criticism.

Aland, Kurt, and Barbara Aland. *The Text of the New Testament: An Introduction to the Critical Editions and to the Theory and Practice of Modern Textual Criticism.* 2nd ed. Grand Rapids: Eerdmans, 1995.

This volume is the NT counterpart for Würthwein's *The Text of the Old Testament.* Written by two preeminent NT scholars associated with the Nestle-Aland critical edition, it is a thorough introduction to NT textual criticism.

Black, David Alan. *New Testament Textual Criticism: A Concise Guide.* Grand Rapids: Baker, 1994.

Black's guide is "a simple and direct introduction" that "packages up ... and delivers" countless workshops he has presented to pastors and lay people on the topic of textual criticism. He overviews what errors occur and how, details the history of NT textual criticism, and illustrates the text-critical process on several NT texts.

Comfort, Philip. *Encountering the Manuscripts: An Introduction to New Testament Paleography & Textual Criticism.* Nashville: Broadman & Holman, 2005.

Comfort's introduction combines the study of textual criticism with paleography, the dating and study of ancient writings and inscriptions. He details the role of scribes and various methods of recovering the original Greek NT. He also includes an annotated list of significant Greek manuscripts.

Epp, Eldon Jay, and Gordon D. Fee. *Studies in the Theory and Method of New Testament Textual Criticism.* Grand Rapids: Eerdmans, 1993.

This collection of seventeen essays written by two leading NT scholars contains both introductory articles and more specialized analyses. Epp and Fee critique theories and methods, consider the Greek papyri in light of the text-critical method, and offer guidelines for text-critical use of the church fathers' writings.

Finegan, Jack. *Encountering New Testament Manuscripts: A Working Introduction to Textual Criticism.* Grand Rapids: Eerdmans, 1980.

Finegan's noteworthy contribution to the array of books on NT textual criticism is his inclusion of twenty-four near-actual-size photographs of some important manuscripts among the earliest NT witnesses. He leads readers through transcription of the texts and consideration of the comparative evidence.

Greenlee, J. Harold. *The Text of the New Testament: From Manuscript to Modern Edition.* Grand Rapids: Baker, 2008.

Greenlee's book provides a brief introduction to the development of the NT. Written for a nonscholarly audience, the work covers several matters from the physical appearance of ancient manuscripts to traditional methods of NT textual criticism to modern Bible translations.

Metzger, Bruce M. *A Textual Commentary on the Greek New Testament.* 2nd ed. New York: United Bible Societies, 1994.

Metzger explains the text-critical decisions made by the translation committee of the UBS4. It is an invaluable guide to understanding the selection of variants as detailed in the critical apparatus.

Metzger, Bruce M., and Bart D. Ehrman. *The Text of the New Testament: Its Transmission, Corruption, and Restoration.* 4th ed. New York: Oxford University Press, 2005.

A standard among introductory materials in the field of NT textual criticism since 1964, *The Text of the New Testament* provides a comprehensive survey of ancient manuscripts and a substantial section on the art of producing books. It also details the theory and practice of textual criticism. The fourth edition is Ehrman's revision of Metzger's classic work.

Parker, David C. *An Introduction to the New Testament Manuscripts and Their Texts.* Cambridge: Cambridge University Press, 2008.

Written by one of today's leading NT text critics, Parker's book introduces readers to the methodology and history of the discipline. He examines a wide range of matters including the various NT manuscripts and witnesses, the skills necessary for the discipline, the different critical editions, and current scholarly research on each of the major sections of the NT.

Royse, James R. *Scribal Habits in Early Greek New Testament Papyri*. New Testament Tools, Studies, and Documents 36. Leiden: Brill, 2007.

A published version of his 1981 doctoral dissertation, Royse's work has become a landmark study on the writing habits of scribes. The book examines six early papyri—P45, P46, P47, P66, P72, and P75—to explore the significance of scribal practices among early Christian manuscripts.

Vincent, Marvin R. *A History of the Textual Criticism of the New Testament*. New York and London: Macmillan, 1899.

A classic work on NT textual criticism, Vincent's book traces the development of the discipline from the writing of the original manuscripts through the scholarship of the nineteenth century. It also includes extensive explanations of terms and definitions, making it a valuable resource for students and pastors.

5
—
TEXTUAL CRITICISM AND THE BIBLE TODAY

We began chapter 1 by quoting a committed Christian who was disturbed by the differences between the KJV and the NIV at Romans 8:1. She assumed her preferred version was the correct one and seemed to disparage the other—as if the NIV translators had intentionally omitted something they should not have.

By now you should recognize that a better way to deal with discrepancies between English translations is to ask why a particular difference exists; is it a translation decision or a text-critical issue? If the latter, you now know how to proceed: determine the variation unit, evaluate the merits of each variant, and then make a reasoned decision about which variant is more likely to represent the oldest form of the text. In the case of Romans 8:1, marginal notes in your English Bible should indicate that some manuscripts have a longer or shorter reading, depending on what they have decided to record in the text.[1] The footnotes in your English version inform you of every variation unit that affects the translation and provide enough information to prompt a text-critical investigation.

Although textual criticism is primarily the task of translators and specialists, anyone who reads and studies the Bible will benefit from a foundational understanding of the field's issues and practices. As a Bible reader, and especially if you teach and preach the Bible, you should be aware of text-critical issues and be able to understand the basic meaning of them.

---

1. For example, the ESV and HCSB note that some manuscripts **add** "*who walk not after the flesh, but after the spirit,*" while the NKJV notes that some manuscripts **omit** this text.

We hope this book has helped you understand why textual differences exist and how to evaluate them.

5.1 TEXTUAL CRITICISM AND ENGLISH TRANSLATIONS

Translators of the Bible face the complex task of faithfully reflecting the language and meaning of the ancient Hebrew or Greek text in intelligible English. Most of their decisions result from translation philosophy and, to a lesser extent, interpretative theory. However, translators also make decisions at points where their source texts, the ancient manuscripts, disagree. These are text-critical decisions.

Translation committees first decide which Hebrew and Greek texts to use as the base text for their translation. The majority of English Bibles are based on the latest edition of the *Biblia Hebraica* (currently *BHS*) for the OT and the text of the NA or UBS editions for the NT. But translation committees do not then automatically use the text decided on by the editorial committee of the critical edition they use as their base text. The translators must give attention to the variant readings provided in the apparatus, choose which variant to translate into their main text, and decide whether to include alternative readings in a footnote. The text-critical methodology used by the translation committee is generally included in a Bible's preface. Below is a summary of the text-critical approaches of several popular English translations, as described in their prefaces.

King James Version (KJV). The 1611 KJV used the Second Rabbinic Bible as a base text for the OT and incorporated some variants from the Septuagint and Vulgate. Their NT base text appears to have been one or more of the relatively similar Greek editions that were in turn based on the manuscript evidence available at the time. These editions tend to be grouped under the category of Textus Receptus.

New King James Version (NKJV). For its OT base text, the NKJV uses *Biblia Hebraica Stuttgartensia (BHS)*, though the committee says they also consulted the Second Rabbinic Bible, the Septuagint, Vulgate, and Dead Sea Scrolls. In the NT, the Textus Receptus remained the base text, although the committee acknowledges that better manuscripts are available. The committee chose to retain the Textus Receptus as the base text because of the historical value of the KJV, of which the NKJV is the fifth major revision.

New American Standard Bible (NASB). The translators of the 1960 NASB used *Biblia Hebraica Stuttgartensia* as their OT base text, along with what they call "the most recent light from lexicography, cognate languages, and the Dead Sea Scrolls."[2] However, the preface does not indicate to what extent they actually incorporate variants from these sources. The twenty-third edition of NA was the base text for the NT. In 1995 the NASB was reissued to allow for an updating of the language. Limited revisions were made to the OT text, and the NA26 was closely followed as the new Greek base text.

New International Version (NIV). The NIV 2011 uses *Biblia Hebraica Stuttgartensia* as a base text, but its translators also "occasionally followed" variant readings from ancient witnesses "where the Masoretic Text seemed doubtful and where accepted principles of textual criticism" favor a particular variant as the correct reading. As in the NASB, the extent to which the NIV translators actually incorporated variants from these other sources is unclear. For the NT, the translators use the latest editions of the NA and UBS GNTs, making their choices from the variants listed "in accordance with widely accepted principles of New Testament textual criticism."[3]

English Standard Version (ESV). The translators of the ESV used *Biblia Hebraica Stuttgartensia* as their base text for the OT, and they adhere to the Masoretic Text unless they consider a reading unusually difficult—meaning they can't make sense of the Masoretic Text. In such cases, they consult one of the ancient witnesses. Their philosophy in the NT is similar with respect to their base text: NA27 or UBS4.[4]

---

2. Editorial Board of the Lockman Foundation, "Preface to the New American Standard Bible," *New American Standard Bible* (La Habra, CA: The Lockman Foundation, 1977).

3. The quotes in this paragraph come from the preface to the NIV translation (The Committee on Bible Translation, "Preface," *New International Version* [Grand Rapids: Zondervan, 2011]. The comments on the textual basis of the translation are also available online: https://www.thenivbible.com/textual-basis/).

4. The Translation Oversight Committee, "Preface to the English Standard Version," *English Standard Version* (Wheaton, IL.: Good News Publishers, 2001).

New Revised Standard Version (NRSV). The NRSV used *Biblia Hebraica Stuttgartensia* in its translation of the OT. However, when the translators judged that scribal errors had been made in the manuscripts that became the Masoretic Text, they drew on witnesses that predate the work of the Masoretes, including the Septuagint, Targums, Peshitta, Vulgate, and Dead Sea Scrolls. When none of the sources provided a "satisfactory restoration"[5] of a problematic text, the scholars reconstructed it. For the NT, the committee followed UBS3, varying from it only in rare instances.

New English Translation (NET). Beginning with a beta version of the NT released in 1998, the NET Bible was created with the intention of providing a trustworthy text in print that was also available free on the Internet. The value of the translation for text criticism comes from the inclusion of over sixty thousand translators' notes, explaining grammatical, syntactical, and text-critical choices made in translation. The textual basis for the Old and New Testament texts was the best currently available Hebrew, Aramaic, and Greek texts (not specifically named).

This overview illustrates the spectrum of text-critical approaches that lie behind English translations. You should look at your English Bible's introductory material for information about the theory and style of translation, the base texts, and the committee's level of comfort with deciding to follow a variant reading rather than their base texts.

5.2 TEXTUAL CRITICISM AND THE AUTHORITY OF SCRIPTURE

Many people are uncomfortable with the idea that discrepancies exist in the biblical text. Why wouldn't God have preserved his Word with greater care? How can we really know what God has said when there are variations in the wording? These are important questions for people who believe the Bible to be God's inspired, authoritative Word. To answer them, we must consider what Christians believe and have believed about the nature of the Bible—our doctrine of Scripture.

---

5. Bruce Metzger, "To the Reader," *New Revised Standard Version* (New York: National Council of the Churches of Christ in the U.S.A., 1989).

Evangelical Christians generally consider the Bible to be "the completely true and trustworthy, final and authoritative, source for theology."[6] Many Christians also use the word "inerrant" (literally "without error") to describe the Bible. However, this term can hold different meanings. For some, inerrancy means there are no errors of any kind in our Bible—God has preserved it as perfectly as he inspired it. For others, inerrancy extends only to the autographs of the Bible, while the manuscripts (and our English translations) that descended from them are understood to contain variation in readings, from scribal mistakes to theological emendations. People also associate the word "infallible" with the Bible—another word that holds varying meanings. Some equate it with "inerrant," while others consider infallibility a broader category that refers to the overall trustworthiness of Scripture's teaching.[7]

The doctrine of Scripture has developed over time, as have all theological doctrines. Early on, the church fathers recognized variants among their biblical manuscripts. However, they did not seem to view these variants as damaging to Scripture's authority. Differences in texts became more problematic after the advent of the printing press. For the first time, Christians were able to have a fixed text—but *which* text should be fixed? Later, as European scholars in the eighteenth century sifted through a plethora of newly discovered biblical manuscripts, they began to understand how the biblical text had developed over time.

By the nineteenth century, scholars had begun to engage in textual criticism with the goal of determining the "original text." At the same time, some biblical scholars questioned the veracity and historicity of the Bible. This convergence of questions and scholarly investigation led many critical scholars to dismiss the Bible as a flawed, ancient document with no value for modern faith and practice. In response, Christians rose to defend

---

6. Stanley J. Grenz, "Nurturing the Soul, Informing the Mind: The Genesis of the Evangelical Scripture Principle," in *Evangelicals & Scripture: Tradition, Authority and Hermeneutics*, ed. Vincent Bacote, Laura C. Miguélez, and Dennis L. Okholm (Downers Grove, IL: InterVarsity, 2004), 22.

7. Kevin Vanhoozer distinguishes between inerrancy, a subcategory of infallibility that pertains to propositional statements, and infallibility, which applies to the "full variety of Scripture's utterances" (see Vanhoozer, "Semantics of Biblical Literature," in *Hermeneutics, Authority, and Canon*, ed. D. A. Carson and John D. Woodbridge [Grand Rapids: Zondervan, 1986], 49–104).

the Bible. In the process, though, some conservative Christians came to view the discipline of textual criticism as "another scholarly weapon in the many-sided attack against Scripture."[8] The most extreme position—beginning with the widely held evangelical belief that the autographs of the biblical text were inspired and inerrant—argued that "God must have faithfully preserved these autographs throughout the history of the church and that the original text [can] be found in the TR [Textus Receptus]."[9] Proponents of this view today are typically "King James only" Christians and consider textual criticism a "theologically suspect and completely unnecessary" endeavor.[10]

Most Christian scholars believe that while God did inspire the content of Scripture, he also chose to entrust human authors with its composition and copyists with its transmission. Even though God superintended the preservation of Scripture, he was pleased to reveal his word through human imperfection. When we consider that the Bible was transmitted by hand and in harsh climates for thousands of years, we can only marvel that, even though there is variation in the text, most of these variants are insignificant copying errors, and nearly all variants involve no significant doctrinal issues.[11]

Ultimately, we can have confidence that the Bible we use reflects an extraordinary degree of accuracy and integrity. The variants in biblical manuscripts are not challenges to the authority of God's word. Rather, they reflect God's use of human instruments in the divine process of authoring and preserving his sacred text. Through the efforts of textual critics, God continues to employ human agents in preserving his Word.

---

8. John J. Brogan, "Can I Have Your Autograph? Uses and Abuses of Textual Criticism in Formulating an Evangelical Doctrine of Scripture," in *Evangelicals & Scripture*, ed. Bacote, Miguélez, and Okholm, 96.

9. Brogan, "Can I Have Your Autograph?" 97.

10. Brogan, "Can I Have Your Autograph?," 98. KJV-only proponents are normally supporters of the Majority Text, and they make the same arguments in defense of that text. This is different from the conservative scholars who provide text-critical reasoning for their support of the Majority Text.

11. You can check this for yourself by looking at the footnotes of your English Bible, which should indicate variation units that have significance for translation.

5.3 RESOURCES FOR FURTHER STUDY

Alexander, Archibald. *Evidences of the Authenticity, Inspiration and Canonical Authority of the Holy Scriptures*. Philadelphia: Presbyterian Board of Publication and Sabbath-School Work, 1836.

In this book nineteenth-century theologian Archibald Alexander defends Scripture's reliability and credibility. Topics of discussion include inspiration, the nature of Scripture, the veracity of miracles, the fulfillment of prophecy, and the canon of Scripture.

Bacote, Vincent, Laura C. Miguélez, and Dennis L. Okholm, eds. *Evangelicals & Scripture: Tradition, Authority and Hermeneutics*. Downers Grove, IL: InterVarsity, 2004.

The twelve articles in this edited volume explore the evangelical doctrine of Scripture and wrestle with the inherent difficulties of a divine-human book. The essays originated at the 2001 Wheaton Theology Conference and consider the evangelical tradition of Scripture, evangelical exegesis, and evangelicals in the postmodern context.

Beale, G. K. *The Erosion of Inerrancy in Evangelicalism: Responding to New Challenges to Biblical Authority*. Wheaton, IL: Crossway, 2008.

Beale writes in response to Peter Enns' book *Inspiration and Incarnation*. He contends that Enns' presuppositions and conclusions are opposed to the authority and inspiration of Scripture, and he addresses several contradictions in the Bible in light of his own view of inspiration and inerrancy.

Carson, D. A. *Collected Writings on Scripture*. Compiled by Andrew David Naselli. Wheaton, IL: Crossway, 2010.

This collection includes five essays by Carson related to the doctrine of Scripture and nine book reviews he wrote on books about the inspiration and authority of the Bible.

Carson, D. A., and John D. Woodbridge, eds. *Scripture and Truth.* Grand Rapids: Baker, 1992.

> This collection of twelve apologetic essays first appeared in 1983 and divides into three sections: (1) addressing concerns about the Bible itself; (2) considering contemporary interpretations of historical positions on Scripture; and (3) examining theological issues related to the reliability of the Bible.

Enns, Peter. *Inspiration and Incarnation: Evangelicals and the Problem of the Old Testament.* Grand Rapids: Baker, 2005.

> Enns considers three issues that challenge traditional views of Scripture and specifically the OT: (1) its similarity to other literature of the ancient Near East; (2) the diversity of its theological views; and (3) the NT use of the OT. Enns takes the divine-human nature of the text seriously and proposes an "incarnational model" to explain Scripture's authority.

Feinberg, P. D. "Bible, Inerrancy and Infallibility of." Pages 156–59 in *Evangelical Dictionary of Theology.* Edited by Walter A. Elwell. 2nd ed. Grand Rapids: Baker, 2001.

> Feinberg provides a helpful overview of the inerrancy issue. He defines the term and outlines the arguments for the position as well as the objections against it.

Marshall, I. Howard. *Biblical Inspiration.* Milton Keynes, UK: Paternoster, 1982.

> Marshall aims "to try to produce a positive statement of the nature of the Bible in light of the difficulties that readers face today."[12] He begins by surveying theories on the nature of inspiration. Then he considers the Bible's trustworthiness, the inerrancy debate, and the authority, meaning, and significance of Scripture for today.

---

12. I. Howard Marshall, *Biblical Inspiration* (Milton Keynes, UK: Paternoster, 1982), 12.

Nichols, Stephen J., and Eric T. Brandt. *Ancient Word, Changing Worlds: The Doctrine of Scripture in a Modern Age.* Wheaton, IL: Crossway, 2009.

> Nichols and Brandt discuss the historical development of the doctrines of inspiration and inerrancy. They also include collections of excerpts from nineteenth- and twentieth-century writings on both issues and appendices with historical doctrinal statements, key biblical texts, and a guide for further reading.

Ryrie, Charles C. *What You Should Know about Inerrancy.* Chicago: Moody Press, 1981.

> Ryrie's defense of inerrancy is a classic resource in the debate. He traces the development of ideas over the authority of Scripture and discusses inerrancy with respect to God's character, Christ's incarnation, human authorship, and contradictions in the text.

Sproul, R. C. *Can I Trust the Bible?* Lake Mary, FL: Reformation Trust, 2009.

> This brief book is a commentary on "The Chicago Statement of Biblical Inerrancy," which was drafted in 1978 by the members of the International Council for Biblical Inerrancy. It includes the full statement and chapters on the Bible's authority, revelation, inspiration, inerrancy, and truth.

Wright, N. T. *Scripture and the Authority of God.* London: SPCK, 2005.

> Wright considers what it means for Scripture to be "authoritative." He briefly reviews the Bible's place historically and within contemporary culture before proposing what it means for the "authority of Scripture" to be shorthand for "the authority of the triune God, exercised somehow *through* scripture."[13]

---

13. N. T. Wright, *Scripture and the Authority of God* (London: Society for Promoting Christian Knowledge, 2005), 17.

GLOSSARY

accentuation A system of symbols developed by the Masoretic scribes to mark clauses and stressed syllables in the Masoretic Text.

Aleppo Codex A Masoretic manuscript in the Ben Asher tradition dating to the mid-tenth century AD; most of the Pentateuch was reportedly destroyed in a 1947 fire in Aleppo, Syria; the base text for the Hebrew University Bible Project.

Alexandrian text-type Or Alexandrian textual tradition. One of several textual streams or groupings among NT manuscripts; regarded highly by many scholars as being likely to contain the oldest form of the text.

Aquila A second-century AD Jewish convert who produced a Greek translation of the OT.

Aramaic A Semitic language that is closely related to Hebrew; spoken widely in the ancient Near East from the seventh century BC to the seventh century AD; the language of the Targums (Targumim), part of the OT, and most of the Talmud.

archetype The common ancestor of a group of closely related manuscripts. Establishing the text of an archetype is one possible goal of textual criticism.

Ausgangstext German for "beginning text" or "start text"; sometimes translated as "initial text." This term is used in NT textual criticism to reflect the process of examining all variant readings for a variation unit, and discerning which reading is the starting point for all of them.

autograph The original manuscript or document of a writing. The Greek word *autographos* literally means "written in one's own hand." No autographs of biblical books have survived.

base text The single text or manuscript from which a translation (or a diplomatic critical edition) is made.

ben Asher tradition A system of vocalizing and accenting the OT text practiced by the ben Asher family of Tiberian Masoretes. The Aleppo Codex is in the ben Asher tradition; the Leningrad Codex was corrected toward the ben Asher tradition.

ben Naphtali tradition A system of vocalizing and accenting the OT text practiced by the ben Naphtali family of Tiberian Masoretes.

***Biblia Hebraica* (BHK)** Diplomatic critical editions of the Masoretic Text edited by Rudolf Kittel; the first and second editions, published between 1906 and 1913, were based on the Second Rabbinic Bible. Beginning with the third revision (1929–1937), the text was based on the Leningrad Codex.

***Biblia Hebraica Quinta* (BHQ)** The fifth revision of the *Biblia Hebraica* critical text, producing a diplomatic edition of the Masoretic Text based on the Leningrad Codex. This ongoing project is edited by Adrian Schenker. The first fascicle appeared in 2004, and six others have been published between 2006 and 2015.

***Biblia Hebraica Stuttgartensia* (BHS)** The fourth revision of the *Biblia Hebraica* critical text, producing a diplomatic edition of the Masoretic Text based on the Leningrad Codex. The edition was edited by Karl Elliger and Wilhelm Rudolph between 1967 and 1977. The current published version of *BHS* is the fifth, corrected edition, edited by Adrian Schenker, and published in 1997.

Byzantine text-type Or Byzantine textual tradtion. One of several textual streams or groupings among NT manuscripts; includes the majority of extant manuscripts, most of which were produced during the prolific period of copying between the ninth and fifteenth centuries. The Byzantine text provided the basis for the Textus Receptus, the Greek edition behind the KJV.

Caesarean text-type Or Caesarean textual tradition. The existence of this textual grouping is disputed, but the label refers to a collection of manuscripts that have unusual readings in common, though not consistently.

Cairo Codex of the Prophets A Masoretic manuscript of the Former and Latter Prophets in the Ben Asher tradition, dating to AD 895.

Cairo Genizah A medieval collection of thousands of worn-out or flawed sacred manuscripts found in a storage room of an old synagogue in Cairo, Egypt.

canonical criticism A method of biblical interpretation that focuses on the final canonical form of a biblical book and considers the text in terms of its reception and function within communities that accept it as authoritative Scripture.

codex Bound sheets, much like a modern book, which became prominent in the fourth century AD.

Codex Alexandrinus An important fifth-century majuscule manuscript that contains most of the Bible.

Codex Ambrosianus A sixth/seventh-century manuscript of the Peshitta that is the base text for the Leiden Peshitta.

Codex Bezae A fifth-century majuscule manuscript of the NT containing the Gospels and Acts; the leading representative of the Western textual tradition.

Codex Sinaiticus An important fourth-century majuscule manuscript that contains most of the OT and all of the NT; a good representative of the Alexandrian textual tradition.

Codex Vaticanus An important fourth-century majuscule manuscript that contains most of the Bible; a good representative of the Alexandrian textual tradition.

colophon A statement written at the end of a manuscript that relates details of the manuscript's production such as the name of the scribe or the date the manuscript was completed.

Complutensian Polyglot The first printed polyglot of the Bible (1514–1517), containing Hebrew, Latin, Greek, and Aramaic. See also **polyglot**.

conflation The combining of two elements to create one new product; used in textual criticism to describe when a copyist took two differing readings and combined them into one new text.

Coptic The language of Egyptian Christians from the first century through the Middle Ages.

critical apparatus The data that accompanies a critical edition of the Bible (usually in footnotes) and identifies the sources of variant readings; also called a textual apparatus.

critical edition A printed biblical text created by textual critics that either primarily represents the text of a single manuscript (a diplomatic edition) or presents the best hypothetical original text of the Bible (an eclectic version); created by evaluating and selecting superior textual variants according to the standards of textual criticism; includes a critical apparatus detailing the variants and editorial choices.

Dead Sea Scrolls A large collection of ancient Jewish manuscripts found in caves on the northwest end of the Dead Sea at various times between 1946 and 1956. These texts in Hebrew, Aramaic, and Greek date from 250 BC to AD 70. They represent the oldest existing copies of the OT (including almost all OT books) and include religious texts outlining the practices of a Jewish sect.

deuterocanonical Means "part of the second canon" and refers to books that were in the Greek OT that were not part of the Hebrew Bible; also called the "apocryphal books."

Diaspora Literally means "dispersion." A term used to refer to Jewish communities outside the land of Israel, especially in Babylon, Egypt, Persia, and Asia Minor (1 Pet 1:1).

diplomatic edition A critical edition of a text that primarily reproduces a single manuscript; the *BHS* is a diplomatic edition of the Leningrad Codex.

dittography A manuscript error that results from the unintentional duplication of a letter, syllable, or word. It is the opposite of haplography.

dynamic equivalence An approach to translation that values conveying the sense or meaning of the source text using words and expressions native to the target language over preserving foreign aspects of the source language's formal structure. Also called sense-for-sense or thought-for-thought translation. Often contrasted with **formal equivalence**.

eclectic edition A critical edition of a text that combines the most accurate readings of multiple manuscripts to create a hypothetical original manuscript. The Hebrew Bible: A Critical Edition project (formerly the Oxford Hebrew Bible) is an eclectic edition. The Nestle-Aland Greek New Testament is an eclectic edition.

editor Scribe of the biblical text during its literary development and early transmission who shaped the text prior to its final form.

Erasmus A sixteenth-century humanist who produced a Greek NT that became the basis for the **Textus Receptus**.

exemplar The source document that lay before a scribe as he or she produced another copy of that text.

external evidence Manuscript evidence in textual criticism that relates to the age, grouping, quantity, and distribution of the biblical manuscripts.

family A group of manuscripts that are so closely related that it is possible to create a family tree, called a **stemma**, showing how they all descend from a common textual ancestor.

form criticism A method of biblical study that focuses on classifying the literary units or "forms" that make up a larger text and connecting those pieces with an original social or historical setting called the "setting in life" or *Sitz im Leben*.

formal equivalence An approach to translation that values preserving aspects of the linguistic form of the source text as much as possible. A formal translation may use phrasing that is wooden or awkward in the target language because it is closely following the linguistic structure of the source text, not adapting it to the natural phrasing of the target language. Also called word-for-word or literal translation. Often contrasted with **dynamic equivalence**.

genizah A room where worn-out or flawed sacred manuscripts were stored until they could be properly disposed of; see also **Cairo Genizah**.

gloss A short explanation, usually written in the margins or between the lines of biblical text.

Göttingen Septuagint A critical eclectic edition of the Septuagint with multiple volumes.

Griesbach, Johann Jakob The NT scholar (1745–1812) who first classified NT manuscripts according to the three text-types (Alexandrian, Western, and Byzantine) and established guidelines for textual criticism that are still used today.

haplography A manuscript error that results from the unintentional omission of a letter, syllable, or word. A letter, word, or phrase is written only once when it should be written more than once. It is the opposite of dittography.

harmonization In textual criticism, a change to the biblical text where one passage is made to align more closely with another related passage.

Hebrew University Bible Project (HUBP) A critical, diplomatic edition of the OT based on the Aleppo Codex.

Hexapla Origen's six-column document that included the Hebrew text, Origen's Greek transliteration of the Hebrew, Greek translations of Aquila, Symmachus, Theodotion, and an annotated column that compared the Hebrew with the Greek (the fifth column); dates to the third century; survives only in other documents and fragments.

historical criticism An approach to biblical interpretation that emphasizes the historical context of the world depicted in the biblical text. Historical criticism looks at the broader historical and cultural context of the ancient Near East and Mediteranean world to understand biblical events and ancient customs.

homophony Two words that sound alike but are spelled differently; in textual criticism it can refer to the possible reason for a scribal error.

internal evidence Manuscript evidence in textual criticism that relates to the habits of scribes and the stylistic and theological bent of the author. See also **intrinsic probability** and **transcriptional probability**.

intrinsic probability The textual critic's assessment of a variant's likelihood based on the author's style, language, or theological argument; a component of internal evidence.

Irenaeus A second-century church father and apologist.

itacism A type of pronunciation shift, especially in Greek, where the pronunciation of certain vowels and diphthongs converged. Scribal errors may result from itacism because of the confusion of similar sounds.

Jerome A Christian biblical scholar of the fourth and fifth centuries AD (331–420); translator of the Latin **Vulgate**.

Kaige recension An early Greek version of the OT in which the translator used the Greek phrase καί γε (*kai ge*) for all occurrences of the Hebrew גם (gam); also called the proto-Theodotion recension.

Karaites A Jewish sect known for its emphasis on the Hebrew Bible (and not oral tradition) as its only authority.

kethiv Literally, "what is written." A word in the consonantal text of the **Masoretic Text** that should be read with the vowels of a different word (*qere*) in the margin.

lectionaries Liturgical books with selected Scripture readings for a given day or occasion on the Christian or Jewish calendar.

Leiden Peshitta A critical edition of the Peshitta (the Syriac translation of the OT) prepared by the Peshitta Institute in Leiden (the Netherlands).

Leningrad Codex The oldest complete Masoretic manuscript, dating to AD 1009; the base text for *Biblia Hebraica Stuttgartensia*.

Letter of Aristeas A pseudepigraphal document that purports to give the history of the Septuagint translation—that in the third-century BC, seventy-two Jewish delegates translated the Pentateuch in seventy-two days with complete agreement.

London Polyglot The most extensive printed polyglot of the Bible (1654–1657).

Maimonides A preeminent medieval Jewish scholar and philosopher.

Majority Text The text of the majority of extant NT manuscripts, also called the Byzantine text; several manuscripts belonging to this grouping were the basis for Erasmus' Greek NT, the **Textus Receptus**, which is the Greek text behind the KJV.

majuscule A script that uses only capital letters; used in Greek (and Latin) manuscripts in antiquity well into the ninth century AD;

also refers to manuscripts written in this script. The script and
the manuscripts are sometimes called uncials.

Masorah A collection of textual notes made by the Masoretes to
regulate the copying of OT manuscripts.

Masoretes The group of Jewish scholars who preserved the Hebrew text
of the OT in the early Middle Ages.

Masoretic Text Refers to any Hebrew text of the OT preserved by the
Jewish scholars known as Masoretes in the early medieval period.
This standard Hebrew text of the OT is also referred to as MT and
is usually based on the copy from the Leningrad Codex, the oldest
complete Masoretic manuscript dating from AD 1009.

matres lectionis Latin phrase meaning "mothers of reading"; refers to
Hebrew consonants used to indicate vowels in the biblical text to
help readers.

metathesis A scribal error in which one letter or word is transposed
with an adjacent one.

minuscule A cursive script used in Greek manuscripts beginning in
the ninth century AD; also refers to manuscripts written in
this script.

Nestle-Aland A critical edition of the Greek NT, in several editions,
edited by E. Nestle and K. Aland; the base text for most modern
English translations; the Greek text matches that of the UBS, but
the apparatuses of the two editions differ.

nomen sacrum Latin for "sacred name"; pl. *nomina sacra*; designates the
abbreviated forms found in some New Testament manuscripts
as shorthand for about fourteen names or words relating to the
names of God or "holy" entities such as "Israel," "Jerusalem," or
"David." For example, θεός (*theos*, "God") might be written as θς
(*ths*), which in a majuscule manuscript (one in all capital letters)
would look like ΘΣ.

Old Greek The earliest Greek translations of the Hebrew OT; they
predate Christianity.

Old Latin Latin translations of the Bible that are independent of the
Latin Vulgate.

Origen A Christian scholar and theologian of the early third century AD who typified the allegorical interpretation of Scripture; he also produced the **Hexapla**.

palimpsest A document that was erased to make the parchment available for another writing.

papyrus A writing material made from the papyrus plant; in textual criticism, plural "papyri" refers to biblical manuscripts on papyrus.

parablepsis A textual error in which the scribe's eye skips over text and accidentally omits it.

parchment A writing material made from prepared animal skin; technically synonymous with vellum, which usually denotes higher quality.

pericope A selection from a larger literary work. In biblical studies, a pericope is a distinct section of text analyzed as a literary unit.

Peshitta The Syriac translation of the Bible. It may date to as early as the second century AD.

pharyngeal A type of consonant sound created when air is constricted as it passes through the pharynx, the space between the mouth and the larynx; the Biblical Hebrew ח *het* is a pharyngeal (also called a guttural).

polyglot A printed edition of the Bible that contains three or more languages side by side.

proto-Masoretic Text The Hebrew manuscript tradition that became the Masoretic Text.

proto-Theodotion An early Greek version of the OT that aligns well with a later version by Theodotion; also called the Kaige recension.

pseudepigraphal Anonymous writings that were attributed to famous or authoritative figures from the past to lend additional authority or credibility to the writing—often written by the dead person's disciples based on what they taught (or supposedly taught).

qere A scribal notation in the margins of biblical Hebrew manuscripts usually offered as a correction of the written text or as a way to note an alternative textual tradition.

qere perpetuum A word in the written text of the Hebrew OT that
    is always to be read another way, though no scribal notation
    indicates this. See also **qere** and **kethiv.**

Rahlfs An eclectic edition of the Septuagint named for its initial editor,
    Alfred Rahlfs.

recension A revision of a text or document; a term in textual criticism
    to describe manuscripts that modified earlier manuscripts.

redaction criticism An approach to biblical interpretation that focuses
    on how a biblical passage or entire biblical book was edited into
    its final literary form.

Samaritan Pentateuch A sacred text that includes only the Torah and
    reflects the ideology of the Samaritan community.

scribe A copyist or writer who copied texts prior to the invention of the
    printing press.

scriptio continua Latin for "continuous script"; refers to the practice
    of writing Greek manuscripts in all capital letters and with no
    spaces between the words.

Second Rabbinic Bible A sixteenth-century Jewish edition of the OT
    that became the authoritative version for Judaism; the base text
    for the first two editions of *Biblia Hebraica* by Kittel.

Septuagint The Greek translation of the Hebrew Old Testament
    (Genesis–Malachi) begun around 250 BC. Sometimes abbreviated
    with the Roman numeral for seventy (LXX) based on the tradition
    that seventy translators participated.

sigla Abbreviations or symbols used to identify specific manuscripts;
    singular "siglum."

source criticism The method of analyzing biblical texts that attempts
    to identify separate sources that may have been used to form the
    final composition.

source language The language of a text being translated.

stemma A sort of family tree that maps the relationship among textual
    witnesses.

Symmachus A second-century AD translator who produced a Greek
    translation of the OT.

Synoptic Gospels Refers to Matthew, Mark, and Luke because of the large degree of overlap in language and descriptions of events. Mark was likely a source for Matthew and Luke.

Syriac A dialect of Aramaic used in early Christian texts and the Peshitta translation of the OT.

Syro-Hexapla A Syriac translation of Origen's **Hexapla** produced during the seventh century.

target language The language of a text being produced from a text in another language (source language).

Targum An Aramaic translation of a book from the Hebrew Bible.

text-type The older term for a grouping of NT manuscripts based on their similarity of text; the term is thought by many current textual critics to be misleading because it implies clearer boundaries than actually exist between the groupings. The names of the "text-types" (Alexandrian, Byzantine, Western, or Caesarean) are typically still used in text-critical discussions, but they are called groupings, streams, or traditions.

textual critic A scholar who examines variants in the biblical text to determine the most authentic readings.

textual criticism The process of evaluating variants in the biblical text to determine which reading was likely the earliest.

textual emendation A correction to a biblical manuscript based on a superior reading (variant) or on a textual critic's conjecture (conjectural emendation).

Textus Receptus A label eventually applied to editions of the Greek NT published by Erasmus in the sixteenth century and the text behind the KJV; often confused with the **Majority Text**.

Theodotion An early church father of the Alexandrian school; a second-century AD translator of the Hebrew Bible into Greek; his translation was in the sixth column of Origen's **Hexapla**.

tiqqune sopherim Hebrew for "corrections of the scribes"; refers to around eighteen minor changes in the text of the Hebrew Bible traditionally attributed to scribes who perceived the original text to be irreverent. The changes are sometimes likened to replacing an offensive term or image with a euphemism. Since the Hebrew manuscripts typically have the "correction" in the main text, it is difficult to say with certainty what the "original" reading may have been.

Tischendorf, Constantin von A nineteenth-century German Protestant theologian who published critical editions of the Greek NT and discovered Codex Sinaiticus.

Torah Another name for the Law of Moses or Pentateuch. In Jewish tradition, "Torah" can also refer to the legal parts of the Pentateuch, the entire Hebrew Bible, or the written Scripture plus the later traditions interpreting Scripture contained in the Mishnah and Talmud.

transcriptional evidence Text-critical evidence related to the practices of scribes.

transcriptional probability A text-critical term referring to the likelihood of a scribe making certain types of copying mistakes.

translation technique A general term for the various methods that make up a translator's approach to the source text including word choice, how closely they follow the source text in word order or syntax, what grammatical categories they use to represent different categories in the source language, etc.

UBS Greek New Testament United Bible Society's edition of the Greek NT, currently in its fifth edition; the most widely used critical edition of the Greek NT and the base text for most English Bible translations.

Urtext The hypothetical earliest form of a biblical text that textual critics may try to reconstruct.

variant A term of textual criticism describing the different wording of one text when compared with another; also called a variant reading.

variation unit A place in the text where there is variation in the wording of the ancient manuscripts. A specific different reading in a variation unit is called a **variant**.

versification The introduction of verse numbers in the Bible during the Middle Ages.

vocalization The addition of vowel symbols by the Masoretes to the consonantal text of the OT.

Vorlage The source document behind a translation or a recension (a German word meaning "what lies before").

Vulgate The late fourth-century AD Latin translation of the Bible completed largely by St. Jerome.

Westcott and Hort A nineteenth-century critical edition of the Greek NT produced by B. F. Westcott and F. J. A. Hort; a classic work in the field of NT textual criticism.

Western text-type Or Western textual tradition. One of several textual streams or groupings among NT manuscripts; represented by only a few Greek manuscripts and much of the Latin, having the reputation for paraphrasing the text rather than careful reproduction.

witness A particular manuscript, translation, or quotation that is cited as evidence of a variant reading in a variation unit.

BIBLIOGRAPHY

GENERAL

Abegg, Martin, Peter Flint, and Eugene Ulrich. *The Dead Sea Scrolls Bible: The Oldest Known Bible Translated for the First Time into English.* New York: HarperOne, 1999.

Akin, Daniel L. *1, 2, 3 John.* NAC 38. Nashville: Broadman & Holman, 2001.

Aland, Barbara, and Kurt Aland, eds. *Das Markusevangelium.* Vol. 1/1 of *Text und Textwert der Griechischen Handschriften des Neuen Testaments IV. Die Synoptischen Evangelien.* Berlin: de Gruyter, 1998.

Aland, Kurt, and Barbara Aland. *The Text of the New Testament: An Introduction to the Critical Editions and to the Theory and Practice of Modern Textual Criticism.* 2nd ed. Grand Rapids: Eerdmans, 1995.

Alexander, Archibald. *Evidences of the Authenticity, Inspiration and Canonical Authority of the Holy Scriptures.* Philadelphia: Presbyterian Board of Publication and Sabbath-School Work, 1836.

Allen, Leslie C. *Psalms 101–150.* Rev. ed. WBC 21. Dallas: Word, 2002.

Anderson, Amy S. *The Textual Tradition of the Gospels: Family 1 in Matthew.* Leiden: Brill, 2004.

Anderson, Robert T. "Samaritans." *AYBD* 5:940–47.

Andrews, Herbert T. "The Letter of Aristeas." Pages 83–122 in vol. 2 of *The Apocrypha and Pseudepigrapha of the Old Testament in English.* Edited by R. H. Charles. Oxford: Clarendon, 1913.

Arnold, Clinton E. "Ephesians, Letter to the." *DPL* 238–48.

Aune, David E. *Revelation 1–5.* WBC 52A. Dallas: Word, 1997.

Bacote, Vincent, Laura C. Miguélez, and Dennis L. Okholm, eds.
    Evangelicals & Scripture: Tradition, Authority and Hermeneutics.
    Downers Grove, IL: InterVarsity, 2004.

Bagnall, Roger S. *Early Christian Books in Egypt.* Princeton: Princeton
    University Press, 2009.

Barker, Kenneth. *The Balance of the NIV: What Makes a Good Translation.*
    Grand Rapids: Baker, 2000.

Barrera, Julio Trebolle. *The Jewish Bible and the Christian Bible: An
    Introduction to the History of the Bible.* Translated by Wilfred G E.
    Watson. Leiden: Brill, 1998.

Bauer, Walter, Frederick W. Danker, William Arndt, and F. Wilbur
    Gingrich, eds. *A Greek-English Lexicon of the New Testament
    and Other Early Christian Literature* [BDAG]. 3rd ed. Chicago:
    University of Chicago Press, 2000.

Beale, G. K. *The Book of Revelation: A Commentary on the Greek Text.* NIGTC.
    Grand Rapids: Eerdmans, 1999.

———. *The Erosion of Inerrancy in Evangelicalism: Responding to New
    Challenges to Biblical Authority.* Wheaton, IL: Crossway, 2008.

Beekman, John, and John Callow. *Translating the Word of God:
    With Scripture and Topical Indexes.* Rev. ed. Dallas: SIL
    International, 2002.

Birdsall, J. N. "Codex Sinaiticus (א)." *ZEB* 1:941–42.

Black, David Alan. *New Testament Textual Criticism: A Concise Guide.*
    Grand Rapids: Baker, 1994.

———, ed. *Rethinking New Testament Textual Criticism.* Grand Rapids:
    Baker, 2002.

Bland, Dave. *Proverbs, Ecclesiastes, & Song of Songs.* College Press
    NIV Commentary. Joplin, MO: College Press Publishing
    Company, 2002.

Blenkinsopp, Joseph. *Isaiah 40–55: A New Translation with Introduction
    and Commentary.* AYBC 19A. New York: Doubleday, 2002.

Brannan, Rick, Ken M. Penner, Israel Loken, Michael Aubrey, and Isaiah
    Hoogendyk, eds. *The Lexham English Septuagint.* Bellingham, WA:
    Logos Bible Software, 2012.

———. *The Lexham English Septuagint: Alternate Texts.* Bellingham, WA:
    Logos Bible Software, 2012.

Brenton, Lancelot C. L. *The Septuagint with Apocrypha: Greek and English.* Peabody, MA: Hendrickson, 1986.

Brock, Sebastian. *The Bible in the Syriac Tradition.* Piscataway, NJ: Gorgias, 2006.

Brogan, John J. "Can I Have Your Autograph? Uses and Abuses of Textual Criticism in Formulating an Evangelical Doctrine of Scripture." Pages 93–111 in *Evangelicals & Scripture: Tradition, Authority and Hermeneutics.* Edited by Vincent Bacote, Laura C. Miguélez, and Dennis L. Okholm. Downers Grove, IL: InterVarsity, 2004.

Brotzman, Ellis R. *Old Testament Textual Criticism: A Practical Introduction.* Grand Rapids: Baker, 1994.

Brotzman, Ellis R., and Eric J. Tully. *Old Testament Textual Criticism: A Practical Introduction.* 2nd ed. Grand Rapids: Baker, 2016.

Brown, Derek R., Miles Custis, and Matthew M. Whitehead. *Lexham Bible Guide: Ephesians.* Edited by Douglas Mangum. Bellingham, WA: Lexham Press, 2012.

Brown, Francis, Samuel R. Driver, and Charles A. Briggs. *A Hebrew and English Lexicon of the Old Testament.* Oxford: Clarendon, 1906.

———. *Enhanced Brown-Driver-Briggs Hebrew and English Lexicon.* Electronic ed. Oak Harbor, WA: Logos Research Systems, 2000.

Bruce, F. F. *The Epistles to the Colossians, to Philemon, and to the Ephesians.* NICNT. Grand Rapids: Eerdmans, 1984.

Bush, Frederic W. *Ruth, Esther.* WBC 9. Dallas: Word, 1996.

Carson, D. A. *Collected Writings on Scripture.* Edited by Andrew David Naselli. Wheaton, IL: Crossway, 2010.

Carson, D. A., and John D. Woodbridge, eds. *Hermeneutics, Authority, and Canon.* Grand Rapids: Zondervan, 1986.

———. *Scripture and Truth.* Grand Rapids: Baker, 1992.

Carson, D. A., John D. Woodbridge, and Kevin Vanhoozer. "Semantics of Biblical Literature." Pages 49–104 in *Hermeneutics, Authority, and Canon.* Grand Rapids: Zondervan, 1986.

Charlesworth, James H., ed. *The Old Testament Pseudepigrapha.* 2 vols. New York: Doubleday, 1983–1985.

Christensen, Duane L. *Deuteronomy 21:10–34:12.* WBC 6B. Dallas: Word, 2002.

Collins, John J., and Craig A. Evans. *Christian Beginnings and the Dead Sea Scrolls*. Grand Rapids: Baker Academic, 2006.

Comfort, Philip W. *Early Manuscripts and Modern Translations of the New Testament*. Grand Rapids: Baker Books, 1990.

———. *Encountering the Manuscripts: An Introduction to New Testament Paleography & Textual Criticism*. Nashville: Broadman & Holman, 2005.

Comfort, Philip W., and David P. Barrett. *The Text of the Earliest New Testament Greek Manuscripts*. Wheaton, IL: Tyndale House, 2001.

Committee on Bible Translation. Preface to the *New International Version*. East Brunswick, NJ: International Bible Society, 1983.

Cross, Frank M. "The Evolution of a Theory of Local Texts." Pages 306–20 in *Qumran and the History of the Biblical Text*. Edited by Frank M. Cross and Shemaryahu Talmon. Cambridge: Cambridge University Press, 1975.

Dahood, Mitchell J. *Psalms III: 101–150*. AYBC 17A. Garden City, NY: Doubleday, 1970.

DeMoss, Matthew S. *Pocket Dictionary for the Study of New Testament Greek*. Downers Grove, IL: InterVarsity, 2001.

Dines, Jennifer M. *The Septuagint*. London: T&T Clark, 2004.

Doble, Peter, and Jeffrey Kloha, eds. *Texts and Traditions: Essays in Honor of J. Keith Elliott*. Leiden: Brill, 2014.

Donaldson, Amy M. "Explicit References to New Testament Variant Readings among Greek and Latin Church Fathers." PhD diss., University of Notre Dame, 2009. https://curate.nd.edu/show/571m615k50.

Dotan, Aaron. "Masorah." Pages 1418–19 in vol. 14 of the *Encyclopedia Judaica*. Edited by Cecil Roth and Geoffrey Wigoder. New York: Macmillan, 1971.

Dunn, James D. G. *Romans 1–8*. WBC 38A. Dallas: Word, 1998.

Duvall, J. Scott, and J. Daniel Hays. *Grasping God's Word: A Hands-On Approach to Reading, Interpreting, and Applying the Bible*. 2nd ed. Grand Rapids: Zondervan, 2005.

Editorial Board of The Lockman Foundation. Preface to the *New American Standard Bible*. La Habra, CA: The Lockman Foundation, 1977.

Ehrman, Bart D. *The Orthodox Corruption of Scripture: The Effect of Early Christological Controversies on the Text of the New Testament.* Oxford: Oxford University Press, 1993.

Ehrman, Bart D., and Michael W. Holmes, eds. *The Text of the New Testament in Contemporary Research: Essays on the Status Quaestionis.* Grand Rapids: Eerdmans, 1995.

Ehrman, Bart D., and Michael W. Holmes, eds. *The Text of the New Testament in Contemporary Research: Essays on the Status Quaestionis.* 2nd ed. Leiden: Brill, 2013.

Elliott, J. K., and Ian Moir. *Manuscripts and the Text of the New Testament: An Introduction for English Readers.* London: T&T Clark, 2003.

Enns, Peter. *Inspiration and Incarnation: Evangelicals and the Problem of the Old Testament.* Grand Rapids: Baker, 2005.

Epp, Eldon J.. "Codex Sinaiticus: Its Entrance into the Mid-Nineteenth Century Text-Critical Environment and Its Impact on the New Testament Text." Pages 53-89 in *Codex Sinaiticus: New Perspectives on the Ancient Biblical Manuscript.* Edited by Scot McKendrick, David Parker, Amy Myshrall, and Cillian O'Hogan. London: The British Library, 2015.

———. "Critical Editions and the Development of Text-Critical Methods [Part 2]: From Lachmann (1831) to the Present." Pages 13-48 in *The New Cambridge History of the Bible,* vol. 4, *From 1750 to the Present.* Edited by John Riches. Cambridge: Cambridge University Press, 2015.

———. "Critical Editions of the New Testament, and the Development of Text-Critical Methods [Part 1]: From Erasmus to Griesbach (1516-1807)." Pages 110-37 in *The New Cambridge History of the Bible,* vol. 3, *From 1450 to 1750.* Edited by Euan Cameron. Cambridge: Cambridge University Press, 2016.

———. "How New Testament Textual Variants Embody and Exhibit Prior Textual Traditions." Pages 271-88 in *Biblical Essays in Honor of Daniel J. Harrington, SJ, and Richard J. Clifford, SJ: Opportunity for No Little Instruction.* Edited by Christopher G. Frechette, Christopher R. Matthews, and Thomas D. Stegman, SJ. New York: Paulist Press, 2014.

———. "In the Beginning Was the New Testament Text, but Which Text?" In *Texts and Traditions: Essays in Honour of J. Keith Elliott*, edited by Peter Doble and Jeffrey Kloha, 35–70. Leiden: Brill, 2014.

———. *Perspectives on New Testament Textual Criticism: Collected Essays, 1962–2004*. Leiden: Brill, 2005.

———. "Text-Critical Witness and Methodology for Isolating a Distinctive D-Text in Acts." *NovT* 59 (2017): 225–96.

———. "Textual Criticism (New Testament)." *AYBD* 6:412–35.

———. *The Theological Tendency of Codex Bezae Cantabrigiensis in Acts*. Cambridge: Cambridge University Press, 2005.

———. "The Twentieth Century Interlude in New Testament Textual Criticism." *JBL* 93.3 (1974): 386–414.

———. "Why Does New Testament Textual Criticism Matter? Refined Definitions and Fresh Directions." *The Expository Times* 125, no. 9 (2014): 417–31.

Epp, Eldon J., and Gordon D. Fee, eds. *Studies in the Theory and Method of New Testament Textual Criticism*. Grand Rapids: Eerdmans, 1993.

Evans, Craig A., and Emanuel Tov, eds. *Exploring the Origins of the Bible: Canon Formation in Historical, Literary, and Theological Perspective*. Grand Rapids: Baker Academic, 2008.

Fee, Gordon D. "The Majority Text and the Original Text of the New Testament." In *Studies in the Theory and Method of New Testament Textual Criticism*, edited by Eldon J. Epp and Gordon D. Fee, 183–208. Grand Rapids: Eerdmans, 1993.

———. "Textual Criticism of the New Testament." Pages 417–33 in *The Expositor's Bible Commentary*, vol. 1, *Introductory Articles*. Edited by Frank E. Gaebelein. Grand Rapids: Zondervan, 1979.

———. *To What End Exegesis?: Essays Textual, Exegetical, and Theological*. Grand Rapids: Eerdmans, 2001.

Feinberg, Paul D. "Bible, Inerrancy and Infallibility of." Pages 156–59 in *Evangelical Dictionary of Theology*. Edited by Walter A. Elwell. Grand Rapids: Baker Academic, 2001.

Fernández Marcos, Natalio. *The Septuagint in Context: Introduction to the Greek Version of the Bible*. Translated by W. G. E. Watson. Leiden: Brill, 2000.

Finegan, Jack. *Encountering New Testament Manuscripts: A Working Introduction to Textual Criticism*. Grand Rapids: Eerdmans, 1974.

Fitzmyer, Joseph A. *The Gospel according to Luke I–IX: Introduction, Translation, and Notes*. AYBC 28. Garden City, NY: Doubleday, 1970.

———. *Romans: A New Translation with Introduction and Commentary*. AYBC 33. New York: Doubleday, 1993.

Flesher, Paul V. M., and Bruce Chilton. *The Targums: A Critical Introduction*. Waco, TX: Baylor University Press, 2011.

Flint, Peter W., and Tae Hun Kim, eds. *The Bible at Qumran: Text, Shape, and Interpretation*. Grand Rapids: Eerdmans, 2001.

Fox, Michael V. "Editing Proverbs: The Challenge of the Oxford Hebrew Bible." *JNSL* 32.1 (2006): 1–22.

———. *Proverbs 10–31: A New Translation with Introduction and Commentary*. AYBC 18B. New Haven: Yale University Press, 2009.

Freedman, David Noel, ed. *The Leningrad Codex: A Facsimile Edition*. Grand Rapids: Eerdmans, 1998.

Friedman, Matti. *The Aleppo Codex: A True Story of Obsession, Faith, and the Pursuit of an Ancient Bible*. Chapel Hill, NC: Algonquin Books, 2012.

Gamble, Harry Y. *Books and Readers in the Early Church*. New Haven: Yale University Press, 1995.

Gentry, Peter J. "1.3.1.2 Pre-Hexaplaric Translations, Hexapla, Post-Hexaplaric Translations." Pages 211–34 in *Textual History of the Bible*, edited by Armin Lange. Leiden: Brill, 2016.

———. "The Text of the Old Testament." *JETS* 52.1 (2009): 19–45.

German Bible Society. "The Septuaginta-Edition from A. Rahlfs and Its History." *Academic-Bible.com: The Scholarly Bible Portal of the German Bible Society*. http:www.academic-bible. comenhomescholarly-editionsseptuaginthistory-of-the-lxx.

Ginsburg, Christian D. *Introduction to the Massoretico-Critical Edition of the Hebrew Bible*. London: The Trinitarian Bible Society, 1897.

Gooding, D. W. "Texts and Versions: The Septuagint." *NBD* 1169–72.

Goodrich, Richard J., and Albert L. Lukaszewski, eds. *A Reader's Greek New Testament*. Grand Rapids: Zondervan, 2003.

Gordis, Robert. *The Biblical Text in the Making—A Study of the Kethib-Qere*. Philadelphia: Dropsie College for Hebrew and Cognate Learning, 1937. Repr., New York: Ktav, 1971.

Goshen-Gottstein, Moshe, ed. *The Aleppo Bible Codex: The Crowning Achievement of the Master of the Massora ben Asher*. Jerusalem: Magnes Press/The Hebrew University, 1976.

Goshen-Gottstein, Moshe. "The Aleppo Codex and the Rise of the Massoretic Bible Text." *Biblical Archaeologist* 42.3 (1979): 145–63.

———. "Editions of the Hebrew Bible—Past and Future." Pages 221–42 in *Sha`arei Talmon: Studies in the Bible, Qumran, and the Ancient Near East Presented to Shemaryahu Talmon*. Edited by Michael Fishbane, Emanuel Tov, and W. W. Fields. Winona Lake, IN: Eisenbrauns, 1992.

Gottingen Academy of Sciences and Humanities. "Septuaginta-Unternehmen: History." *Gottingen Academy of Sciences and Humanities* website. http://adw-goe.de/en/research/research-projects-within-the-academies-programme/septuaginta-unternehmen/history/.

Greenlee, J. Harold. "Texts and Manuscripts (NT)." ZEB 5:801–22.

———. *The Text of the New Testament: From Manuscript to Modern Edition*. Grand Rapids: Baker, 2008.

Greenspoon, Leonard J. "Theodotion, Theodotion's Version." AYBD 6:447–48.

Grenz, Stanley J. "Nurturing the Soul, Informing the Mind: The Genesis of the Evangelical Scripture Principle." Pages 21–41 in *Evangelicals & Scripture: Tradition, Authority and Hermeneutics*. Edited by Vincent Bacote, Laura C. Miguélez, and Dennis L. Okholm. Downers Grove, IL: InterVarsity, 2004.

Gurtner, Daniel M., Juan Hernandez Jr., and Paul Foster, eds. *Studies on the Text of the New Testament and Early Christianity*. Leiden: Brill, 2015.

Hatch, Edwin. *Essays in Biblical Greek*. Oxford: Clarendon, 1889.

Hatch, William Henry Paine. *Facsimiles and Descriptions of Minuscule Manuscripts of the New Testament*. Cambridge, MA: Harvard University Press, 1951.

Hendel, Ronald. "The Oxford Hebrew Bible Project: Its Aims and a Response to Criticisms." *Hebrew Bible and Ancient Israel* 2.1 (2013): 63–99.

———. "The Oxford Hebrew Bible Project: Prologue to a New Critical Edition." *VT* 58 (2008): 324–51.

Henry, Matthew. *Matthew Henry's Commentary on the Whole Bible: Complete and Unabridged in One Volume*. Peabody, MA: Hendrickson, 1994.

Hillers, Delbert R. *Lamentations: A New Translation with Introduction and Commentary*. 2nd rev. ed. AYBC 7A. New York: Doubleday, 1992.

Holmes, Michael W. "From 'Original Text' to 'Initial Text': The Traditional Goal of New Testament Textual Criticism in Contemporary Discussion." Pages 637–88 in *The Text of the New Testament in Contemporary Research: Essays on the Status Quaestionis*. Edited by Bart D. Ehrman and Michael W. Holmes. 2nd ed. Leiden: Brill, 2012.

———. "New Testament Textual Criticism." Pages 52–74 in *Introducing New Testament Interpretation*. Edited by Scot McKnight. Guides to New Testament Exegesis. Grand Rapids: Baker, 1989.

Houghton, H. A. G., ed. *Early Readers, Scholars and Editors of the New Testament: Papers from the Eighth Birmingham Colloquium on the Textual Criticism of the New Testament*. Piscataway, NJ: Gorgias, 2014.

Hurtado, Larry W. "Beyond the Interlude? Developments and Directions in New Testament Textual Criticism." Pages 26–48 in *Studies in the Early Text of the Gospels and Acts: The Papers of the First Birmingham Colloquium on the Textual Criticism of the New Testament*. Edited by David G. K. Taylor. Birmingham: University of Birmingham Press, 1999.

———. "A Challenge to the Dating of P75." *Larry Hurtado's Blog*, June 22, 2016. https://larryhurtado.wordpress.com/2016/06/22/a-challenge-to-the-dating-of-p75/.

———. "The Date of P66 (P. Bodmer II): Nongbri's New Argument." *Larry Hurtado's Blog*, June 3, 2014. https://larryhurtado.wordpress.com/2014/06/03/the-date-of-p66-p-bodmer-ii-nongbris-new-argument/.

———. *The Earliest Christian Artifacts: Manuscripts and Christian Origins.* Grand Rapids: Eerdmans, 2006.

"Institut für Neutestamentliche Textforschung." *Westfälische Wilhelms-Universität Münster.* http://egora.uni-muenster.de/intf/index_en.shtml.

International Organization for Septuagint and Cognate Studies. "New English Translation of the Septuagint." *New English Translation of the Septuagint* website. http://ccat.sas.upenn.edu/nets.

Jewett, Robert. *Romans: A Commentary on the Book of Romans.* Hermeneia. Minneapolis: Fortress, 2006.

Jobes, Karen H., and Moisés Silva. *Invitation to the Septuagint.* 2nd ed. Grand Rapids: Baker Academic, 2015.

Jones, Brice C. *New Testament Texts on Greek Amulets from Late Antiquity.* London: Bloomsbury, 2016.

Kelley, Page H., Daniel S. Mynatt, and Timothy G. Crawford. *The Masorah of "Biblia Hebraica Stuttgartensia": Introduction and Annotated Glossary.* Grand Rapids: Eerdmans, 1998.

Kilpatrick, G. D. *The Principles and Practice of New Testament Textual Criticism: Collected Essays of G. D. Kilpatrick.* Edited by J. K. Elliott. Leuven: Leuven University Press, 1990.

Kimelman, Reuven. "Psalm 145: Theme, Structure, and Impact." *JBL* 113 (1994): 49–50.

Klein, William W., Craig L. Blomberg, and Robert L. Hubbard Jr. *Introduction to Biblical Interpretation.* Nashville: Thomas Nelson, 2004.

Koehler, Ludwig, Walter Baumgartner, and Johann Jakob Stamm, eds. *The Hebrew and Aramaic Lexicon of the Old Testament* [*HALOT*]. Translated and edited under the supervision of M. E. J. Richardson. 5 vols. Leiden: Brill, 1999–2000.

Koptak, Paul E. *Proverbs.* NIVAC. Grand Rapids: Zondervan, 2003.

Kraus, Hans-Joachim. *Psalms 60–150.* Translated by Hilton C. Oswald. CCS. Minneapolis: Fortress, 1993.

Liddell, Henry George, ed. *An Intermediate Greek-English Lexicon Founded upon the Seventh Edition of Liddell and Scott's Greek-English Lexicon.* Oxford: Oxford University Press, 1888.

Liddell, Henry George, Robert Scott, Henry Stuart Jones, and Roderick McKenzie, eds. *A Greek-English Lexicon*. 9th ed. revised with supplement. Oxford: Clarendon, 1996.

Lincoln, Andrew T. *Ephesians*. WBC 42. Dallas: Word, 1990.

Logos Bible Software. *Biblical Dead Sea Scrolls: Bible Reference Index*. Bellingham, WA: Lexham Press, 2011.

MacRae, A. A. "Texts and Manuscripts (OT)." ZEB 5:785–801.

Marshall, I. Howard. *Biblical Inspiration*. Milton Keynes, UK: Paternoster, 1982.

———. *The Gospel of Luke: A Commentary on the Greek Text*. NIGTC. Grand Rapids: Eerdmans, 1978.

McCarter, P. Kyle. *Textual Criticism: Recovering the Text of the Hebrew Bible*. Guides to Biblical Scholarship. Old Testament Series. Philadelphia: Fortress, 1985.

McCarthy, Carmel. *The Tiqqune Sopherim and Other Theological Corrections in the Masoretic Text of the Old Testament*. Gottingen: Vandenhoeck & Ruprecht, 1981.

McKnight, Scot. *Introducing New Testament Interpretation*. Guides to New Testament Exegesis. Grand Rapids: Baker, 1989.

McKnight, Scot, and Grant R. Osborne, eds. *The Face of New Testament Studies: A Survey of Recent Research*. Grand Rapids: Baker Academic, 2004.

McLay, Tim. "Theodotion." EDB 447–48.

Metzger, Bruce M. *The Canon of the New Testament: Its Origin, Development, and Significance*. Oxford: Clarendon, 1987.

———. *The Early Versions of the New Testament: Their Origin, Transmission, and Limitations*. Oxford: Clarendon, 1977.

———. *Manuscripts of the Greek Bible: An Introduction to Greek Paleography*. New York: Oxford University Press, 1981.

———. *The Text of the New Testament: Its Transmission, Corruption, and Restoration*. 3rd enl. ed. New York: Oxford University Press, 1992.

———. *A Textual Commentary on the Greek New Testament*. London: United Bible Societies, 1971.

———. *A Textual Commentary on the Greek New Testament*. 2nd ed. Stuttgart: Deutsche Bibelgesellschaft, 1994.

———. "To the Reader." In *New Revised Standard Version*. New York: National Council of the Churches of Christ in the U.S.A., 1989.

Metzger, Bruce M., and Bart D. Ehrman. *The Text of the New Testament: Its Transmission, Corruption, and Restoration*. 4th ed. New York: Oxford University Press, 2005.

Mincy, John C. "Preservation of the Copies." Pages 123–62 in *God's Word in Our Hands: The Bible Preserved for Us*. Edited by James B. Williams and Randolph Shaylor. Greenville, SC: Emerald House, 2003.

Morris, Leon. *The Epistle to the Romans*. PNTC. Grand Rapids: Eerdmans, 1988.

Murphy, Roland E. *Proverbs*. WBC 22. Dallas: Word, 1998.

Nichols, Stephen J., and Eric T. Brandt. *Ancient Word, Changing Worlds: The Doctrine of Scripture in a Modern Age*. Wheaton, IL: Crossway, 2009.

Nongbri, Brent. "Grenfell and Hunt on the Dates of Early Christian Codices: Setting the Record Straight." *Bulletin of the American Society of Papyrologists* 48 (2011): 149–62.

———. "The Limits of Palaeographic Dating of Literary Papyri: Some Observations on the Date and Provenance of P. Bodmer II (P66)." *Museum Helveticum* 71 (2014): 1–35.

———. "Reconsidering the Place of Papyrus Bodmer XIV–XV (P75) in the Textual Criticism of the New Testament." *JBL* 135.2 (2016): 405–37.

Omanson, Roger L. *A Textual Guide to the Greek New Testament: An Adaptation of Bruce M. Metzger's Textual Commentary for the Needs of Translators*. Stuttgart: Deutsche Bibelgesellschaft, 2006.

Orsini, Pasquale, and Willy Clarysse. "Early New Testament Manuscripts and Their Dates: A Critique of Theological Palaeography." *Ephemerides Theologicae Lovanienses* 88.4 (2012): 443–74.

Parker, David C. *Codex Bezae: An Early Christian Manuscript and Its Text*. Cambridge: Cambridge University Press, 1992.

———. *Codex Sinaiticus: The Story of the World's Oldest Bible*. Peabody, MA: Hendrickson, 2010.

———. *An Introduction to the New Testament Manuscripts and Their Texts*. Cambridge: Cambridge University Press, 2008.

————. *The Living Text of the Gospels*. Cambridge: Cambridge University Press, 1997.

Paulson, Gregory S. "An Investigation of the Byzantine Text of the Johannine Epistles." *Review and Expositor* 114.4 (2017): 580–89.

Perrin, Jac. *Family 13 in St. John's Gospel: A Computer Assisted Phylogenetic Analysis*. Leiden: Brill, forthcoming.

Pietersma, Albert. "A New English Translation of the Septuagint." Pages 217–28 in *X Congress Volume of the IOSCS, 1998*. Edited by B. A. Taylor. Chico, CA: Society of Biblical Literature, 2001.

Pietersma, Albert, and Benjamin G. Wright, eds. *A New English Translation of the Septuagint*. New York: Oxford University Press, 2007.

Plummer, Alfred. *A Critical and Exegetical Commentary on the Gospel according to Saint Luke*. ICC. London: T&T Clark, 1896.

Porter, J. Scott. *Principles of Textual Criticism, with Their Application to the Old and New Testaments*. London: Simms and M'Intyre, 1848.

Porter, Stanley E. *How We Got the New Testament: Text, Transmission, Translation*. Grand Rapids: Baker, 2013.

Read-Heimerdinger, Jenny. *The Bezan Text of Acts: A Contribution of Discourse Analysis to Textual Criticism*. London: Sheffield Academic Press, 2002.

Roberts, C. H., and T. C. Skeat. *The Birth of the Codex*. Oxford: Oxford University Press, 1987.

Royse, James R. *Scribal Habits in Early Greek New Testament Papyri*. Leiden: Brill, 2007.

Ryrie, Charles Caldwell. *What You Should Know about Inerrancy*. Willow Grove, PA: Woodlawn Electronic Publishing, 1998.

Sanders, James A. "The Hebrew University Bible and *Biblia Hebraica Quinta*." *JBL* 118.3 (1999): 518–36.

Schmid, Ulrich. "Reassessing the Palaeography and Codicology of the Freer Gospel Manuscript." Pages 227–49 in *The Freer Biblical Manuscripts: Fresh Studies of an American Treasure Trove*. Edited by Larry W. Hurtado. Leiden: Brill, 2006.

Schnabel, Eckhard J. "Textual Criticism: Recent Developments." Pages 59–85 in *The Face of New Testament Studies: A Survey of Recent*

Research. Edited by Scot McKnight and Grant R. Osborne. Grand Rapids: Baker Academic, 2004.

Scott, William R. *A Simplified Guide to the BHS.* North Richland Hills, TX: BIBAL Press, 1987.

Shutt, R. J. H. "Letter of Aristeas." *OTP* 2:7–34.

Sperber, Alexander, ed. *The Bible in Aramaic Based on Old Manuscripts and Printed Texts.* 3 vols. Leiden: Brill, 2004.

Sproul, R. C. *Can I Trust the Bible?* Lake Mary, FL: Reformation Trust Publishing, 2009.

Swete, Henry Barclay. *An Introduction to the Old Testament in Greek.* Cambridge: Cambridge University Press, 1914.

Talmon, Shemaryahu. "Old Testament Text." Pages 159–99 in vol. 1 of *Cambridge History of the Bible.* Edited by P. R. Akroyd and C. F. Evans. Cambridge: Cambridge University Press, 1975.

Tawil, Hayim, and Bernard Schneider. *Crown of Aleppo: The Mystery of the Oldest Hebrew Bible Codex.* Philadelphia: Jewish Publication Society, 2010.

Taylor, D. G. K., ed. *Studies in the Early Text of the Gospels and Acts: The Papers of the First Birmingham Colloquium on the Textual Criticism of the New Testament.* Birmingham, UK: The University of Birmingham Press, 1999.

Tigay, Jeffrey H. *Deuteronomy.* The JPS Torah Commentary. Philadelphia: Jewish Publication Society, 1996.

Tov, Emanuel. *The Greek and Hebrew Bible: Collected Essays on the Septuagint.* Leiden: Brill, 1999.

———. *Textual Criticism of the Hebrew Bible.* 2nd rev. ed. Minneapolis: Fortress, 2001.

———. *Textual Criticism of the Hebrew Bible.* 3rd rev. exp. ed. Minneapolis: Fortress, 2012.

Translation Oversight Committee. Preface to the *English Standard Version.* Wheaton, IL: Good News Publishers, 2001.

Tsedaka, Benyamim, trans. *The Israelite Samaritan Version of the Torah: First English Translation Compared with the Masoretic Version.* Edited by Benyamim Tsedaka and Sharon J. Sullivan. Grand Rapids: Eerdmans, 2013.

Ulrich, Eugene. *The Dead Sea Scrolls and the Origins of the Bible*. Grand Rapids: Eerdmans, 1999.

"United Bible Societies." *United Bible Societies* website. No pages. http://www.unitedbiblesocieties.org.

VanderKam, James C. *The Dead Sea Scrolls Today*. Grand Rapids: Eerdmans, 1994.

Vincent, Marvin R. *A History of the Textual Criticism of the New Testament*. New York: Macmillan, 1899.

Wallace, Daniel B. "The Majority Text and the Original Text: Are They Identical?" *BSac* 148 (April 1991): 151–69.

———. "The Majority-Text Theory: History, Methods and Critique." *JETS* 37.2 (June 1994): 184–215.

———. "Some Second Thoughts on the Majority Text." *BSac* 146 (July 1989): 270–90.

———. "Textual Criticism of the New Testament." *LBD*.

Waltke, Bruce K. "Aims of Old Testament Textual Criticism." *WTJ* 51 (1989): 92–108.

———. "Textual Criticism of the Old Testament." Pages 209–28 in *The Expositor's Bible Commentary*, vol. 1, *Introductory Articles*. Edited by Frank E. Gaebelein. Grand Rapids: Zondervan, 1979.

———. "Textual Criticism of the Old Testament and Its Relation to Exegesis and Theology." *NIDOTTE* 1:51–67.

Warfield, Benjamin B. *An Introduction to the Textual Criticism of the New Testament*. London: Hodder and Stoughton, 1890.

Wasserman, Tommy, and Peter J. Gurry. *A New Approach to Textual Criticism: An Introduction to the Coherence-Based Genealogical Method*. Atlanta: SBL Press, 2017.

Wegner, Paul D. *A Student's Guide to Textual Criticism of the Bible: Its History, Methods & Results*. Downers Grove, IL: InterVarsity, 2006.

Weis, Richard D. "*Biblia Hebraica Quinta* and the Making of Critical Editions of the Hebrew Bible." *A Journal of Biblical Textual Criticism* 7 (2002): http://rosetta.reltech.org/TC/vol07/Weis2002.html.

Weitzman, Michael. *The Syriac Version of the Old Testament: An Introduction*. Cambridge: Cambridge University Press, 1999.

Welsby, Alison. *A Textual Study of Family 1 in the Gospel of John*. Berlin: de Gruyter, 2013.

Westcott, B. F., and F. J. A. Hort. *Introduction to the New Testament in the Original Greek*. New York: Harper and Brothers, 1882.

Williams, James B., and Randolph Shaylor, eds. *God's Word in Our Hands: The Bible Preserved for Us*. Greenville, SC: Emerald House, 2003.

Wonneberger, Reinhard. *Understanding BHS: A Manual for the Users of "Biblia Hebraica Stuttgartensia"*. 2nd rev. ed. Subsidia Biblica 8. Translated by Dwight R. Daniels. Rome: Pontificio Istituto Biblico, 1990.

Wright, N. T. *Scripture and the Authority of God*. London: Society for Promoting Christian Knowledge, 2005.

Würthwein, Ernst. *The Text of the Old Testament: An Introduction to the "Biblia Hebraica"*. 2nd ed. Translated by Erroll F. Rhodes. Grand Rapids: Eerdmans, 1995.

Würthwein, Ernst, and Alexander Achilles Fischer. *The Text of the Old Testament: An Introduction to the "Biblia Hebraica."* 3rd ed. Translated by Erroll F. Rhodes. Grand Rapids, Eerdmans, 2014.

Yeivin, Israel. *Introduction to the Tiberian Masorah*. Edited and translated by E. J. Revell. Masoretic Studies 5. Missoula, MT: Scholars Press, 1980.

CRITICAL EDITIONS

NEW TESTAMENT

Aland, Barbara, Kurt Aland, Johannes Karavidopoulos, Carlo M. Martini, and Bruce M. Metzger, eds. *The Greek New Testament*. 5th rev. ed. Stuttgart: Deutsche Bibelgesellschaft, 2014.

Aland, Kurt, Barbara Aland, Johannes Karavidopoulos, Carlo M. Martini, and Bruce M. Metzger, eds. *Novum Testamentum Graece*. 28th ed. Stuttgart: Deutsche Bibelgesellschaft, 2012.

Aland, Kurt, Matthew Black, Carlo M. Martini, Bruce M. Metzger, Allen Wikgren, Barbara Aland, and Johannes Karavidopoulos, eds. *The Greek New Testament*. 4th rev. ed. Stuttgart: Deutsche Bibelgesellschaft, 2000.

Hodges, Zane Clark, and Arthur L. Farstad. *The Greek New Testament according to the Majority Text*. 2nd ed. Nashville: Thomas Nelson, 1985.

Holmes, Michael W., ed. *The Greek New Testament: Society of Biblical Literature Edition*. Atlanta: SBL Press; Bellingham, WA: Logos Bible Software, 2011.

Institute for New Testament Textual Research. *Novum Testamentum Graecum: Editio Critica Maior*. Volume III: The Acts of the Apostles. Part 1.1: Text: Chapters 1–14. Part 1.2: Text: Chapters 15–28. Part 2: Supplementary Material. Part 3: Studies. Edited by Holger Strutwolf, Georg Gäbel, Annette Hüffmeier, Gerd Mink, and Klaus Wachtel. Stuttgart: Deutsche Bibelgesellschaft, 2017.

———. *Novum Testamentum Graecum: Editio Critica Maior*. Volume IV: Catholic Letters, 1st ed. Installment 1: James. Part 1: Text. Part 2: Supplementary Material. Edited by Barbara Aland, Kurt Aland, Gerd Mink, and Klaus Wachtel. [1997]. Installment 2: The Letters of Peter. Part 1: Text. Part 2: Supplementary Material. Edited by Barbara Aland, Kurt Aland, Gerd Mink, and Klaus Wachtel. [2000]. Installment 3: The First Letter of John. Part 1: Text. Part 2: Supplementary Material. Edited by Barbara Aland, Kurt Aland, Gerd Mink, and Klaus Wachtel. [2003]. Installment 4: The Second and Third Letter of John and the Letter of Jude. Part 1: Text. Part 2: Supplementary Material. Edited by Barbara Aland, Kurt Aland, Gerd Mink, Holger Strutwolf, and Klaus Wachtel. [2005]. Stuttgart: Deutsche Bibelgesellschaft, 1997–2005.

———. *Novum Testamentum Graecum: Editio Critica Maior*. Volume IV: Catholic Letters, 2nd ed. Part 1: Text. Part 2: Supplementary Material. Edited by Barbara Aland, Kurt Aland, Gerd Mink, Holger Strutwolf, and Klaus Wachtel. Stuttgart: Deutsche Bibelgesellschaft, 2013.

———. *Novum Testamentum Graecum: Editio Critica Maior*. Parallel Pericopes: Special Volume Regarding the Synoptic Gospels. Edited by Holger Strutwolf and Klaus Wachtel. Stuttgart: Deutsche Bibelgesellschaft, 2011.

Jongkind Dirk, and Peter J. Williams, eds. *The Greek New Testament, Produced at Tyndale House, Cambridge*. Wheaton, IL: Crossway, 2017.

Nestle, Eberhard, Erwin Nestle, Kurt Aland, and Barbara Aland, eds. *Novum Testamentum Graece*. 27th ed. Stuttgart: Deutsche Bibelstiftung, 1993.

Robinson, Maurice A., and William G. Pierpont. *The New Testament in the Original Greek*. Southborough, MA: Chilton Book Publishing, 2005.

Scrivener, F. H. A., ed. *The New Testament in Greek according to the Text Followed in the Authorised Version Together with the Variations Adopted in the Revised Version*. Cambridge: Cambridge University Press, 1908.

Tischendorf, Constantine von, ed. *Novum Testamentum Vaticanum (Codex Vaticanus)*. Leipzig: Giesecke and Devrient, 1867.

Tregelles, Samuel Prideaux, ed. *The Greek New Testament, Edited from Ancient Authorities, with Their Various Readings in Full, and the Latin Version of Jerome*. London: Bagster; Stewart, 1857–1879.

Westcott, Brooke F., and Fenton J. A. Hort. *The New Testament in the Original Greek*. American ed. New York: Harper & Brothers, 1881.

OLD TESTAMENT

Masoretic Text

Ginsburg, Christian D. *Massoretico-Critical Text of the Hebrew Bible*. London: The Trinitarian Bible Society, 1894.

Kennicott, Benjamin. *Vetus Testamentum Hebraicum cum varus lectionibus*. 2 vols. Oxford: Clarendon, 1776, 1780.

de Rossi, Johannis B. *Scholia Critica in V. T. Libros seu supplementa ad varias sacri textus lectiones*. Parma: Ex Regio Typographeo, 1798.

———. *Variae Lectiones Veteris Testamenti, ex immensa MSS. Editorumq. Codicum Congerie haustae et ad Samar. Textum, ad vetustiss. versiones, ad accuratiores sacrae criticae fontes ac leges examinatae opera ac studio Johannis Bern de Rossi*. 4 vols. Parma: Ex Regio Typographeo, 1784–1788.

Schenker, A., ed. *Biblia Hebraica Quinta*. Stuttgart: Deutsche Bibelgesellschaft, 2004–.

———. *Biblia Hebraica Stuttgartensia.* Electronic ed. Stuttgart: Deutsche Bibelgesellschaft, 2003.

Peshitta

Peshitta Institute, Leiden, eds. *Leiden Peshitta.* Electronic ed. Leiden: Peshitta Institute Leiden, 2008.

———. *The Old Testament in Syriac according to the Peshitta Version.* 14 vols. Leiden: Brill, 1972–2013.

Samaritan Pentateuch

Gall, A. F. von, ed. *Der hebräische Pentateuch der Samaritaner.* 4 vols. Giessen: Töpelmann, 1914. Repr., Berlin, 1966.

Sadaqa, Avraham, and Ratson Sadaqa. *Jewish and Samaritan Version of the Pentateuch—With Particular Stress on the Differences between Both Texts.* Tel Aviv: Ruben Mass, 1961.

Tal, A., ed. *The Samaritan Pentateuch, Edited according to MS 6 (C) of the Shekhem Synagogue.* Texts and Studies in the Hebrew Language and Related Subjects 8. Tel Aviv: Chaim Rosenberg School, 1994.

Tal, Abraham, and Moshe Florentin, eds. *The Pentateuch: The Samaritan Version and the Masoretic Version.* Tel Aviv: The Haim Rubin Tel Aviv University Press, 2010. [Hebrew]

Septuagint

Brooke, Alan E., Norman McLean, and Henry St. John Thackeray. *The Old Testament in Greek according to the Text of Codex Vaticanus.* 9 vols. Cambridge: Cambridge University Press, 1906–1940.

Holmes, Robert, and James Parsons. *Vetus Testamentum Graecum, cum variis lectionibus.* 5 vols. Oxford: Clarendon, 1798–1823.

Rahlfs, Alfred. *Septuaginta.* Stuttgart: Deutsche Bibelgesellschaft, 1935, 1979.

Rahlfs, Alfred, and Robert Hanhart. *Septuaginta.* Electronic ed. Stuttgart: Deutsche Bibelgesellschaft, 2006.

Swete, Henry Barclay. *The Old Testament in Greek: According to the Septuagint.* Cambridge: Cambridge University Press, 1909.

Göttingen Septuagint

Hanhart, R., ed. *Esdrae liber I.* 2nd rev. ed. Septuaginta: Vetus
Testamentum Graecum 8/1. Göttingen: Vandenhoeck &
Ruprecht, 1991.

———, ed. *Esdrae liber II.* Septuaginta: Vetus Testamentum Graecum 8/2.
Göttingen: Vandenhoeck & Ruprecht, 1993.

———, ed. *Esther.* 2nd rev. ed. Septuaginta: Vetus Testamentum Graecum
8/3. Göttingen: Vandenhoeck & Ruprecht, 1983.

———, ed. *Iudith.* Septuaginta: Vetus Testamentum Graecum 8/4.
Göttingen: Vandenhoeck & Ruprecht, 1979.

———, ed. *Maccabaeorum liber III.* 2nd rev. ed. Septuaginta: Vetus
Testamentum Graecum 9/3. Göttingen: Vandenhoeck &
Ruprecht, 1980.

———, ed. *Tobit.* 2nd rev. ed. Septuaginta: Vetus Testamentum Graecum
8/5. Göttingen: Vandenhoeck & Ruprecht, 1983.

Kappler, W. ed. *Maccabaeorum liber I.* 3rd ed. Septuaginta: Vetus
Testamentum Graecum 9/1. Göttingen: Vandenhoeck &
Ruprecht, 1990.

Kappler, W. and R. Hanhart, eds., *Maccabaeorum liber II.* 3rd rev. ed.
Septuaginta: Vetus Testamentum Graecum 9/2. Göttingen:
Vandenhoeck & Ruprecht, 2008.

Quast, U., ed. *Ruth.* Septuaginta: Vetus Testamentum Graecum 9/3.
Göttingen: Vandenhoeck & Ruprecht, 2006.

Rahlfs, A. ed., *Psalmi cum Odis.* 3rd unchanged ed. Septuaginta:
Vetus Testamentum Graecum 10. Göttingen: Vandenhoeck &
Ruprecht, 1979.

Rahlfs, A. and D. Fraenkel, eds., *Supplementum: Verzeichnis der
griechischen Handschriften des Alten Testaments: Die Überlieferung
bis zum VIII. Jahrhundert.* Septuaginta: Vetus Testamentum
Graecum 1/1. Göttingen: Vandenhoeck & Ruprecht, 2004.

Wevers, J. W., ed., *Deuteronomium.* 2nd ed. Septuaginta: Vetus
Testamentum Graecum 3/2. Göttingen: Vandenhoeck &
Ruprecht, 2006.

———, ed. *Exodus.* Septuaginta: Vetus Testamentum Graecum 2/1.
Göttingen: Vandenhoeck & Ruprecht, 1991.

————, ed. *Genesis.* Septuaginta: Vetus Testamentum Graecum 1. Göttingen: Vandenhoeck & Ruprecht, 1974.

————, ed. *Leviticus.* Septuaginta: Vetus Testamentum Graecum 2/2. Göttingen: Vandenhoeck & Ruprecht, 1986.

————, ed. *Numbers.* Septuaginta: Vetus Testamentum Graecum 3/1. Göttingen: Vandenhoeck & Ruprecht, 1982.

Ziegler, J. ed. *Duodecim prophetae.* 3rd rev. ed. Septuaginta: Vetus Testamentum Graecum 8. Göttingen: Vandenhoeck & Ruprecht, 1984.

————, ed. *Ezechiel.* 3rd ed. Septuaginta: Vetus Testamentum Graecum 16/1. Göttingen: Vandenhoeck & Ruprecht, 2006.

————, ed. *Iob.* Septuaginta: Vetus Testamentum Graecum 11/4. Göttingen: Vandenhoeck & Ruprecht, 1982.

————, ed. *Isaias.* 3rd ed. Septuaginta: Vetus Testamentum Graecum 14. Göttingen: Vandenhoeck & Ruprecht, 1983.

————, ed. *Jeremias, Baruch, Threni Epistula Jeremiae.* 3rd ed. Septuaginta: Vetus Testamentum Graecum 15. Göttingen: Vandenhoeck & Ruprecht, 1957.

————, ed. *Sapientia Iesu Filii Sirach.* 2nd rev. ed. Septuaginta: Vetus Testamentum Graecum 12/2. Göttingen: Vandenhoeck & Ruprecht, 1980.

————, ed. *Sapientia Salomonis.* 2nd rev. ed. Septuaginta: Vetus Testamentum Graecum 12/1. Göttingen: Vandenhoeck & Ruprecht, 1980.

————, ed. *Susanna, Daniel, Bel et Draco.* 2nd ed. Septuaginta: Vetus Testamentum Graecum 16/2. Göttingen: Vandenhoeck & Ruprecht, 1999.

Vulgate

Weber, Robertus, and R. Gryson, eds. *Biblia Sacra iuxta Vulgatam versionem.* 2nd ed. Stuttgart: Deutsche Bibelgesellschaft, 1975.

————. *Biblia Sacra iuxta Vulgatam versionem.* 5th rev. ed. Stuttgart: Deutsche Bibelgesellschaft, 2007.

SUBJECT INDEX

SCRIPTURE INDEX

Old Testament

New Testament

Printed in the United States
By Bookmasters